THE CASSOULET SAVED OUR MARRIAGE

THE CASSOULET SAVED OUR MARRIAGE

TRUE TALES OF FOOD, FAMILY, AND HOW WE LEARN TO EAT

Enjoy the feast!

Edited by Caroline M. Grant & Lisa Catherine Harper

ROOST BOOKS
Boston & London 2013

Roost Books
An imprint of Shambhala Publications, Inc.
Horticultural Hall
300 Massachusetts Avenue
Boston, Massachusetts 02115
roostbooks.com

"Lobster Lessons" first appeared in *Gourmet* (August 2009).
"Still Life on the Half-Shell" first appeared in *Gastronomica: The Journal
of Food and Culture* (10:2).

Diligent efforts were made in every case to obtain rights from copyright
holders. The efforts were not all successful. The editors and the publisher
are grateful for the use of this excerpted material.

9 8 7 6 5 4 3 2 1

First Edition
Printed in the United States of America

♾ This edition is printed on acid-free paper that meets the
American National Standards Institute Z39.48 Standard.
♻ This book is printed on 30% postconsumer recycled paper.
For more information please visit www.shambhala.com.

Distributed in the United States by Random House, Inc.,
and in Canada by Random House of Canada Ltd

Designed by Daniel Urban-Brown

LIBRARY OF CONGRESS CATALOGING-IN-PUBLICATION DATA
The cassoulet saved our marriage: true tales of food, family, and how
we learn to eat / [compiled by] Caroline M. Grant and Lisa Catherine
Harper.—First edition.
Pages   cm
ISBN 978-1-61180-014-2 (pbk.: alk. paper) 1. Cooking. 2. Dinners and
dining—Social aspects. 3. Gastronomy. I. Grant, Caroline, 1967– II.
Harper, Lisa Catherine, 1966–
TX714.C3764 2013
641.01'3—dc23
2012026370

For Ben, Eli, Ella, and Finn, who inspired
this project, and for Tony and Kory,
who sustained us along the way.

Nothing is more interesting than that something that you eat.

—GERTRUDE STEIN

CONTENTS

FOR STARTERS ...

A child should be encouraged, not discouraged as so many are, to look at what he eats, and think about it.

—M. F. K. FISHER

The grilled fish he ate with his father in a rustic seaside restaurant. The vinaigrette they drizzled over their soup, or the oysters they ate together the first night in their new city. The chicken Milanese her brother taught her to cook after weight-loss surgery. The cassoulet that anchored and saved their marriage.

Food is never simply about what you eat.

Since 2008, we've been writing on our blog, *Learning to Eat*, about how we feed our families: practical recipes for busy weeknights, special meals for celebrations, snack foods, and desserts. We've written about holiday traditions and everyday meals, what we keep in the pantry and what we hoard in the freezer. We write about cocktails and appetizers, even junk food. But we also consider bigger questions: Does family dinner, every night, *really* matter? Who cooks, cleans up, and sets the table? Why is Caroline's family vegetarian? Should Lisa serve meat? Where do we shop and how do we economize? What family food traditions do we maintain, which do we abandon, and how do new ones arise?

Like generations of food writers before us—Brillat-Savarin, M. F. K. Fisher, Elizabeth David, Julia Child—we believe that eating is not a singular experience, nor has there ever been one right way to eat. How we eat reflects what we find important about our family, our culture, and our particular time and place in the world. Food is fundamental in our lives, but how we *should* eat is not necessarily obvious. How else can we explain the way our national food culture has stirred up such controversy? From foodies obsessed with sourcing the most rarefied ingredients to ordinary families putting something on the table every day, how we eat has become the subject of feverish debate and scrutiny. In the midst of these heated conversations, most of us are just trying to get our families fed. Why should we care so much? The answer is not as simple as you think.

The Cassoulet Saved Our Marriage broadens the conversation we began on our blog. In the stories and essays that follow, everyday people—parents, professional food writers, chefs, and others—answer a basic question for fellow everyday people: Why does family food matter? Like our blog, *The Cassoulet Saved Our Marriage* goes beyond the "local, sustainable, organic" mantra to offer an intimate look at the way real families eat. From favorite meals to the relationships forged (or broken) at our tables to the social, cultural, and ethical lessons inherent in our family traditions, this book explores the profound connection between food and family.

Over a century ago, Jean Anthelme Brillat-Savarin famously proclaimed, "Tell me what you eat and I will tell you what you are." Stories of family food are similarly revealing, and the writers in our first section, "Food," show us the many ways that food—whether or not it's healthy or homemade—can make the family. One bite of carrot exposes a mother's deepest desires and anxieties for herself and her son; a Midwestern casserole conjures a lost memory; a poached egg restores an exhausted parent. Family food reflects where we live and how we arrived there; it expresses how we've been raised, how we treat others, what we remember, and even what we find funny. We've all eaten something, like Proust's madeleine, that evokes, with startling, sensory immediacy, our first or dearest home and everything that place means. It might not be healthy: French Toast Sandwiches with Toffee-Chocolate Crumble? Blackaroni and Cheese? It might not make sense: Shrimp at a kosher table? Lobsters boiled in seawater? But sometimes—the carrot sweetens the red sauce; the zucchini melts into the risotto—something ineffable occurs, and the dish is no longer just part of the meal but something that defines the family and symbolizes home. If you think your family has no food traditions, these stories will make you think again.

Part Two, "Family," continues the conversation with stories that show how deeply food reflects the dynamic of a family's life. At every meal, food connects us to our parents, siblings, and extended family. Who cooks for us? Who do we cook for? Who eats around our table? Whose place stands empty? In fact, these stories show clearly that our family meals do more than nourish us; day in and day out, they help create and define our relationships.

As adults, we remake our families in many ways, but cooking for and eating with those we love most remain some of the best ways we celebrate them. And since families are spared neither grief nor conflict, *Cassoulet* writers show how these also play out around the table—whether it's set with a feast or stands bare. It's not surprising that stories about mothers are everywhere in this section. They are good cooks and terrible ones. They are present and absent and ill. But we also find fathers and husbands and brothers whose presence in the kitchen is equally life-changing. These men cook elaborate feasts and mystically good gravy. They comfort their sisters, support their wives, and teach their sons. These writers show us that Brillat-Savarin was not completely right: It's not just what you eat but whom you cook for and eat with that tells you who you are.

The writers in Part Three know that "Learning to Eat" is no simple matter. We might teach our children to eat—literally—one bite at a time: a bit of banana, anything non-white, something other than sweet potato, *please!?*, but as we feed them, we offer deeper lessons, too. While what we learn at our family table includes (hopefully) a set of nutritional values that may help when dealing with the school lunch lady, our family's food can also communicate how we feel about animals, or the environment, or other cultures, or table talk, or even pleasure. These writers dig deep to show how their family food reveals their particular point of view about the world. They share their politics and religious traditions, including whether to serve meat or keep kosher. And they show how food connects us to the community beyond our family, from our friends at the lunch table to our colleagues at the PTA to the strangers who wait in line with us for our morning coffee. A sliver of herring, a shot of orange liqueur, an elaborate tournedos Rossini—each of these expresses our priorities and reflects something about how we choose to live in the world.

The Cassoulet Saved Our Marriage is not a book about being a foodie, though some of our writers certainly are. And it's not a guide to how you should feed yourself and your family—though some of our writers think they know that, too. Nor is this a book about the apocalypse of modern American food culture. It's a book that begins a new conversation, while sharing many excellent recipes. We're asking you to think beyond caveats and calorie counting, mandates and manifestos. All our writers are saying one important thing: This is what food means in our families. What does it mean in yours?

—Caroline M. Grant & Lisa Catherine Harper

PART ONE

FOOD

STILL LIFE ON THE HALF-SHELL

K. G. SCHNEIDER

A football game crackles on the television set, and as is often the case the twins—two middle-aged women in wheelchairs—are filling up on raw oysters and fried grouper. Otherwise it is so quiet in the Shell Oyster Bar on this blustery January afternoon in Tallahassee that I can hear the rhythmic scraping of sharp metal against calcite as the shuckers crack open oysters and joke among themselves about the abysmal performance of the local college football team. Two men at the counter lean over plastic trays, dripping Crystal hot sauce on freshly shucked oysters and downing them as fast as they appear.

Maria, the server, steps toward us, menus in hand. She's a handsome middle-aged woman with a chin-up esprit de corps I've seen at Café des Artistes and Chez Panisse. "How are you girls today?" she asks.

Though my partner and I have not been girls for several decades, we always say, "Fine, and you?" and ask to be seated in our favorite cubbyhole near the oyster counter, where we can watch the action. Sandy and I had finished our Saturday morning housework, which meant it was now time to tuck into plates of raw oysters so fresh, "they make you wanna slap your granny," as our electrician describes any food he likes.

We've been here a year and a half, ever since we ended five years of on-again, off-again employment in Northern California with a job offer Sandy couldn't refuse.

"Lived in the South before?" asked one friend.

No, we hadn't. The friend, who had, said nothing.

———————

Our first weekend in Tallahassee—Labor Day weekend in 2006—was also the occasion of my forty-ninth birthday. That Sunday evening we left the house we had purchased two days before to go out and celebrate, figuring as the house (and thus, kitchen) was empty, we'd hunt down a nice meal.

We puttered along the spokes of this old market city, first tooling up and down forest-dark roads where canopies of ancient trees formed natural shelter from the sun, then criss-crossing six-lane asphalt highways flanked by strip malls and chain restaurants. We drove past the lawns of ranch bungalows with ballerina-slender crape myrtles dusted with dark pink blossoms. We drove past graceless McMansions squeezed shoulder to shoulder, with two-car garages planted where gardens should be. We drove through downtown, then midtown, then uptown, and after a couple of hours we realized what everyone in Tallahassee knows: Most restaurants here are closed on Sunday.

"That's all right," I said in a high voice. *I will have a good time tonight, damn it.*

We ate bad Thai food in a dark, dusty, suspiciously odiferous restaurant.

"Is this shrimp local?" I asked. *Please, let the shrimp be local.*

For the previous three months, we had been spinning this move to everyone, including ourselves, into anything but what it was, a move to an unknown part of the country prompted by blunt economic realities; I needed the magic for one more night. I knew the Gulf of Mexico was less than thirty miles from where we sat, and that Apalachicola Bay, a lagoon and estuary that mingles freshwater and seawater in perfect balance for intertidal seafood such as oysters, was just an hour's drive from the southern end of town.

The waiter, a small, gaunt man of indeterminate age, shuffled his feet. "I don't know."

Sandy looked up from her menu and stretched her hand halfway across the table, our clandestine version of hand-holding in places where prudence dictates two women do not hold hands. I wiggled my fingers at her. Fifteen years of love and adventure: We were in this together—whatever "this" might be.

The shrimp were small, soggy, and wan. If they had come from A-Bay, it was during another presidential administration, but I suspected they were from far away; they had the mealiness of fish that have traveled thousands of miles. We ordered Thai beer and tried to be cheerful, then went home to sleep on a borrowed inflatable mattress. The enormity of our decision to move to this alien land lay heavily on us.

The next day we wheeled a shopping cart around the local grocery store.

"Where's the citrus? Isn't this Florida?" Sandy asked, her forehead creased with confusion.

On our house-hunting trip, Publix had seemed reassuringly large, bright, and clean. In the sober aftermath of our cross-country move, it was still all that, but not much more. For all the available produce, we could have been in a Midwestern grocery store in the deep winter.

Drifting slowly through the fluorescent-bright produce section sharp with the ammonia odor of fresh-mopped floors, we were confronted with mounds of waxed apples, dyed navel oranges, and row after row of packaged lettuce lined up in the refrigerated case. Nearly everything was packaged, tucked into little Styrofoam trays with plastic stretched over it as tight as pantyhose. Sandy lifted a package of onions, turned it in her hands, then gently set it down. This grocery store's tidy efficiencies ensured no nose would consider the tuft of an onion, no fingers would run across the ridges of an English cucumber or explore the bottom of a red pepper. No palm would be dusted with the coarse, crumbly honesty of a few grains of topsoil clinging to a russet potato.

I pushed the cart toward the limes—thankfully, the possibility of sealing them in plastic hadn't occurred to anyone at Publix yet—and picked one up to sniff. I had a thin, shaky hope that the lime would yield a seductive fragrance evocative of the sour oranges from South Florida that John McPhee had written about so affectingly. For years I had tasted these sour oranges in my fantasies, baking luscious pies that, I imagined, Sandy would insist I take to work so she wouldn't be tempted to make lunch of the leftovers. Wouldn't that be one of the perks of moving to Florida? But the lime was hard and lifeless in my hand, having surrendered its volatile oils many thousands of miles ago—somewhere between here and Mexico, according to its tiny label.

We were quiet and did not look at each other as our cart wobbled to the fish counter, where the shrimp, Sandy observed, were labeled "previously frozen." The two or three types of fish fillets on display looked weary, the flesh dull and a little shriveled. The oysters, sold by the jar, were from Washington State. We drove home, unpacked our sterile wares, and talked of other things.

Life toiled on, a dull quotidian stream of work, errands, and frozen vegetables.

Then one spring day, on a narrow old road, kitty-corner to the service entrance of a pharmacy chain, we discovered the farmer.

A battered pickup truck sat in front of the local oil-change station. MELONS, shouted its hand-lettered sign, though that was evident. The truck bed was a green mountain of the summer's first watermelons—a little shy on flavor but dense and not mealy. With the melons were fat, ruddy tomatoes that were heavy in the hand and tasted like a late spring day, rich and sunny.

As the season progressed, we became familiar with—even proprietary about—"our" truck farmer, this sanguine man in a Gators jersey who held forth boxes of dark red cherry tomatoes as if they were jewels. Logically, I knew we shared him with everyone who drove past that corner or lived in that neighborhood. But his parking lot was tiny, so we never saw another customer when we stopped to buy his goods, and he treated us as if he had been personally delivered by our creator to save us from grocery-store produce. "Snuppercongs," Sandy would say, cupping a bag of dark, delicate, wildly flavorful grapes in her hands while I let them dissolve on my tongue. "Scuppernongs," our truck farmer would gently correct her, and then they would banter about sports.

We were a little sad in late September, when the weather broke and the truck with its hand-lettered sign was there no more—very like the sadness I feel every January when we bundle up our Christmas ornaments, an emotion sown with a seed of anticipation for the day we will see them again. The guy who parks his truck in front of the shopping center at the other end of the canopy road to sell pretty much the same produce our farmer sells is perfectly fine, but he's not our truck farmer.

When the truck farmers disappeared, I became aspirational, and began thumbing through the local newspaper and prowling the public library's bulletin board, searching for other local food sources. To my surprise, I found local farmers' markets humble affairs by some yardsticks, and trafficked by a handful of fresh-food devotees and Northern ex-pats, yet better than the stores. In the dark, rainy days of January, the Tallahassee "market" can be two coolers in the back of a pickup truck in the parking lot of the American Legion. But even at the two peaks of Florida's growing season—the earth takes a deep breath in the middle of the very hot summer—the market is not much more than two rows of folding tables.

There are no fancy signs at these tables. Actually, there are no signs at all; if you want to know who you're buying tomatoes from, you introduce yourself. And unlike some of the tonier markets in the Bay Area we were used to, there are no massage therapists, musicians, pâté vendors, or bakery stands. There are just farmers, selling their prized food. In Tallahassee, the fellow who grows oyster mushrooms will encourage you to flip through his photo album of—what else?—his oyster farm. One farmer sells bags of trimmed, diced turnips—gorgeous pumpkin-orange cubes that simmer up firm and toothsome—with a handful of turnip greens at the bottom of each bag. "I peel 'em so y'all don't have to!" she says, tilting us a winning smile as she hands them to us: Southern Organic Locavore Fast Slow Food.

The farmers' market scene in Tallahassee is a little rough, and a little plain. But when Jack from Crescent Moon Farms in Sopchoppy pushes back the hood of his yellow slicker as he hands me parsley and spinach while Sandy throws breadcrumbs to the fat ducks waddling in the gray wintry drizzle, I feel joy and even awe. Not only that we will dine tonight on spinach pulled from the ground that morning—no small feat in the winter months, given the temperatures hover above freezing—but that we have become part of the loop of that spinach, and part of Jack's loop, as well. Our cold, wet hands touch briefly, our eyes catch each other's for a flash.

On a rubbernecking Sunday drive our first spring, as we pass through Saint Mark's en route to Panacea, Sandy shouts, "Pull over." I stop at a truck where a very old man hawks delicate tupelo honey. The honey is harvested from beehives sent on flats into river swamps where the squat, glossy-leaved tupelo trees grow. Though his coastal patois is such a thick burr I can barely understand him, he pulls out a well-thumbed stack of photographs and shows us all the people who have posed with him and his wares. He then hands his camera to Sandy and poses with me, shoulder to shoulder. With our faces framed by jar after jar of golden honey glimmering in the sunshine, we grin toward the lens.

In the fall, when the tupelo trees blush red and the heat has broken a bit, we drive south again toward Panacea a couple of times, hoping to see him, but he isn't there. We pull over for a moment on the spot where we met him; we are alone, but together, and while the autumn light glitters through the tupelo trees, Sandy's hand creeps into mine, and we conjure up stories about the honey man. Maybe he found an even more felicitous place to hawk honey, or maybe his pickup truck is bumping along canopy roads in the great tupelo forest in the sky; regardless, I am glad to have been a picture in his album.

Shortly after our move, I had returned to California just long enough to see our worldly goods bundled onto a truck, and to my credit I flew back to Florida anyway, blinking back tears as my beloved Bay Area shrank and then disappeared from my horizon.

My first full day in Florida we had no food in the house. There was a frog-strangler that September morning, a rain so strong that as I drove us toward Adams Street long green clumps of Spanish moss splatted on our car.

Could that be the Shell everyone had been raving about, that small, squat building, gray and vanishing into the rain, set back in an alley next to a car repair shop, on a nondescript street in the not-so-nice part of town? I squeezed between the pickup trucks in the tiny parking lot. We ran toward the building and pushed our way into a two-rump foyer cluttered with dust-shouldered gallon jugs of marinating peppers and wet umbrellas. The walls were blanketed with yellowed clippings and photos of everyone who has been anyone in Florida for the last seventy years; the welcome mat seemed to be made from frayed squares of carpet samples.

I was relieved when I pushed open the door into the restaurant proper. The Shell is, perhaps, not pretty. Its small, windowless dining room seats fifty at best, and is a pragmatic place with prefab blond paneling, cafeteria furniture, artificial plants, and one seven-stool counter facing the shucking operation. But the Shell is immaculate and well-lit, its well-fanned air redolent of the cool aquatic fragrance of truly fresh oysters—some weeks they run through several thousand, brought directly from Buddy Ward's, the biggest and oldest oyster operation on A-Bay—with a high note or two of fresh fried food to tickle the senses. There are two TVs perennially tuned to sports. (Around here, if you don't like football you act like you do anyway.)

That first day, our maiden voyage at the Shell, when we opened menus and saw oysters for $6.50 a dozen, raw, fried, or "nuked" (microwaved), we almost got up and left, worried that oysters that cheap wouldn't be any good. We didn't know that $6.50 could even be considered pricey in an area that features twenty-five-cent oyster nights at the local student dives.

We were two hungry ladies in a strange city. We knew the oysters came from somewhere south of Tallahassee. We could see and smell their freshness. We needed those oysters to restore a little of the dream that had carried us here, a dream that already was dwindling into the flat prose of the quotidian. Sandy's hand crept across the vinyl tablecloth; I inched a hand in her direction, pretending to examine the table condiments. "Can I have horseradish?" asked Sandy. Maria brought it without comment, and without a smile.

The oysters came on paper plates, with forks wrapped in plastic. We had ordered hush puppies, and nibbled them; they were ghastly, soaked with oil, half cold, and flavorless. The coleslaw lacked spark and was swimming in mayonnaise, so it seemed churlish to object that the portion was miniscule.

But then I ate an oyster, tipping it into my mouth after letting a little of the seawater-cold liquor run in first. The meat—a pale silver, well-contained mound—was crisp, creamy, and flavorful, a little coppery and a little sultry. I looked at Sandy, and saw happiness and relief in her face, not only that I was happy, but that she was, too. We slowly swallowed oyster after oyster, then lingered at the table, tucked in the shell of our love.

————

The January rain thrums on the roof of the Shell. Maria brings us our hush puppies and coleslaw. It's Year 3 of the Great Tallahassee Experiment. The pups are bad as always; I feel somehow reassured. The coleslaw has greatly improved—it's grated now, with very little mayonnaise, and bright bits of green stuff—and that reassures me, too. Sandy stares hard at the menu, which except for the prices has not changed in decades, if ever. The shrimp is succulent, the clams toothsome, the mixed-fry special wickedly tempting, but we order raw oysters anyway. Sandy asks for horseradish, but Maria, ever intent on training Sandy in Southern ways, once again "forgets" to serve it (and in collusion with Maria, I "forget" to remind her).

The oysters arrive, small hillocks of joy. We reach for the Crystal sauce and saltines.

I've grown up eating oysters in all kinds of hoity-toity restaurants where I learned to fork oysters from the shell, reluctantly abandoning the liquor; I've also eaten in places where I felt comfortable delicately tilting the shell toward my mouth, sipping a little oyster juice, then allowing the oyster to discretely slip into my mouth. But though some people do all that—and when I travel to exotic places such as New York City I do so, as well—this is how we eat them in the Gulf.

Open a packet of fresh, fresh saltines.* Hold one saltine horizontal. Place an oyster on the cracker. Eat. (One bite, two bites, three—let the size of the oyster determine the experience.)

The crisp cracker stuccoed with sharp grains of salt is a perfect textural foil for the oyster's tender meat; there is salt, and more salt, of different kinds and flavors, sea salt and table salt and the ambient saltiness of food itself; the oven-baked, bland mellowness of the cracker's flavor toys with the creamy oceanic sweetness of the oyster. But best of all (and there is no polite way to describe this), the oyster stays in your mouth longer by sheer dint of being anchored to a cracker.

However far they may travel once harvested, the life of an oyster includes no cross-country moves; they are sessile, bound to their birthplace. Many oysters in the United States are the same variety—*Crassostrea virginica*—but take on distinct regional characteristics from the waters that give them

---

* The Shell uses Lance brand, which along with Keebler I prefer becaue they're a little more dense and flavorful than Nabisco.

life. A-Bay oysters are sometimes snubbed by connoisseurs—Apalachicola supplies 10 percent of the national oyster supply and 90 percent of Florida's, so they are hardly rare or precious—but having tasted quite a few oysters in my day, I prefer them to all others; they are a perfect balance of sweet and salt, resilience and tenderness. To pass a fresh-shucked A-Bay oyster under my nose is a trip to the Gulf itself, conjuring up a crisp ocean wind buffeting our faces while Sandy and I stand beneath the shadow of the old lighthouse at Saint Mark's, our hands "accidentally" brushing now and then, gazing from the crook of Florida's Big Bend to a brilliant blue horizon that over six hundred miles later touches the beaches of Cancun before spreading its apron of possibilities around the globe.

Then again, I think any oyster tonged one hour's drive from my mouth is going to taste pretty damn good.

DEEP WINTER OYSTER CHOWDER

Sometimes I like a thin, uncomplicated chowder: not much more than rich milk and barely heated oysters. Other times I want something more involved and rib-sticking, like this one. The trick is to never overwhelm the star: the oyster. If you find ingredients at local dairies and farms and steam fresh clams for the juice, the wine, salt, and pepper can be the only imports.

MAKES 2 HEARTY MAIN-DISH PORTIONS
(LEAVE OUT THE POTATO AND YOU HAVE 4 FIRST-COURSE SERVINGS)

3 slices bacon (Niman Ranch is a good choice)
1 baking potato, about the size of 2 fists
2 cups chopped leeks, white and pale green parts only
1 tablespoon all-purpose flour
1 8-ounce bottle clam juice or water
1 pint half-and-half
1 to 2 tablespoons chopped fresh thyme, or a pinch of dried thyme
½ cup good dry white wine, such as sauvignon blanc or pinot grigio
1 pint shucked oysters, with oyster liquor
Salt and freshly ground black pepper
Crusty bread and hot sauce for serving

Dice the bacon and stir it gently in a large sauté pan over medium heat until its fat has rendered out and it has begun to crisp. While the bacon is cooking, peel the potato and chop it into ¼-inch dice. (You can leave a little of the peel on.) When the bacon has browned, remove it from the pan and set aside; do not discard the bacon fat.

Add the chopped leeks to the fat in the pan and sauté until wilted, 3 to 5 minutes. Stir in the flour and cook for 30 seconds, then slowly stir in the clam juice and 1½ cups of the half-and-half. Add the diced potato and thyme.

If no one is looking, take a long drink of the oyster liquor—it's delicious. Otherwise, pour all of the oyster liquor into the chowder, then stir in the wine.

Simmer the chowder for about 10 minutes, until the potatoes are tender. Stir now and then so the chowder doesn't burn and so the surface doesn't develop a skin. If the chowder gets too thick, add a little half-and-half and water. Stir in the oysters and cook for 3 minutes more, until the oysters have heated through. While the oysters are heating, taste the broth; add salt if necessary.

Serve the chowder in wide bowls, topped with the reserved bacon and a little pepper, with crusty bread and some hot sauce on the side for those who enjoy a splash of it in their chowder.

AN AMERICAN OMELET IN BROOKLYN

SARAH SHEY

When I think of my mother's merry lunches full of winks and laughter, she is standing guard over the men hired to work on our farm, the sturdy legged chairs pushed in and out, the dog yipping outside to show his approbation, the sunflower wallpaper bombarding the room with cheer. My mind is filled with wonder at my mother's generosity and her idea of hospitality. I think how lucky I was to grow up with that cozy scene, the rare intimacy between boss and hands. The round table that hosted these gatherings occupied a bright corner in her kitchen. Double-hung windows let in light and air and offered views of the corncrib, the old garage, the scarlet barn, and birdfeeders dangling from maple trees like earrings. Men's elbows vied for space among the coffee pot, platters, and plates. Worn boots rested below the table. Hands wiped mouths clean. My mother, who spent her childhood on a farm, was at ease with these men: She knew their wives, the pickups they drove, the pews they did (or did not) sit in at church. The men's coarseness and pungent odors, along with my mother's kindness and food, made her kitchen rowdy and alive.

Twenty years later I found myself in Brooklyn, New York. I had moved to the city to attend graduate school. In almost every possible way it was different from my parents' farm in northern Iowa. It took me a long time to find my way. I missed the sky. I missed small-town courtesies. My Cobble Hill neighbors seemed baffled by my bold friendliness. *What does she want?* their eyes seemed to ask. When I shared extra cookies from a fresh-baked batch, they responded as if I had given them a concrete sculpture for their living room instead of a treat. I came to realize they weren't used to random deliveries of goods they didn't order or pay for, goods that came from someone else's kitchen for no apparent reason. I was being a neighbor the only way I knew how (as were they). We each seemed puzzled by the other.

My husband and I had lived in our apartment for almost seven years, when twelve construction workers arrived to restore the cornice on the 1882 co-op building we shared with twenty-six other families. I knew too well what construction entailed and was grumpy at the idea of spending a summer with workers who would treat me as if I were the bothersome houseguest and not the other way around. I worked at home as a mom and a writer; I could not escape. Then I met the foreman. His name was Wojtek. He had a captain's stance, gaze, and height, not to mention a fine, chiseled chin. He inspired his workers to walk fast—and to sweep at the end of the day. The door to the courtyard I shared with two other families was kept closed—without reminders. The foreman conveyed to everyone that he was hosting this noisy event.

I asked Wojtek where he was from.

"Poland," he said.

"*Jaksiemasz?*" I asked. (How are you?)

"*Bardzodobrze,*" he said. (Very well.)

I shouldn't have been surprised to meet someone from Poland in New York City, but I was. It had been over a decade since I had spoken Polish. One year after college graduation, long before marriage and motherhood, I taught in rural Poland. Eastern Europe had needed English teachers in the early nineties. I had wanted a cheap overseas adventure. So off I went. I wasn't a very good teacher, but I proved an able eater. When the foreman mentioned his home country, I recalled piquant tomato soup; cake topped with sparkly Jell-O (looking like a plump countess with a tiara); fresh, angelic bread I sprinkled with sugar because jam was too expensive; severe unfiltered coffee served in glasses on honorary occasions; ten o'clock "second breakfasts" of tasty ham and butter sandwiches wrapped in wax paper; and the old man who wore a navy blue beret and presented me with pears from his tree propped throughout with ladders for harvesting. I remembered my Polish hosts, who understood how to welcome a stranger into their homes: with a smile and something they had baked or had grown.

When my young son and I set out to become acquainted with the workers, it was as if my voyage in Poland had not ended after all. I could attach new faces to the names I still loved hearing: Bogdan, Mariusz, Roman, Marcin, Jacek, Przemek, Pawel, Slawek. As I got to know the men, I recognized something about them that I treasured from my rural roots. The workers were unguarded and refreshing; they laughed a lot. They didn't care where I went to school or what my father did for a living. They were helpful in traditional ways: unscrewing the lid to my ice cream maker; tightening on the spare tire when my car got a flat; replacing a broken doorknob. And they kicked off a scent I adored: a heady mixture of cigarette smoke, sweat, and sun-baked hay. Before long I was pining to feed the outdoor help. It was what my family had always done.

My mother's mother, Lena, fed anyone who worked on her Iowa farm. It was modest in all aspects except for its swagger of hollyhocks, bridal wreath bushes, and peonies—and for its lavish tabletop of food. Her most exhausting efforts took place in August when she cooked for one-and-a-half days during the threshing run. Seven to eight men, all neighbors, worked together to thresh each other's oat fields. The oats first had to be cut down and stacked in bundles. The men loaded the bundles onto hayracks and sacrificed them to the two threshing machines parked in the yard. The unwieldy looking contraptions separated grain from the stalks.

Lena served the big meal at noon: chicken butchered in the morning and fried by twelve o'clock; hot corn or green beans; potatoes and gravy; homemade white bread served with jam and butter; cherry or apple pie or chocolate cake. She and her sister Mary cooked while my mother and Mary's daughter Sally snuck rides on the hayracks. The men feasted on the dishes in shifts so someone was always tending to the thresher. Before sitting down, they washed up outside under a tree, where a metal bowl, soap, comb, and towel had been set on a bench.

My mother's unique chore took place later in the afternoon. Lena fitted a crimson wagon with a cream can of iced lemonade and bologna sandwiches made with white bread. My mother left the wagon under a shade tree, near where the men stacked the straw spat out by the thresh-ers. The men ate. The women dried dishes in the kitchen and tossed the squeezed lemons into a field. The little girls played.

When my mother moved with my father to their own farm, a dozen men were hired several times over the year to put up hay, make silage, or har-vest the corn and soybeans. My mother served her lunches at 4 P.M. to tide the help over until supper. She and I layered white bread with bologna and mayonnaise and figured one-and-a-half sandwiches per man. She served chocolate cake made with a capful of vinegar. Homemade pick-les. Potato chips. A refreshment of orange juice mixed with 7Up. Weak coffee. In cooler weather she made barbecued turkey for sandwiches with pickles on the side or the hot casserole we favored as children, exotically referred to as goulash: macaroni, browned ground beef, and tomato juice baked under a blanket of mozzarella cheese and pepperoni slices. Her unfussy menus went a long way in making her company feel satisfied and cared for; we always hoped for leftovers.

My mother trucked the food to the field—depending on the weather, the men might not want to stop—or the men gathered around my mother's kitchen table. There was a perfection attained in those meals, in those moments, in those plates freckled with just crumbs by the end. I learned by watching. But I did not see then as I did later that serving lunches was a skill I would one day use or be proud of. Until the construction workers showed up in Brooklyn.

———————

The more I longed to feed the workers, the more I realized it wasn't done in the city. My gesture, like my small-town friendliness, might be taken the wrong way. Besides, the men might not want to be fed. They, like many New Yorkers who had precious little personal space, might want to be left alone. I let the matter drop. Then my son turned five. My husband and I threw a birthday gathering under the scaffold outside. A dozen adults and their children joined us on a sweltering June afternoon. We prayed for but received no breeze.

"Are the workers coming?" my son asked. His hazel eyes looked con-cerned.

"They don't come on Sundays," I said. "They're home with their families."

My husband pronounced that my egg casserole—packed with cheddar cheese, potatoes, and an indispensable teaspoon of mustard—was amazing, but it was hardly touched. Neither were the other savories. Leftovers colonized my fridge. (I knew next time to serve cold food for a hot day.) What would I do with all the uneaten food? In my desire to not waste, I became courageous. I called my mom and asked her about reheating the eggs.

"I might serve it to the workers," I said to her. My little family could never finish the nine-by-thirteen pan of eggs, so I worried that it would go uneaten for a second time.

"Oh, what a neat idea," she said. "They'll love it. Fifteen minutes at three-fifty should be fine." My mother's enthusiasm encouraged me. It was decided. I would feed the workers. And I had more than an inkling of how to do it.

On Monday, my son helped me. He carried the sturdy stuff: napkins, melamine plates, and real silverware. The other supplies filled his rusty wagon. I pulled it to where the workers ate their lunches, in a courtyard that mirrored ours on the other side of the building. I draped a three-foot-tall toolbox with a Provençal tablecloth. I placed on top sixteen bottles of soda; the egg casserole; a pasta dish of caramelized onions, tomato, and turkey sausage; birthday cake; and salt and pepper shakers. I added a jar of dill pickles and a bowl of apples and nectarines to keep the meal from being too heavy. My son played airplane with a stick and waited with me for the workers.

The men showed up at noon and took turns washing their hands and faces with a hose. I could tell my banquet confused them.

"I promise I'm not trying to poison you," I said. "Even though I am mad you took away my hammock." (My concrete "yard" had been sacrificed to a yellow box that hoisted supplies to the roof.) I finished arranging the buffet. The foreman looked bemused. He said something in Polish to his crew.

"My son's birthday was yesterday," I said, "and he wanted the construction workers to come, too." At the mention of his birthday, my son clutched my right leg.

"Thank you," said the foreman.

"*Smacznego,*" I said. After I wished the men the Polish version of *bon appétit,* I squeezed my son's hand and together we left.

The verdict about my cooking would be delivered after their lunch, in about thirty minutes. As I had never cooked for such a large group of men before—and all strangers to me—I was a little nervous. This seemed, in my naïveté, the most important meal I had ever made.

It was time to distract myself. "Come on," I said to my son. "We're going to the store." I did not want to be home to greet any returned bowls of unwanted food. My son and I walked to Smith Street and I wondered as he nattered if the men whose hunger stemmed from outdoor work would find my food tasty. I wondered, too, if my efforts had been a success, if I had tapped the farm wife's hospitality I inherited but had never used before as an adult.

There was a delightful surprise waiting for us when we got home. My plates and dishes were in an organized pile at my front door. My tablecloth was folded. My dishes and pans were washed clean (even the egg dish). I called my mother to tell her that no food was returned. Not an apple. Not a pickle. Not a peppercorn. "Twelve men can eat a lot of food," she said. It was a fine moment.

I saw Artur later in the afternoon. He was the only worker who hung around my stoop when the foreman wasn't looking so I could "learn him English." He was outside in his *kuchnia* (kitchen), as I called his outdoor work area, where he mixed mortar for bricks.

"Oh, Sarah, Sarah," he said rolling the *R*s of my name. "A good cook." He rubbed his stomach with both hands. "What was that? American omelet?"

"Sort of," I said. I explained in detail, even though Artur didn't understand that much English, that the egg dish was my mother's recipe, one she has made for years for Sunday brunches after church. It was a classic. "Casserole," I said. "A Midwest sort of deal."

Artur gazed into space as if contemplating my culinary triumph. He shoveled some sand and then regarded me with ardor. "I love American omelet."

———

That lunch inspired me. All those empty plates went to my head. My dated ivory-colored kitchen no longer seemed dull but invigorated and modern, full with possibilities. I reminded myself that I was no longer that little girl on a farm in Iowa. I had my own kitchen, and it was time to see what it could do. I hoped to captivate these men from Poland, as if I had always known them, their sons and daughters, their wives, their pets, the dents in their pickups. It was as if I had been bewitched by my kitchen and had surrendered to its remarkable ways.

The next week I tried out a toffee-bar recipe that came from an old cousin who grew up on a farm in southern Iowa. They were devoured. A week later, when my son was playing soccer with his father, I made a chocolate cake using pure cocoa and buttermilk. ("You can't go wrong with buttermilk," my mother always said.) Such a rich dessert was only half-eaten, however.

Next, to use up blackened bananas, I baked banana cake that called for sour cream (can't go wrong with sour cream, either). It was devoured. To use up chocolate candy bars, I cut them into pieces and mixed them into a pumpkin muffin batter. After they had cooled from the oven, I poured milk chocolate frosting over them. Devoured. To use up the rest of the pureed pumpkin, I made muffins again, but this time with swankier frosting (made from heavy cream, powdered sugar, and dark chocolate). Devoured as well. I got a jolt from seeing an empty pan at the day's end instead of watching it dwindle, bar by bar, on the countertop as our little family ate it over several days. I was on a roll.

The workers did not volunteer opinions about Cobble Hill gastronomy. I asked the crew's best English speaker—he was also the skinniest—for his views. Tomek deemed the banana cake (*ciasto bananowe*) "beautiful" and admitted a fondness for the milk chocolate–frosted pumpkin muffins.

This effort I made for strangers seemed different from my usual exertions. At first I thought that cooking for the crew was about the essence of hospitality: to please for the sake of pleasing, to treat guests so well that they never want the meal to end. But as time went on, I wondered whether my baking escapades really had that much to do with tending to others. It seemed more selfish than that, and in a good way. I liked my projects in the kitchen and began to look forward to my time there with a bowl, a spoon, and an obliging oven. I started reading cookbooks again, and noticing which ingredients in my pantry needed to be finished off. I liked using my hands and not thinking too much about anything else—just how many teaspoons of this and cups of that. I liked holding family recipes, many written in my mother's hand, and seeing the names of departed family members in the upper right hand corner. And I liked being alone. Not since my son was born had I baked uninterrupted. I had forgotten how much I enjoyed it. I felt powerful in my kitchen, and I loved it.

My confectionary tales delighted my mother and friends. My husband took to the pieces I always saved for him with a devotee's earnestness; he could find no fault with them. It seemed my streak would not end. Which was why what happened next was so startling. One morning, I baked muffins using applesauce to sneak some vitamin C into my son's pasta-heavy diet. My son, who helped stir, assured me that he'd love them. He didn't. I had ten muffins left over. I set them out for the workers early, at 7:30—so the men would see them as the ideal pairing for their morning cigarettes and coffee. The day ended. My green melamine plate failed to turn up at its usual place on top of my outdoor table. In the dark, in a downpour, I searched for my plate. I found it abandoned next to the toolbox, on the ground, the plastic covering soaked. Only one had been eaten. A pie spatula had been jabbed into my stomach. Or so I dramatically sighed to my friend Nancy.

"Don't you want to know the truth?" she asked.

"No," I said. "I just want an empty plate."

She harrumphed.

To salvage the muffins, I poured my signature frosting over them; my husband gobbled them up. But it didn't matter. My ego was bruised; it was a cook's nightmare for her food to go uneaten. It took me a couple of days to realize that I needed to do something to make myself feel better, something theatrical. I had only to look to my mother for ideas. She loved being mischievous. Her prankster repertoire included, but was not limited to, serving dessert on plates placed upside down; presenting a donut the size of a basketball; and "baking" a cake that was a six-pack of beer in a frosting disguise. I thought to myself, "What do these men love? What do these men love so much that they will give me back an empty plate?"

I bought my first pack of cigarettes at the nearest deli. I arranged twelve of them on the usual plate, covered it with plastic, and set it out the next morning. At the end of the day, the plate appeared on my outdoor table, empty. My stoop was swept clean. We were even—almost.

The following week, I visited the men at noon.

"I made chocolate chip cookies this morning," I said.

The men murmured pleasant sounds and looked toward me.

I presented my plate. It held one chocolate chip cookie.

"You can divide it among you," I said. One of the workers guffawed. A few smiled. Most of them looked confused. (Problems with the language barrier.)

After work, the men returned my green plate, empty.

The renovation came to an end. I seemed to be one of the few in the co-op sad to see the men and their blue scaffolding leave. Every day, the project, the noise, the baked goods, and the Polish dozen had called to mind my childhood—and the little community that a farm created. I had grown to like it.

"What are you going to do for them?" Nancy asked. "Bake them break-fast?"

My son and I drove to Greenpoint, a Polish neighborhood in Brooklyn, to a slim bakery that could fit four standing adults and one stroller. A stack of foot-long loaves rose to the ceiling. Plump pastries adorned the window. A glass case showed off striped cakes and airy unknown wonders.

"I need something really Polish," I said to the strawberry-blond teenager. She held a raspberry-colored cell phone to her ear while tending the store.

"Everything is Polish here," she said.

"But these men are really, really Polish."

She whispered something into the phone and set it down.

The next morning, I set out egg bread crowned with cherries and a cake layered with Jell-O on the toolbox. It was my last offering. My note said, "I give up. Polish bakers can best take care of Polish men."

The world I had known for seven months was gone. It had been packed away onto trucks that bulged with gear and onto subways that slinked underneath the city to the workers' homes. Soon I forgot my sadness and the hammers' clacking and the scaffolded sky, and I forgot, too, the men. I did not relinquish my kitchen avocation, however, nor my neighborly ways. Baking satisfied my hunger.

EGG CASSEROLE

SERVES 10 TO 12, DEPENDING ON THE SIZE OF THE PIECES AND
THE SIDES THAT ARE SERVED (TOAST AND FRUIT AND A MEAT
ARE RECOMMENDED)

12 eggs, beaten
1 cup milk
½ teaspoon prepared mustard
2 tablespoons melted butter
½ to 1 cup grated cheese (we used American cheese growing up, but now I
  use cheddar)
Salt and freshly ground black pepper

Preheat the oven to 350°F and grease a 9 × 13-inch baking pan.

Combine all the ingredients in a large bowl. Pour the mixture into the prepared pan. Place in the oven and bake for 30 minutes until set. Remove from the oven and serve.

My mother's note: You may add cut-up ham or hash browns with peppers.

My note: You may add chicken sausage and a few cut-up boiled potatoes.

A CASE FOR SOUL FOOD

DEESHA PHILYAW

When I was kid, spinach came in cans, dark green slop with a suspect aroma. Collard greens were cooked with fatback or ham hocks for Sunday dinner, and my grandmother slathered the occasional midweek string beans with mayonnaise. The nonstarchy vegetables of my childhood were woefully overcooked and mostly afterthoughts. I didn't have broccoli that wasn't grayish and limp until I left my native Florida for college in the Northeast. My family went on a salad kick when I was in junior high, but the iceberg we ate has the lowest nutritional value of all lettuce.

When I was expecting my first child, I made the decision to feed my newly pregnant body better. Now, over a decade later, my eating and cooking habits remain radically different from those I developed during my childhood. Now I buy fresh spinach at the organic grocery store. I've also added Brussels sprouts—something I'd only ever heard of on eighties sitcoms—to our dinner menu.

Given this history, I considered it a triumph when my older daughter, Taylor, then nine, built her own salad on a bed of romaine. My girls have healthier eating habits than I had at their ages—or even in my early twenties. I've helped them become savvy eaters and consumers, less susceptible to the lure of junk food and its attendant marketing. But watching Taylor decide between kidney beans and garbanzo beans—with the garbanzos on the losing end because of the "slime" factor—I realized just how far from my Southern soul food roots I have traveled. I saw, too, that these roots could wither and die with me.

Wellness, by some measures, comes at a price. It costs more to eat healthier, to buy organic instead of conventional foods, or to create a home-cooked meal instead of ordering off a fast-food chain's ninety-nine-cent "value" menu. But these are the conventional arguments. I go further, measuring the cost of my family's healthier lifestyle in the currency of cultural touchstones and family lore, not just dollars.

To wit: The fried chicken at B's, a local, family-owned restaurant, tastes just like my grandmother Nay-Nay's chicken. The sight and smell of it make me nostalgic and mournful. If memory and wanting were all that mattered, I would eat at B's every day. Instead, I treat my family and houseguests to B's wings a few times a year, and rather than dwelling on the salt and the fat, I reminisce. I remember how Nay-Nay made a science of frying chicken—science that tasted like art.

Nay-Nay was the resident fried chicken expert in our family; my mother prided herself on what I call "blackaroni and cheese." Growing up, I saw white families in commercials eating Day-Glo orange macaroni and cheese out of a box. This looked nothing like the macaroni and cheese I was used to eating: casserole-style pasta made with three cheeses, butter, eggs, and evaporated milk. It pains me that my children have eaten organic mac and cheese out of a box twenty-five times more often than they have eaten blackaroni and cheese. When I do make blackaroni and cheese, my girls rank the box stuff a close second: too close for my comfort and my cultural and culinary pride.

Most of the time, I don't think about the cultural costs of feeding my children the way I do. But there are moments when the cost looms large and problematic. One time, Taylor asked me, "What's soul food?" I was stunned. How could *my* child not know about soul food? I responded by rattling off the names of foods I'd made before and that she'd eaten on visits to our family in Florida. Giving examples still didn't explain what soul food was. I felt sad, at a loss for words to convey the personal significance of foods we rarely ate.

I have tallied it up and decided that this is a price I'm willing to pay for my children's good health. But I also wondered if good health and embracing our heritage must be mutually exclusive. With some creativity and flexibility, could I plant my culinary roots in different ground?

Growing up in the 1970s, food was an Experience in my family and in the community of black folks to which I belonged. Eating and cooking weren't just about staving off hunger; they were celebration, culture, and identity.

Feeding people was an act of love. To refuse a home-cooked meal was a slap in the face to the cook. A child known to be a picky eater was considered spoiled and ungrateful, her parents indulgent and negligent. "Good" eaters, like me, had hearty appetites and cleaned our plates; we reflected well on our parents.

A woman who had a reputation for knowing her way around the kitchen—"She put her foot in those greens!" or "Her pound cake will make your tongue slap your tonsils!"—could be the biggest gossip or liar, but her cooking forgave a multitude of sins. Conversely, a black woman with a reputation for being a bad cook was viewed as a sort of freak of nature, an object of pity and occasional ridicule. She would find herself with lots of no-shows and leftovers on Thanksgiving. At family get-togethers, she would be asked to contribute paper products and drinks.

My paternal Grandma Pauline was well-known for her cooking. Bountiful Sunday dinners drew three generations to her house every week. Before she went to church on Sunday morning, Grandma would make barbecue or fried chicken; boiled or fried cabbage; rice and gravy; black-aroni and cheese; candied yams; cornbread; and maybe banana pudding or a German chocolate cake for dessert. After church, Grandma, Granddaddy, and various members of their brood would gather around the table, most of us kicking our shoes off before digging in. Weekday dinners at Grandma's were impressive in their own right: smothered pork chops or fried liver and onions, with mashed potatoes and gravy, green peas, and biscuits.

My grandmothers, my mother, and practically every black woman I knew cooked big, delicious spreads, almost daily, and effortlessly, it seemed. Even when they ate at someone else's table, they often cooked their own meal at home, either out of habit or to make sure they could fix a plate for anyone who happened to stop by unannounced. Those were the days before cell phones, hyper-busy lives, and scheduled play dates, days when there was always an extra seat at the dinner table, just in case.

Those were also the days when a coffee can of used shortening was de rigueur in every household, conveniently located on the back of the stove or between the back burners. After frying, the used grease would be poured back into the can to solidify, and then scooped out and reused again and again. (A separate can was kept for fish grease.)

A few years ago, some friends and I reminisced about the grease cans. Like plastic slipcovers on living room furniture, stereo systems the size of small caskets, and the ubiquitous framed pictures of the Black Holy Trinity—Jesus, MLK, and JFK—the grease can was a hallmark of our childhoods, a reminder of simpler times.

My friends and I agreed that the absence of grease cans in our kitchens (and for the most part, the grease) marks the end of an era. Our kitchens are generally healthier places than the kitchens of our youth. Whole wheat bread replaces white. "Fat-free" is a familiar phrase on condiment labels. Turmeric, curry powder, and anise sit alongside Lawry's Seasoned Salt in our spice racks. Our kitchens reflect how we straddle two worlds: the present, where we are parents trying to raise healthy kids; and the past, where our parents and grandparents raised us the best they knew how, where kitchens were more than just places to cook and eat.

Nay-Nay was a natural teacher: patient and welcoming of my curiosity. When I asked, at age six, to be taught to cook, Nay-Nay insisted that she could not teach me directly, but that I would learn by watching closely as she maneuvered around the kitchen of our multigenerational household.

And she was right. When Nay-Nay finally let me try my hand at the stove at about age nine, I instinctively knew what to do. I had my share of mishaps, though, like the time I made a gravy that resembled white Play-Doh. Or when I tried to make peach cobbler with only half the ingredients I needed . . . in a tiny frying pan. "It's OK, baby," Nay-Nay said to me as she scraped the burnt mess into the garbage. "But I know you can do better than that."

Nay-Nay's response was always gentle, but she never wavered on what she called the Basics: *Don't be heavy-handed with the salt. Pay attention.*

Clean the kitchen as you go along. In time, I became a self-assured cook, worthy of privileges in Nay-Nay's kitchen.

A few things eluded me. I didn't learn to make a decent turkey neck gravy until just a few years ago; I'm much better at making crepes than I am at making cobblers; and I'd have to search online for a recipe for black-eyed peas the way Nay-Nay made them. But I grasped important stuff, like how high the gas flame should be under a pot of greens at different stages of cooking, and how long to cook potatoes for mashing versus for potato salad.

I learned by sight and taste how much and what type of seasoning to add to different dishes. Nay-Nay never measured anything, and I can't write down recipes for the dishes I make because I rarely measure anything either. My daughters will have to learn how much black pepper to sprinkle on homemade hash browns, and how much red bell pepper to add to three bunches of kale, by watching me.

Watching Nay-Nay, Grandma Pauline, and my mother cook and serve food taught me that eating and cooking were as much about good times, community, and handing down tradition and skill as they were about physical sustenance. Other than a full, happy belly and occasional indigestion, the physical consequences of our daily diet were rarely discussed when I was a child. No one ever talked outright about heart disease. When men in the family were diagnosed with high blood pressure we said they needed to "watch the salt." If they did start watching it, I never knew it. Grandma Pauline's diabetes, her "sugar," as she called it, was something mysterious and personal and seemingly had no bearing on how Grandma herself cooked and ate.

Ten years ago, my mother and Nay-Nay were diagnosed with breast cancer and colon cancer, respectively. They didn't change their eating habits significantly, despite my suggestions and offers regarding whole and organic foods. I felt helpless in the face of their resistance, and in hindsight, I believe I subconsciously started to mourn them, even as they began rounds and rounds of chemo and radiation, and though they would not succumb to the cancers for three years after diagnosis.

When my father died of a massive stroke that same year, I learned that he was not taking any of the three medications he'd been prescribed for high blood pressure. My last clear memory of him is of breakfast at his house when he proudly made fried whiting, grits, and homemade cat's head biscuits, so named for their size.

One argument against soul food—as if the high rate of hypertension, obesity, and heart disease among blacks isn't argument enough—is that it is an unfortunate legacy of American chattel slavery. Some culinary historians believe that the origins of soul food can be traced back to Africa as early as the fourteenth century. These foods—black-eyed peas, greens, and gumbo—were celebrated by the black liberation movement in the 1960s. But popular wisdom states that enslaved blacks had to make do with whatever ingredients they could find or scraps given to them by their masters—like leftover, undesirable parts of cows and pigs. Even today, some blacks still have a fondness for pigs' intestines, or chitlins (the dictionary calls them *chitterlings*). While eating the white man's rejects is hardly a legacy worth passing on to future generations, such eating—also known as "Southern poverty cooking"—is also cited as evidence of the slaves' resourcefulness, their artfulness at "makin' a way out of a no way," in the words of an old Negro spiritual.

Then I came across a slim pamphlet, "Domestic Cook Book: Containing a Careful Selection of Useful Receipts for the Kitchen," published in 1866 by Malinda Russell. This earliest known cookbook by a black woman details "complex, cosmopolitan food inspired by European cuisine"— *not* what we have come to know traditionally as soul food. It forced me to wonder: What if I had been settling for a narrow definition of our culinary heritage?

I imagine some naysayers would look askance at any suggestion that *soul food* cuisine is not synonymous with *black* cuisine. Is it so odd that black cuisine could be defined by its European influences, for example? We gave birth to jazz, blues, R&B, and rock and roll, so why should our cooking, itself an art form, be derivative?

On the flipside, I am also a big fan of broad definitions of "blackness," of how it's a social construct and yet inclusive of a powerful political movement and a rich cultural and social history. It bothers me when "blackness" is reduced to stereotypes promoted by small-minded people, some of them black.

So I considered Malinda Russell's cookbook—her recipes for puff pastry, rose cake, catfish fricassee, and sweet onion custard, with no mention of sweet potato pie or fried okra—and wondered if my desire to pass my soul food cooking prowess on to my daughters, however well meaning, is perpetuating a stereotype. After all, black folks have a long, and sometimes uncomfortable, public history with foods like fried chicken and watermelon. I know several black adults who won't eat either in "mixed" company because of infamous depictions of blacks as comically voracious consumers of these foods.

When my children are old enough to understand, we will talk about the unsavory social history associated with the fried chicken they enjoy so much. I will give them a heads-up about imagery that denigrates black people under the cloak of "nostalgia," but I will not teach them to shy away from publicly eating any foods they enjoy. To do so gives a victory to racists in their efforts to instill shame and fear, and to stifle freedom.

Malinda Russell's cookbook symbolizes freedom—the freedom to pick and choose and savor the best of what we find in our world. In light of her cookbook, I wondered, too, if I am more my mother's daughter than I realized, wanting to teach my girls *the* right "black" way to cook, which isn't very freeing at all.

I find myself at a crossroads about my food heritage: What to keep, and what to leave behind?

———

Some years ago at our house, we instituted monthly Soul Food Nights, evenings when I forget about calories and arteries. I take solace in the fact that I'm not telling my kids, "Black people *love* fried chicken, and this is the *right* way to fry it." Instead as I cook, I tell my girls stories about how Nay-Nay taught me to make the dishes we're having, and the ups and downs I experienced learning to cook as a child. I tell them to watch as I conjure memories with my hands. Watch, as I add just the right amount of garlic powder, Old Bay seasoning, Lawry's, and black pepper to the chicken. With Peyton standing on a chair and Taylor tall enough now not to need one, I hand them the shakers, so their hands can start to forge these memories.

Using water to test the grease first (if the drops set off sizzling, it's hot enough), we add the chicken, careful not to splash or to fry our fingertips. This takes skill and patience, both of which Peyton lacks. She huffs, convinced that the "white chicken" will never turn brown because it is taking too long.

Eventually, the transformation begins. As the chicken browns, the aroma reminds me of summertime, of playing in my backyard with friends who sniff Nay-Nay's cooking in the air and ask if they can stay for dinner; of Sundays after church; of bus trips to the beach, with fried chicken and biscuit lunches wrapped in aluminum foil.

Some of our new Soul Food "Nights" take place on Sunday afternoons. This early dinner means that the girls, who cook with me straight through lunchtime, are ravenous by the time we drain the oil from the chicken onto paper towels. We sit down quickly at the table, remembering how good the chicken is when eaten as hot as we can stand it.

I douse my chicken wings in hot sauce, and declare, as always, the skin the best part. Peyton agrees, but Taylor, who prefers drumsticks, does not. "The meat," she insists. "That's the best part. We made it juicy." Our fried chicken is good, but it's not quite Nay-Nay's. With each batch, though—a little more garlic powder maybe, the heat lower for slower cooking—we get closer.

One Sunday the girls and I admired the spread before us—potato salad, blackaroni and cheese, fried cabbage, biscuits—and I told them, "This is how your Grandma P. cooked, and how my grandmothers cooked. . . ." I am my children's only living link to my side of their family. There's no homestead to return to for the holidays, no reunions in the summertime; just sporadic visits to my mother's and grandmother's headstones. Besides fragile, fading photographs, food is the only tangible tie I can give my children to their roots—to their mama's people, as Nay-Nay would say. My girls keep eating, and I know I cannot feed them my childhood, my memories. I can only offer them a taste, and savor the new memories we're creating together.

BLACKARONI AND CHEESE

SERVES 6 TO 8

1 16-ounce box macaroni

½ cup (1 stick) butter, softened

13 ounces canned evaporated milk

1 egg, beaten

16 ounces sharp cheddar cheese, cubed

1 12-ounce box Velveeta cheese, sliced

½ cup chopped jalapeño peppers

Salt (I recommend Lawry's Seasoned Salt) and pepper

8 ounces mild cheddar cheese (or 8 ounces more sharp cheddar, depending on personal taste), grated, sliced, or cubed

Preheat the oven to 350°F. Cook the macaroni in a large saucepan of boiling water for about a minute less than instructed on the package.

Drain but do not rinse the macaroni. Return the macaroni to the saucepan while it is still hot. Turn the heat to medium-low and add the butter, milk, egg, sharp cheddar cheese, and Velveeta cheese.

Stir the macaroni mixture until the butter and cheeses are melted. Add the jalapeños and season with salt and pepper.

Pour the mixture into a large baking dish and top the macaroni with the mild cheddar cheese. Bake for about 35 minutes, until the top is browned.

RED SAUCE DAYS

CHRIS MALCOMB

When I was a child, my mother made her Italian red sauce once a month, waking the house with clanking metal pans and steel blades on the wooden cutting board. I would drift downstairs just as the warm kitchen started to fill with familiar scents: simmering salt pork, soup bones, onions, garlic, spices. She never measured anything, tossing ingredients into her dented metal pot on instinct. Before long, empty cans of tomatoes—whole, paste, and puree—littered the countertop like open clamshells, and the bubbling, blood-colored liquid had turned the white stovetop into a small Jackson Pollock painting. Once the sauce was boiling, my mother set the burner to "low" and left it to simmer for most of the day.

Later that evening, I would find her at the kitchen sink, bathed in the dim light of a single bulb, stooped over a food mill (or "strainer" as she called it). She used this instrument to grind the sauce to velvet smoothness, removing tomato seeds, pieces of bone, and strips of meat she hadn't already fished out by hand and popped into her mouth. When each batch was complete she poured it into tall, rectangular plastic containers. These she would seal, label, and hand to me to stack in the freezer.

I maintain a fantasy about the origins of my family's red sauce. A dark-eyed woman, her salt-and-pepper hair tied back in a bun, stands in the sunny kitchen of an Italian country cottage. On the grooved wooden table in front of her, she chops several plump, red Roma tomatoes and fresh sprigs of parsley from her garden. I see a little barefoot boy, my great-grandfather Pasquale, leaning over the table, chewing on a basil leaf while he watches his mother toss ingredients into a dented pot on the back of the stove. The kitchen fills with the aromas of simmering garlic, tomatoes, and olive oil. The boy absorbs it all, unaware that years later, in a faraway land, he will re-create the very sauce that was so essential to his childhood.

It's a comforting image, for sure. But is it true? "Well, I believe it *is* a traditional sauce," my grandfather Theodore Jeveli says, noting the similarities between the recipe he uses at the East Boston restaurant founded by Pasquale in 1924 and *ragù di carne*, the classic meat-and-tomato Neapolitan ragù from Italy's Campania region, our ancestral home. In that authentic ragù, filets of pork or beef are pounded and rolled, tied with butcher's string, cooked with the sauce, and then removed and served as a main course. The restaurant's sauce, however, calls for braised beef and pork bones—as well as trimmings and fats—for flavor only. After cooking, anything soft enough is ground into the final product; the rest is fished out and discarded.

I sometimes wonder what accounts for this difference. Did economics force my great-grandfather to alter the classic recipe after he emigrated to America? Or had he, in fact, never been exposed to *ragù di carne* while growing up, the price of choice meat putting it beyond his family's reach? Could his mother have actually been cooking a modified ragù, bones only, or even a marinara, no meat at all?

I won't ever learn the answers to these questions. My grandfather never spoke to his father about the sauce's origins, and even if Pasquale *was* re-creating a recipe—traditional Neapolitan or a family adaptation—his sauce was not immune to the evolution of a culinary heirloom passing between generations. He was making his red sauce on a new continent, after years of cooking in American hotel kitchens, which further separated it from its Campanian predecessor.

The family restaurant began as a thirty-seat diner in a corner storefront on Chelsea Street; it was called The Modern Lunch. The original clientele was mostly blue-collar, working-class immigrants, culled largely from the nearby docks, shipyards, and trolley yard. Pasquale fed them American diner fare—steaks and burgers—while dispensing a few basic side dishes like ziti, linguine, and spaghetti with meatballs, each topped with his version of the family red sauce. Yet while Pasquale may have blended traditional knowledge with his own, he was never cooking wholly "authentic" Italian food. He understood that survival meant adaptation, and that to remain purely Italian would have meant failure. So he kept things simple, avoiding the more cumbersome aspects of the old world—classic (and sometimes complicated) Campanian dishes like *risotto*, *gnocchi*, *gattò*, and *timballo*—and tailoring his efforts to the tastes of his new home (and the local Italians). Because his business was to feed people, the story of his red sauce became the story of our family in America. He may not have known it at the time, but my great-grandfather was participating in the invention of an entirely new cuisine—and a new *people*—both of which would come to be called, over time, Italian-American.

Pasquale ran The Modern Lunch for twenty-three years, often with help from his sons Armand, Eddie, Louis, and Theodore, who'd been born the year it opened. After Pasquale's death, Armand took the helm, but soon he and his brothers left to fight in the Second World War, leaving restaurant operations to various extended family members. He returned in 1945 and within a year had purchased another venue, down the street, which he called Armand's. Theodore, who had been working as an airline mechanic after his tour in the Navy, returned to help run this new restaurant. In 1950, Armand suffered a heart attack, stopped serving food at The Modern Lunch, and turned it into a bar. (The restaurant still possesses what may be one of Boston's oldest single-owner liquor licenses, dispensed shortly after Prohibition ended. "When the Depression hit," my grandfather says, "it was no doubt alcohol that kept us from going under.") When Armand died in 1957, my grandfather sold Armand's, bought The Modern Lunch from Armand's wife, and changed the name to Jeveli's Barbeque.

While the menu included some simple Italian staples, Jeveli's Barbeque was mostly a place for meat: tips, chops, chuck, sausages, cutlets, ribs. Most mornings found my grandfather in the basement, slicing up loins with a band saw and selecting the choicest cuts to be grilled over the charcoal pit and sold as that day's $1.99 special. "We were a business," he says, admitting that his early menus, like his father's before him, didn't completely honor his heritage. "Not everyone liked Italian food. You needed other stuff to get people in the door." The neighborhood agreed; customers flocked to the Barbeque.

In the late 1960s my grandfather made another calculated business shift: expansion. Fulfilling the dream hatched when he first took over The Modern Lunch, he purchased the adjoining building, knocked holes in the walls, and filled the space in between with covered archways. He built a new kitchen in the basement, dropped "Barbeque" from the restaurant name, and opened a 120-seat dining room called The Mediterranean Room. This new space allowed him to expand his menu, and he began serving some of the more familiar Italian dishes—*antipasti, manicotti, parmigiana, cacciatore*—that remain on the menu today.

Business boomed. Before long he was serving 250 during lunchtime and twice as many for dinner. Really good days brought nearly 1,200 people to Jeveli's. "There were lines out the door every night," says my mother, who worked part-time as a hostess during those years. "*Every* night."

Today The Mediterranean Room is a warm, carpeted space with handcrafted stained-glass lanterns and wide scallop-backed booths. The walls are marigold stucco, honey-toned wood, and multicolored brick. Scattered throughout the dining room are framed prints: the Ponte Vecchio in Florence, rolling Tuscan vineyards, sleek black gondolas bobbing in green Venetian canals. A third dining room was added in the 1980s, and later redecorated as The Presidential Room after Bill Clinton and his party of sixty dined there in the late 1990s. The original Modern Lunch space is now The Terminal J Lounge: a pub-style gathering place with flat-screen TVs and a Keno screen by the door. Recently Jeveli's was recognized as Boston's oldest family-owned Italian restaurant.

———————

My mother asked my grandfather for the red sauce recipe when she was sixteen. He gave her the fifty-gallon restaurant version, which she copied onto a small sheet of paper and stuffed into her wallet:

36 6 lb. 6 oz. cans ground tomatoes
12 6 lb. 6 oz. cans whole tomatoes in juice
6 6 lb. 6 oz. cans tomato paste
4 gallons water
20 lbs. "braised in oven" beef and pork bones
20 lbs. onions, chopped
10 heads of garlic, chopped
1 round box of salt
3 bunches of parsley, chopped
10 lbs. ground pork fat
20 lbs. beef trimmings

Sauté onions, garlic, and all trimmings. Add tomatoes and water. Simmer for four hours.

For the next thirty years, she carried it everywhere, taping its worn folds and retracing its penciled lines whenever necessary. When it finally became too fragile, she placed it between the pages of her Bible.

Her first attempts to make the sauce were failures. She struggled to reduce the portions to the few servings she wanted to ladle over some spaghetti for friends. Still, she persevered, learning to coax her own version out of her father's ingredients, eventually transforming it into the cornerstone of my childhood diet: ladling it over spaghetti, ziti, or penne; mixing it with browned beef for sloppy joes; warming it in white bowls for dipping bread; and, eventually, slathering it between the layers of her eggplant parmigiana (or "parm" in my family), the meal I have come to most associate with Jeveli's, and my mother.

––––––––––

Eggplant parmigiana is my true comfort food, the meal I most frequently request when I am home visiting my family. Even today I am amazed by how these simple ingredients morph into a taste far exceeding the sum of its parts. The individual flavors—sweet, tangy, earthy—blend effortlessly, revealing a different nuance with each bite. Whether dining with my grandparents in The Mediterranean Room or gathered in my mother's kitchen for a birthday meal, I have always considered this dish reliable, familiar, and unchanging.

Or so I thought.

One summer night as I was finishing up a heaping serving of her eggplant parm, I asked my mother where she bought her cheeses. The traditional recipe calls for a combination of fresh Parmesan and buffalo mozzarella between each layer of eggplant. "Oh, I don't use a mixture," she said casually.

"Wait . . . what?" I said.

She grinned. "I only use one cheese."

"Which one?"

"Provolone."

I set my fork on the plate. I wouldn't have been surprised if she'd said that she'd simply chosen *between* mozzarella and Parmesan—a decision befitting her cautious, yet loyal, rebelliousness—but she'd dropped not one but *two* ingredients. *Defining* ingredients.

"But I thought—"

"That I never changed my father's recipes?"

"Yeah."

"But mine's better, right?"

I wasn't about to answer. "Wait . . . what *other* recipes have you changed?"

She hesitated slightly before standing up and reaching across the table toward my empty plate. "Only one. And just a smidgen."

"One? *Which* one?"

She took my plate and headed toward the sink, laughing.

———

Growing up, I had no reason to question, or even care, if my mother's red sauce was unique. I liked the taste, and I assumed that recipes were recipes, no matter the kitchen or the cook. Now, however, I appreciate how the distinctive taste of her sauce is the product of both history and individuality. My mother's version *is* different from her father's. And while it may share similar roots, it's also not the sauce that Pasquale made in 1924, or that may have bubbled on his mother's stove back in Italy. This, I think, is the true beauty of any family recipe, the cook's ability to blend tradition and personality. My mother not only learned the family recipe, but also made it her own. Just like her father, and just like her grandfather. In doing so, she cemented her position in a line of forward thinkers and risk-takers, people who found a way to both adapt and retain a cultural tradition.

Recently I asked my mother for her red sauce recipe.

"Not if you plan on trying to improve it," she said, half joking.

We chuckled at the irony, knowing that my ties to the "old world" must start in her kitchen but certainly cannot end there.

And so we're formulating a plan for her next visit. First, we'll go shopping: for fresh onions, spices, and cans of tomatoes—whole, paste, puree. At the meat counter, she'll teach me to select the best soup bones and salt pork (she doesn't use fat or trimmings). The next morning, we'll rise early. I'll chop and sauté. I'll open and empty the cans. I'll get everything simmering.

And then I'll do something that my grandfather has never done.

"The carrot goes in right at the beginning," my mother finally told me on the phone the other day. "It keeps the acidity down. It makes the sauce just about perfect."

So in it will go—a whole carrot—just like she's been doing for forty years.

While the sauce is bubbling, I'll visit the kitchen to admire the red dots gathering on my stovetop. I'll ask my mother to retell my favorite family stories: about the time she dropped an entire pot of spaghetti on Jeveli's kitchen floor; about the garlicky meatball she ate while sitting in the circular booth in The Mediterranean Room the day before I was born, the one that—family legend has it—sent her into labor.

Later I'll pour her a glass of red wine, flip on the bulb above my sink, roll up my sleeves, and begin straining my first batch of the family red sauce. I won't let her help. After I'm done pouring the smooth sauce into plastic containers, I'll ask her to do one thing: stack them in the freezer. Most of them. We'll save one in the refrigerator, for the next day's eggplant parm.

MOM'S EGGPLANT PARM

Vegetable oil

2 medium eggplants

2 cups milk

2 cups all-purpose flour

5 eggs, lightly beaten

2 8-ounce packages sliced provolone cheese (mild, not sharp)

2 pints Mom's Red Sauce (recipe follows), more if you want to serve some
on the side (Mom uses 1 to 1½ quarts), warmed

Special equipment needed:

*2-quart, round, flat-bottomed Pyrex casserole dish with lid (or a square
dish)*

Brown paper bags

10 × 10-inch electric skillet

*Note: An electric skillet is ideal for keeping a consistent frying tempera-
ture. If you don't have one, heat the oil in a regular skillet to between 275
and 325°F, checking the temperature with a candy thermometer.*

Cut brown paper bags to make sheets and set aside.

Heat 1 cup vegetable oil in an electric skillet set at between 275
and 325°F, about an inch deep to start with.

Peel the eggplant and slice it ¼ inch thick.

Fill three soup-plate-sized bowls, one with milk, one with flour,
and one with the beaten egg (you can add a little milk to the egg to
stretch it). If you can't fit all the ingredients in your bowls right
away, you may reserve half of the milk, flour, and egg and replenish
bowls as needed. Dredge each slice of eggplant in milk, flour, then
egg, in that order.

Place the eggplant slices in the hot oil and fry each side until
golden, about 2 minutes on each side. Transfer the slices to the paper bag sheet. Cover each layer with another paper bag sheet. Continue frying the eggplant slices until they are all cooked.

Add more milk, flour, and egg to bowls as needed. Add more oil to the pan as needed, letting the oil reach temperature before continuing cooking.

When the last slice of eggplant has been fried, place a final sheet of brown paper on top of the stack of eggplant. Let it sit for a few minutes to absorb the grease. Preheat the oven to 350°F.

ASSEMBLING THE EGGPLANT PARM

You will need:

    Cooked eggplant

    Warmed sauce

    Provolone cheese, enough to cover each layer of egg plant

Spoon a layer of sauce over the bottom of the baking dish.

Cover the sauce with a layer of eggplant, gently pushing it down into the dish.

Cover the eggplant layer with between 1 and 2 slices of cheese (I use round provolone, and depending on the size of the bowl, I generally end up using 1½ slices).

Add another layer of sauce. Continue the above layering until all the eggplant is used, ending with a final layer of sauce.

Cover the dish and bake until bubbly, about 1 hour. Serve warmed extra sauce on the side.

Note: You can also assemble this in a flat baking dish, like a lasagna, which does not make many layers. I prefer to make it with many layers, tall and round.

MOM'S RED SAUCE

Note: Do not try making this recipe without your mom.

Makes about 10 quarts

½ cup vegetable or olive oil

2 large onions, chopped

½ cup chopped salt pork

About 2 pounds beef soup bones

¼ cup dried oregano

¼ cup dried parsley

¼ cup dried marjoram

1 tablespoon ground black pepper

2 shakes of garlic powder

2 bay leaves

9 28-ounce cans crushed tomatoes (Mom likes Redpack and Pine Cone brands the best)

3 29-ounce cans Redpack tomato puree

1 6-ounce can Redpack or Contadina tomato paste

1 large carrot, unpeeled, with ends trimmed

Heat the oil in a large stockpot over medium heat. Add all the ingredients except the tomatoes and carrot. Cook, stirring constantly, about 10 minutes, until the onions are transparent and the bones are browned.

Pour the crushed tomatoes, tomato puree, and tomato paste into the pot.

Fill one empty 28-ounce tomato can one-quarter full with water. Swish the water around to loosen the liquid from the sides of the can. Pour this liquid into the next can. Repeat. Continue pouring the same liquid from can to can until the insides of all cans have been washed. Pour this tomato water into the pot with the sauce.

Add the carrot. Turn up the heat to bring the sauce to a very soft boil, stirring frequently. Once the sauce starts to boil, lower the heat so the sauce cooks just above a simmer. Cook, uncovered, for 8 to 10 hours, stirring the sauce two or three times an hour.

After 8 to 10 hours, let the sauce cool to a warm temperature (don't let it get cold, as that will make it harder to grind).

Remove the carrot. Attach a food mill to the rim of a second large stockpot; place the stockpot and mill on the counter or in the sink. Grind the sauce in small batches, passing bits of meat through the mill but leaving soup bones in the original stockpot.

Reserve 2 to 2½ quarts for the eggplant parm. Pour the rest of the sauce into lidded storage containers and place in the freezer.

LOBSTER LESSONS

ALEKSANDRA CRAPANZANO

Rituals are at once burdens and gifts; this is what makes them worth doing, and having, and keeping. It was a remarkable old woman who taught me this lesson—and how, along the way, not to cook a lobster—and I will never forget it.

John and I had been together a year. I had met his parents and he'd met mine. We had moved in together, traveled together, eaten great meals together, but we had not yet settled into (how could we have?) any enduring rituals. Then when summer arrived, it was time to get serious. Serious, for John, meant introducing me to a tiny beach cottage on the east coast of Nantucket, where he'd spent at least a part of every summer of his life; serious meant our spending a few weeks there with his permanent Other Woman, his great-aunt Margaret, whose cottage it was.

Eighty-two years old and a legend in children's book publishing, Margaret, John had warned me, was a creature of habit. To be precise, dietary habit. I'd already heard tales of her spartan daily regimen, which consisted largely of grapefruit (three), skim milk (two tall glasses), and a tuna-fish sandwich. Dinner was, without variation and without fail, a cold chicken leg (boiled), two red potatoes (also boiled), and a pile of grayish green beans (ditto). I was twenty-one that summer, already something of a food snob, and spartan wasn't really in my repertoire.

The first sign of a new world order came on the day we were supposed to pick Margaret up at the ferry terminal. John, who had never before shown the least interest in cooking, suddenly declared, in the voice of an anxious sergeant, that he knew what his aunt liked to eat and how she liked to eat it—and that while we were all cohabiting, he would take charge of the meals, if that was all right with me. I watched in horror as he filled an entire shopping cart at the A&P with water-packed tuna and low-fat mayonnaise. When I reached for a head of garlic, he simply shook his head in dismay, sensing perhaps the inevitable clash of palates in two of the women he loved best. But it was the margarine that almost brought our relationship to an early end. It would be months before we again crossed the threshold of a supermarket together.

From that first dinner with Margaret in her cottage, I remember her smiling at me as the three of us clinked glasses over the table, making me feel wonderfully welcome. But the food itself? Let's just say that, as with any real trauma, the details are buried deep in my psyche.

The following day, I walked up from the beach to find John waiting for me in Margaret's cherry-red 1967 Buick convertible. "Let's go get the lobsters," he called out over the noisy engine. This was promising. I hopped in. Lobsters, corn on the cob, and baked potatoes: It would be messy and buttery and fun. That evening, I was digging out an old T-shirt, knowing I'd be sprayed and stained by dinner's end, when I looked up and caught sight of John through the window. He was stumbling up from the ocean, through the beach grass, weighted down by an enormous black lobster pot, the water sloshing out by the gallon and running down his legs. As he came up the porch steps, I asked him what he was doing. "If you want your lobsters to taste of the ocean, you have to cook them in ocean water," he explained. Margaret, I learned, had been cooking lobsters this way all her life, as had her parents. It was hard to think of refuting the idea, even when John described the hours and boxes of Brillo it would take to scrub the pot clean.

The smell of boiling brine brought me into the kitchen, where I found Margaret and John standing at the stove. John was holding the lid down on the steaming pot so the lobsters, despite their desperate tail-banging, couldn't escape. Margaret had her hand on top of his and was pressing down with her frail fingers. Years ago, when John was a boy, it would have been Margaret's strength that kept the lid in place. Roles had reversed, but they were still a team. Yet something was terribly wrong. The minutes were ticking by, and the lobsters were still boiling away in the pot. I waited and waited, biting my tongue. After a full twenty-three minutes—not a second more nor less by the stovetop timer—Margaret gave the word and John removed the ruined creatures with a long pair of tongs.

As I silently mourned the soggy ruins on my plate, Margaret washed hers down with plenty of white wine and began telling marvelous stories. She'd been coming to Nantucket since the 1920s and told of riding her bicycle as a girl to fetch ice for her mother's icebox, five miles each way. On sunny days, the ice would start to melt and drip from the basket down her legs and between her toes. She told of the winter when the kitchen—an old farmer's shed—had been drawn by sled all the way across a frozen Sesachacha Pond and attached to the cottage. She told of volunteering in London during the Blitz, when food was rationed, and of the magical day a friend brought a dozen fresh eggs to her as a rare gift. So rare that all her friends and neighbors showed up for a spontaneous "fresh eggs party." As Margaret scrambled them over a makeshift stove, an air-raid siren wailed, but no one left to take shelter. Not before savoring a taste of peace. Not before remembering a better time.

Now, more than fifty years later, at the end of our dinner, Margaret dabbed her lips dry, set down her checkered napkin, and heartily proclaimed: "These lobsters are the best I've ever had." Cheeks rosy from the sun, a glass of wine in hand, her merry blue eyes full of wonder, she seemed impossibly young—and I was smitten.

The thought of those scrambled eggs kept me awake that night. For fifty years, Margaret had held their taste in her memory. Clearly she had an appetite for something beyond her boiled regimen. I decided to feed that hunger and, the very next day, took over the kitchen.

If my plan was to work, I reasoned, I needed to find inspiration, rather than dread, in Margaret's usual fare of milk, tuna, and a narrow range of boiled things. That first night, I simmered a loin of pork in milk with a few sage leaves, a little lemon zest, and a hidden clove of garlic: A dish so comforting and mild, it tasted of childhood. Margaret was transfixed by the golden curdles of milk in the sauce and seemed to suspect me of alchemy. I said nothing to dissuade her of this lovely hypothesis. *Vitello tonnato* for lunch the next day satisfied her need for her daily ration of tuna and begged for a bottle of rosé and a sleepy afternoon. Vacation had finally begun. *Boeuf à la ficelle* had us discussing the health virtues of boiling, and John watched in disbelief as Margaret took, with an enthusiasm bordering on compulsion, to the cornichons I'd set out.

Dinner by dinner, I moved slowly through the classics, rewriting the parameters of Margaret's diet. And while it was sometimes a burden to cook for her, it was also a joy. She responded to good food with an appetite some eighty years in the making but still girlish in its pleasure. I had, it seemed, opened a Pandora's box of tastes.

The following summer, an actual box arrived from Margaret's office the day before her arrival—this one sent via FedEx and containing dozens of recipes that Margaret had clipped from newspapers and magazines throughout the winter months. A short note was attached, in which she expressed her hope that I'd want to take a crack at all of them. With no fancy appliances, no gadgets, a single sharp knife, and a colander with only one remaining leg, I cooked every single dish. It was the stuff of fantasy—asparagus flan and summer pudding, oyster chowder and strawberry soup. Margaret kept religious track of them all, noting the ones she particularly liked and filing them away for future summers. It never occurred to her that she might take a recipe home to New York and try it over the winter. Habits might be broken on holiday, but Labor Day returned life to its proper austerity. Still, the thought of Margaret clipping away—dreaming, really—through the long, cold months conjured the irrepressible hope of a love affair.

The years went by and Margaret's age finally took its long-delayed toll. There was the first summer she could no longer walk the fifty feet to the beach. She'd sit on the porch steps staring at that small, insurmountable distance. And then the summer when her hands were no longer strong enough to crack a lobster shell. John tenderly took the lobster from her, cracked it, and gave it back, continuing the conversation all the while. At the end of dinner, with undiminished fervor, she declared it the best lobster she'd had yet. By then, I'd learned that she graced every lobster dinner with those same words.

Margaret's impatience with her weakening body inevitably turned outward. At five o'clock sharp, she would stomp her cane and call out from the porch: "It's time for a drink!" John and I would scurry, leaving computers, work, sentences half-written—John to get white wine from the fridge, me to get the requisite peanuts. We were older, our obligations had multiplied, summers no longer stretched into fall. Our own frustrations occasionally began to simmer.

One night in particular has stayed with me. Margaret had just arrived, and we were to have our annual lobster feast. It had taken me ten years to scale the boiling time down to a palatable twelve or thirteen minutes, and I'd permanently replaced the dreaded margarine with actual butter. But change is not always a friend. John was in the throes of finishing a new novel and had been at his desk, writing, a solid ten hours by the time he broke for the day. Showered, eager for a glass of wine, he'd already put on fresh khakis, uncorked a good bottle, and settled into the Kennedy Rocker when Margaret appeared with the lobster pot.

The wind was up and we could all hear the ocean roaring on the beach. John asked if this once we might use salted tap water. Margaret's response was a simple enough "No," but the indignation in her voice was unmistakable. John was silent—and as angry as I'd ever seen him. "It just won't do," added Margaret, impatiently tapping her cane on the floor. But John was already rolling up his pants to perform his time-honored chore.

The water was freezing and the sky steel-gray that evening. Margaret sat down on the porch steps and watched John disappear over the dune. I observed her from a few feet away. Far from victorious, she seemed to be questioning herself, wondering, no doubt, if time had made her ways too fixed, irrelevant. I took a seat next to her. Stupidly, I tried to tell her that she was right, even Jasper White, the great New England chef, called for cooking lobsters in ocean water. But that was hardly the point. It was, of course, the ritual, in all its effort, that mattered. It set the meal squarely in her history, some ninety years of it by then, and set it apart from other days and other meals.

John came up the porch steps, bent over his burden. Margaret, surprising us mightily, conceded that next time we might try tap water, but John shook his head. It wouldn't be the same. And seeing him standing there, soaking wet but smiling, his arms trembling under the weight of the huge lobster pot filled with fresh seawater from the Atlantic Ocean, I couldn't help but agree. At the end of dinner, Margaret, true to herself, rose to the occasion—she declared her lobster the very best she'd ever eaten.

This summer Margaret will be ninety-seven. She'll come to Nantucket with a caretaker, an oxygen tank, and a wheelchair. Her short-term memory is under assault, but the past she remembers with intense feeling. Traditions are more important to her than ever. They connect our family. John and I now have a little boy and a large dog. When it's time to collect the ocean water, I imagine I'll give our son a bucket and Margaret and I will watch him traipse after his father, learning the way we have always cooked lobsters.

PORK COOKED IN MILK

This is a tasty dish but not a pretty one. Garnish as you see fit with additional lemon zest and sage leaves. Serve with egg noodles or rice.

SERVES 6

3 pounds pork loin, tied by butcher
2 teaspoons ground sage
2 teaspoons sea salt, preferably Maldon
Freshly ground pepper
1 tablespoon grapeseed or olive oil
6 sprigs of fresh sage
1 to 5 cloves garlic
2 cups heavy cream
1 cup full-fat organic milk
Grated zest of 1 lemon

Rub the ground sage, salt, and pepper into the pork loin and leave to absorb the flavors overnight in the fridge in a large zip-top bag, with the air squeezed out.

Heat a large oval Dutch oven over medium-high heat for 1 minute. Add the oil and tilt the pot so that the oil forms a thin layer over the bottom. Heat another minute, then add the pork, fat side down, and brown. This should take about 20 minutes, estimating about 4 to 5 minutes per side and ends. When the pork is crusted in a rich gold, remove it. Discard the fat from the pot.

Return the pot to the heat and add the fresh sage, garlic, cream, milk, and lemon zest. Bring to a simmer. Return the pork to the pot and return to a simmer. Partially cover and cook until the pork reaches 145°F. This should take about 1 hour and 15 minutes.

Resist the urge to touch the pork while it's cooking. As I mentioned, this is not a pretty dish. The milk curdles, but once those curdles thicken, they turn to a blissful custard. If the curdles have

not thickened to your liking by the time the pork has cooked, simply remove the pork and continue cooking the liquid.

Serve with custard in a gravy boat.

KOSHER. OR NOT.

BARBARA RUSHKOFF

I grew up in a kosher home. We had the whole deal: two sets of silverware, dishes, and cups; no pig products; McDonald's rarely and only on paper plates so it didn't really count. The first time I accidentally ate ham I was six years old, playing at Linda Horn's house surrounded by her enormous family. I gagged on it as if I instinctively knew it was against my religion. I will never forget the stone-cold faces of the Horns when I asked them what kind of salami I just choked on. Did they see me spit it out and hide it in the chair? Were they thinking, "Poor little Jewish girl"? Or was it just me?

Being kosher and eating off special plates and silverware was never explained to me. It's just the way it was. "Do as I say!" was the golden rule, and my siblings and I pretty much did. My six-year-old is not so compliant. We were the only Jewish family on our street, and I think my parents were extra-vigilant about following Jewish laws because of it. They wanted me to know where I came from and to be proud of who I was. Back then, all I understood was G-d forbid I used the wrong fork.

KOSHER REFRESHER COURSE

· Separate tableware is one of the hallmarks of kosher guidelines, which date back to Adam and Eve (who didn't use any tableware at all). But after the flood and Noah's Ark, G-d decided that if the people wanted to eat meat, they'd have to do it in a very ritualistic way, and there were about 493 newer rules to obey if one wanted to chew the flesh. The main dictum was that you can't mix milk and meat. Exodus and Deuteronomy substantiate this: "You shall not cook a kid in its mother's milk." Hence, a cheeseburger, the most delicious diner meal in the world, is banned.

- Meat and milk cannot be cooked together, either. Kosher homes maintain two sets of silverware, glasses, dishes and cookware—one for milk products and one for meat—to prevent any accidental mixing. Because you can't be too careful.
- Certain animals cannot be eaten at all. Birds of prey can't be eaten because they are vicious creatures and you'd be ingesting their bad karma, but they're not usually on the menu (roasted condor, anyone?). Only animals that chew their cuds and have split hooves can be eaten, and only after proper and humane slaughter. Blood must be drained to prevent growth of bacteria, and kosher meat can come only from animals without health problems.
- Foods that are neither meat nor milk, such as vegetables, fruit, or fish, are called *parve*. These are the Switzerlands of kosher foods. Fish is tricky. It can be consumed directly before or after both meat and milk but may not be mixed with meat or even eaten on the same plate as meat. Got that?
- Kosher people cannot eat shellfish, lobsters, or crabs; they can only eat sea creatures with fins and scales, such as tuna, carp, salmon, and herring. For some reason gefilte fish is OK. Reconstituted fish in a jar? Totally fine. Linguine in clam sauce? No, I'm afraid not.
- And if *parve* food is cooked in cookware deemed only for meat, then it automatically can only be eaten with a meat-laden meal (and if cooked in a dairy pot, then same deal). But, then you have to wait. There are varying opinions on how long to wait (a matter of hours) before ingesting meat or dairy after the other. I'd attempt to explain . . . but is your head spinning?

Maybe it's time for some wine. There are rules about that, too.

- Orthodox Jews will not drink wine produced by non-Jews. Period. The reason for this goes back to pagan times, when wine was used for idolatrous purposes. There are loopholes, however, and pasteurized wine, which falls under the category of "cooked wine," is OK. I don't think about this too much when purchasing wine today, as I tend to head for the organic section (sulfates give me a headache), where I also get my meat.

Confession: I buy a lot of meat. Unkosher meat.

You see, I have a six-year-old who eats about ten things. Nine of those things are meat-related. It is very important for me to feed her organic meat, that is, meat without hormones or pesticides, killed in a humane way. This is sounding familiar, no? And while I am not kosher—remember, *I am not kosher*—it is ingrained in me that our meat must be as close to kosher as I can get. Grass-fed beef from cows raised humanely by family farmers: That's how we're doing meat in our family today.

While I am flouting kosher rules, I should also mention that sometimes my daughter has yogurt for dessert. An adventurous eater she is not, so when she decides to have yogurt after her organic chicken nugget entree, I am thrilled. We are working on this dilemma.

So, why do so many people keep kosher? Some Jewish laws are without a reason, and kosher is one of them. It just is. You just do it. Many Jews believe in keeping kosher because it is part of a covenant with G-d. Others feel that the Jewish people have a mission to repair the world, and the special diet reminds them of their mission. In Deuteronomy 14:2–4, the Torah calls Jews a "holy people" and prescribes a holy diet. Jewish mysticism also teaches that nonkosher food blocks the spiritual potential of the soul. According to the Kabbalah, properly offed kosher animals have more "sparks of holiness." The Torah vehemently prohibits cruelty to animals. In the old days animals were literally torn apart, so killing them in the most painless way possible is an improvement, although vegetarians will not find this comforting. So there are many valid, humane, and hygienic reasons to keep kosher. And keeping kosher does teach sensitivity to animals, before you eat them with ketchup anyway.

When I look back on my childhood now, I realize that we ate a whole bunch of other stuff that definitely was not down by kosher laws. We ate shrimp cocktail at the local diner all the time. And that is wrong. We knew it was wrong, but we ate it. I used to ask my mother why we couldn't have those yummy Howard Johnson's fried clams, and she said that they weren't kosher because they are "scavengers of the sea and they eat trash." I still picture those little shrimp and those clams eating their garbage. Delicious, unkosher garbage.

Frankly, we weren't kosher at all, were we? Being partly kosher doesn't count. We ate spareribs from the Chinese restaurant on Christmas. Those jaunts to Burger King and that hidden pepperoni in the vegetable bin in the fridge (yes, I saw that, Mother!) mean that really, we weren't kosher. Being a little kosher is like being a little pregnant; there are no gray areas.

Kosher is a commitment taken very seriously in the Jewish community. Whether or not it was ingrained into me as a child that "we" don't eat pig, I still wouldn't eat bacon because I can't get over that it stays in your system for eight years (which is gross no matter how delectable it tastes).

I think that part is cultural; I don't have the bacon gene, and I'm OK with that. It also helps that I'm deathly allergic to shellfish and drinking milk with my meat just makes my stomach hurt. Kosher by default? Does that still count? No, according to Jewish law, it does not count. I do not make the cut. But according to me, being Jewish is tied to what I eat, or don't for that matter.

Some tell me that I don't know what I'm missing. Don't I know how heavenly bacon is, how divine shrimp scampi is? I'm sure they are fantastic, but there is something in me (besides my mother's voice yelling in my head, "Don't you dare eat that!") that stops me from going there. I'm trying to be the kind of parent who lets my child make her own choices—no ice cream for supper, though. I do hope that one day when she's all grown up and has me over for a meal she cooks for herself, it includes something green and healthy on the plate. And if she serves me a cheeseburger? Well, I'll eat it. Kosher is relative. But I might ask for it on a paper plate.

MY MOTHER'S BRISKET

My mom is one of those people who can look at a pot simmering and just know what to throw in. Sure, she does her taste-testing along the way, but usually she's right on the money. Her brisket is the one dish that I can think about and almost taste. It is so good, so tender, so perfect, and the aroma of it when it is cooking is absolutely tantalizing. So, I'd like to share it with you.

The problem is that my mother cooks from intuition. With that, she mixes in stuff she's gleaned from newspapers (one year she threw a can of Coca-Cola on the brisket—it was surprisingly delicious) and whatever her memory serves. When I approached her about a recipe for her brisket I was met with some very vague instructions, along with some asides that got thrown in for good measure.

First: Get thee to a kosher butcher. "Get a brisket, not too big, not too small."

I wish I could tell you what not too big or not too small is, but you'll have to figure it out for yourself. Get one that has no fat through the middle. Ask the kosher butcher; he will know.

Once you get the brisket home, rinse it in cold water and sprinkle it with salt, pepper, and garlic to taste. I can't give you amounts. As my mother says, "You'll know."

Turn on your oven to 400°F. When I asked my mother if she was sure, she asked me if I had a hot oven. I think so. Ovens are hot, right?

Get a large red onion, slice it, and put it on the bottom of the roasting pan with the meat on top (fat side down). My mother pours two cans of au jus gravy over the whole thing and then something she calls Gravy Master.

"What's that?" I ask.

"It comes in a bottle," she says, not really helping me.

"How much do I use?"

"A little bit."

This is where I suggest nixing the Gravy Master and adding a packet of dry onion soup mix or a mixture of spices you like (example: paprika, garlic powder, salt, pepper). As I said, my mother used a can of Coca-Cola one year.

Cover the meat with a tight lid and put the meat in the oven. My mother likes to "start high" (400°F) and then turn it down after an hour of cooking to 375°F. It all depends on your oven, she says. She has a hot one. Do you?

Overall cooking time is 3 to 3½ hours. How do you know it's done? It's just one of those things that you "know." After 3 to 3½ hours it really *does* finish cooking, and it's perfect. Really.

And then, magically, you open the oven and have a wonderful brisket. Let it cool, slice, remove fat from the gravy, and serve. Enjoy!

FOOD FIGHT

NEAL POLLACK

For a while there, I had a food blog. It ran for several months in 2007 and 2008, on Epicurious.com. At the time, I was still somewhat well-known for my book *Alternadad*, a light satire about my attempts to raise a "cool" kid, so I was asked to post a few times a week about the topic of food and children. I found my preschool-aged son's food habits amusing and, as always, needed the money, so I said yes.

Looking back on the blog now, it reads less like something useful and more like the diary of a Southern California yuppie striver, late-aughts edition. I write about my son's predilection for frozen vegetables and about my attempts to find the best supermarket-brand *mochi*. In the posts, we go out for fish tacos and dim sum and generally avail ourselves of the rich banquet of international cuisine that Los Angeles (where we lived at the time) offers. My wife and I love food. We've tried, with some success, to get our son to appreciate it in all its rich, weird diversity. The blog aimed to get that across. It wasn't a work of art, but it had a cute, sweet, innocent quality, designed to offend no one.

That's not how it worked out.

Early on, I did a short piece about taking my son to Whole Foods, where we sampled cheese. "We're training Elijah for cheese snobbery," I wrote archly. In the piece, he ate a few different types, proclaimed of one, "This cheese is too boring for me," and then decided he liked one that was $17.99 a pound, which I didn't let him get because it was too expensive. That was pretty much the entire post. It ran about four hundred words.

Then Gawker attacked. In a post headlined, "Elijah Pollack Is Going to Be a Horror," the writer described my son as "big, big trouble in the making." He asked, "When is it OK to hate a four-year-old?" It continued, about my son: "He is essentially a formless mass that has been fashioned into what he is by his father. But if we were to come across a sculpture that resembled, for instance, a large penis, we would be remiss not to mention that fact simply because the statue was created by a sculptor and did not form itself."

At the time, Gawker had a bee in its pants about "hipster parents," a subgroup of which I was a convenient avatar and easy target. I responded with outrage at the fact that the writer had compared my son to a penis sculpture. The writer, figuring that this was a chance to make a name, took some more shots. Recriminations flew. Someone created a commenting persona with my son's name and began to post on Gawker. After about a month or so, the fire, having sucked all the oxygen away from the topic, burned itself out. The Internet stopped discussing whether or not my son was a "douchebag."

Years later, the pain has receded from having seen my son's innocence excoriated on the snarkiest gossip website. My food blog died many years ago. But a central question continues to plague me when I pick this particular memory-scab: What is it about food and kids that drives people so crazy?

No parenting topic is more divisive than food. For instance, you either let your kids watch TV or you don't. There aren't a lot of gray areas in that space: Some parents think it's OK in the morning, some restrict it to an hour or less a day, some have no restrictions at all, some only let their kids watch videos. For the most part, though, it doesn't matter and no one really cares.

Discipline is another area where parental responses are all over the board. Some are strict, and some are lenient. There are time-outs and groundings and losses of privilege. Kids run wild and kids sit quietly, but everyone pretty much agrees that even the greatest children can be merely hard-to-control to huge, life-destroying pains. We all do the best we can, goes the mantra. Most people, particularly those who have kids, extend their sympathies.

Not so when it comes to food. Except for maybe certain specialized subjects like vaccination, nothing makes parents, and their critics, sound more neurotic. If you want to bring on quick histrionics, write about your child's diet. The very mention of food habits invites the deluge. When the Gawker potshot about my son ran, it got a lot of comments, including this one: "My husband, an engineer, is quiet much of the time and mows our suburban lawn on Saturdays. He hates all cheese except American. Which he eats with potato chips, peanut butter, and pickles on white bread with mustard." Here I was, trying to teach my kid to eat like an adult, and adults who eat like children were criticizing me. If I'd opened up some kind of weird culture-war gap, I couldn't quite tell how to locate the fissure.

In the realm of Internet nastiness, that comment was very low on the scale, but it left its mark on me. So many value judgments are implied within: Dads should quietly do their chores and not complain. It's good to live in the suburbs. Both of these are arguable sentiments, even if they're far from my reality. But why would someone be considered a real man because he only eats processed cheese and the blandest possible lunch food? Of course, he's not, and neither is the snobbiest turophile who only consumes sustainably farmed vegetables and meats, makes his own pickles, and struts around like the cat who ate the heirloom canary. But people are insecure about their food choices. Or are they too secure? Their eating preferences blot out the sun and lead to a lot of online finger wagging and tongue clicking.

Both extremes can be harmful. The "We eat fast food four times a week and we're fine" crowd, which you can often find grumbling over newspaper articles about federal childhood nutrition standards, arrogantly and deliberately flouts guidelines that don't go far enough. They put their collective head in the sand and deny the very real public-health threat of childhood obesity. Conversely, some families swing the other way, refusing to eat anything "unhealthy" to the extent they turn their children into neurotics. A *New York Times* article in 2009 quoted an eating-disorder counselor as saying, "I have lots of children or adolescent clients or young adults who complain about how their parents micromanage their eating based on their own health standards and beliefs." There you have it.

Meanwhile, parents continue to thwack away at one another online, not to mention in quiet whispers on the playground, certain that their food way is the high road. Ever since my mini-war with the popular gossip site, I've been alert to this, and continually vexed. Though it's socially acceptable for parents to write or talk about their kids' accomplishments in the classroom or in sports or elsewhere, any comment about eating habits is seen as obnoxious.

But why is it OK for your kid to be a precocious reader or soccer player, but not be a good eater? Let's say your children eat all their broccoli, maybe even Chinese broccoli, *broccolini*, or broccoli rabe, and seem to enjoy the process. That's a legitimate point of pride for a parent. It's not a very interesting subject at parties, perhaps, but it's a nice thing. Or, if you've got a kid like mine, who tries beef stomach and chicken feet and has never met an edible tentacle he didn't like, shouldn't that be an acceptable topic of conversation, online or off?

Ideally, more people can relate to food talk than about more rarified childhood accomplishments. Not everyone knows what it's like to be a violin prodigy, but nearly everyone knows what it's like to go out for Chinese food. The problem isn't that we have food opinions and food stories, or even that we share them. It's that our opinions are, more often than not, tainted by harsh personal judgment. These come from our own insecurities at having not done enough as parents, or, even worse, at not having tried hard enough. So we lash out.

You'd have to be obtuse not to see that there's a crisis of childhood nutrition in this country. The evidence is overwhelming. At the same time, there's no reason to be nasty about parents who don't seem to feed their kids properly. Some of them don't have the information to make better choices. Others are weak-willed. And most of us—because no one makes good choices all the time—are just busy and overwhelmed, trying to get through each day as sanely and intelligently as possible, making the best decisions we can in a chaotic, unpredictable atmosphere where we suspect harsh judgment from other people is just around the corner.

The writer Lisa Belkin, in a February 2009 *New York Times Motherlode* blog post titled "Making Kids Crazy about Food," put it beautifully: "Food is just one facet of parenting where so many of us risk becoming dogmatic and extreme . . . 'I would never'—give my baby formula, give my child an Oreo or a Diet Coke, let my child watch THAT program, allow my child to act that way."

Of course, as often happens with such pieces, the comments were sane and measured, to the point where one commenter said, "Cue the comments about how well you feed your kids and give them what they want in moderation." Sure enough, 95 percent of the comments said that they stocked their pantries with whole, unprocessed foods, ate a variety of fruits and vegetables, didn't keep sweets or trans fats in the house, and then, occasionally, just for the hell of it, would go to IHOP or grab a bucket of fried chicken or make a batch of gooey brownies. Altogether these comments gave the impression of an America composed of verdant suburbs inhabited by nutritionally sound families, with *Fresh Air* always on the radio, allowing themselves just the occasional moral peccadillo like a well-dressed businessman letting a fart slip on the elevator up to work.

We don't know how our emotionally overwrought food environment is going to affect our kids. Yes, they should eat their vegetables and avoid processed sugars most if not all of the time. That's the same now as it was a hundred years ago. Our current plague of thirty-year-olds with type 2 diabetes shows, with sharp clarity, that what you put in your body as a kid has a big impact on your adult physical health. But as to whether or not our food choices for our children are going to turn them into hipster asshats, self-satisfied suburban patio men, boring automatons, bloated sugar pigs, or strung-out drug addicts: There's only so much we can control. As one commenter wrote on the now infamous, and now long-buried, post about my post: "Next up, wine appreciation. Flash forward thirty years: fat, constipated, and drunk, with red wine rings around his lips. *Tante belle cose!*"

Maybe that's the best we can hope for as parents. One day, our kids will be adults, and will make their own lousy choices about food and other things. But they might make a few good choices as well. We won't deserve the credit for those any more than we'll deserve the blame for their mistakes. But at least we'll know we gave them some good meals along the way.

RISOTTO WITH ZUCCHINI

ADAPTED FROM MARCELLA HAZAN'S *ESSENTIALS OF CLASSIC ITALIAN COOKING*

I decided to include this recipe because it's something in our dinner rotation that's drawn from an actual recipe, and it's something that Elijah will eat. A lot of our food is improvised. This is one meal that doesn't have to be.

SERVES 6, OR, IF YOU'RE LIKE OUR FAMILY, ABOUT 4

4 medium or 6 small zucchini
3 tablespoons coarsely chopped onion
1 teaspoon very finely chopped garlic
2 tablespoons olive oil
5 cups chicken broth, homemade if you have it
2 cups Arborio or other imported Italian risotto rice
2 tablespoons butter
1 cup freshly grated Parmigiano-Reggiano cheese, plus additional cheese
    for the table
Salt and freshly ground black pepper
1 tablespoon chopped fresh parsley

Essentially, we cut and clean the zucchini. Then we cook it with some onion and garlic in olive oil until it's browned.

Meanwhile, we make risotto. You know how it's done. Throw some steaming broth and some water in with the Arborio rice, a bit at a time, until the rice soaks up the broth. Then you keep adding more liquid and let the rice absorb the flavors. If we're looking for a wild party, we'll toss in some wine, too.

Add some butter and toss in the zucchini. The idea is that the zucchini eventually will vanish into the risotto. It'll become stringy, almost viscous. This is perfect for a kid, because then the vegetable hides itself and you don't have to play one of those stupid "tricks," disguising your food like Tinker Bell or whatever, to get your kid to eat his or her veggies.

Cook for a while, until the zucchini mixes in and the rice is tender. Add some butter and grated Parmigiano, the best quality you can get—the powdered stuff they sell at grocery stores does *not* count—season with salt and pepper, add the parsley, and serve piping hot, with more cheese on the side.

THE SWEET LIFE

KEITH BLANCHARD

My smile is hollow. Oh, the emotion is real enough: I am a happy husband and father, ensconced in suburban simplicity, fulfilled at work, lucky at love. The problem is my teeth: They are hollow. My smile is more or less cavities strung together now, a double-strand necklace of silver and gold beads draped over a few remaining stalactites and stalagmites of original tooth enamel.

How many root canals have I endured . . . seven? Nine? I honestly don't know anymore. I just sit back in that big easy chair next to that tray of drill bits and the unsmiling hygienist and let the magic gas whisk me away.

As much as I'd love to blame it on genetics, or half-assed HMO dentistry, I know the precise cause of this chronic decay. I have always known, because it's been with me all my life.

It's candy.

Sweet, sweet, candy. My sin, my soul . . . candy. Crunchy, nutty, chewy, ooey, sugary, flaky, sticky, gummy candy. Velvety nougat, crisp wafers, springy marshmallow. Caramel, the gooey essence of life: infinitely tensile, mortally adhesive. And good king chocolate, delight of the ancients, mmm, mmm manna for mortal mouths. So sweet on the tongue; but wormwood, dear reader, and bitter to the roots!

My affair with candy predates my wife, my kids, career, everything, and the history of my peppermint tryst is writ all over my jaw. Take #32, middle molar, lower left, which I shattered about ten years ago. Like so much of my mouth, it was already more filling than tooth, a shell so fragile that when I bit into that demon frozen candy bar it was like crushing an aluminum can.

A broken molar sends a shiver of nausea through your system, and I had to sit down or pass out. But that pain was nothing compared to the agony of *removing* the busted tooth. The emergency dentist had to continue breaking it to get it out, wailing away at it with a chisel. And then—oh, we're not done yet, folks—the chisel actually *slipped off and stabbed into my tender gum,* already bleeding in terror of precisely this.

I swore, at that moment, that I was off the sauce forever.

Until on the way out of the dentist's office, I saw a prominently placed bowl of lollipops. . . .

Can I trace the obsession? I came of age at a time when candy was about the only thing marketed to kids at all, and we ate it up—I mean the marketing—and happily regurgitated it. *When Mr. Goodbar met Peppermint Patty she let him touch her Mounds. He put his Chunky in her Bit-O-Honey and they had a Baby Ruth.* I watched those early Almond Joy ads ("Sometimes you feel like a nut . . .") spellbound; I wanted to lay me down naked atop that chilly white coconut bar and close my eyes and feel the hot liquid drizzling down, enveloping me in a blanket of chocolaty goodness.

The reader is sneering her lip in disgust. Does it sound like I don't know how sick this is?

Candy culture is alive for kids. We even had our own candy urban myths, back in the day. Mikey, the kid from that cereal ad, auto-asphyxiated from a deadly cocktail of Pop Rocks and soda . . . remember? And weren't there spider eggs in Bubble Yum? Today's playground must ring with similar discussions.

Our most sacred and profane holiday was Halloween. Obviously. It couldn't touch Christmas for total loot value, of course, but there was something so sneaky and wrong about the world turned upside down, gangs of kids roaming the streets and shaking down the neighborhood. For one glorious day I had a license to steal: three or four hours of efficient collection followed by weeks and weeks of obsessive reorganization of the spoils, brand by brand in soldierly rows, Kit Kats and Milky Ways in constellation, parading around a ragged bonfire of lollipops.

I know, I know: You have that exact memory, too; that is the essence of tradition. The trick is growing out of it.

Candy should not be irresistible to the adult palate. The tongue matures; it loses its taste for simple sweets and seeks out the aged and complex, Belgian ales and foie gras and Stilton and andouille sausage. Yet there they sit: bite-sized and colorful, waiting to be peeled out of their taut little packaging, adorable sugar bombs of temptation. It is pedophilia of the palate, the rocky road to ruin.

But when did shame ever drive away desire?

It's not the kind of compulsion that can be cured at the drugstore. Whatever physic you might find at the pharmacy and drop in your little red handbasket is undone completely by the time you reach the checkout. Right there beneath the registers, four feet high and spanning the length of the room, is the candy rack of all candy racks, a magical panorama splayed before you, positioned at the level of gut and groin, where the brain traditionally bows out of decision-making. You're six feet away, then five, then four, sleepwalking now.

"Next . . . who's next?" And then, from the clerk at the counter: "Did you find *everything you were looking for?*"

It's enough to make you pray for diabetes.

All that candy represents an awful lot of research and development for something so demonstrably useless. Candy has led to no breakthrough technologies, provided no miracle cures, saved no lives. It's barely even food; it just enters your body through the mouth like food. The nutrition statement the FDA requires on all edible products is absurd in this particular aisle, unless you are one of the approximately zero percent of Americans not getting enough refined sugar.

And yet it is a triumph of civilization nonetheless. I believe America will be remembered for her candy long after rock and roll fades and the last pair of blue jeans wears through at the knees. In its endless variety, candy perfectly expresses our nation's steadfast dedication to pointless decadence. *What giants were these,* future archaeologists will marvel, *who twisted red ropes of licorice, hid cherries in chocolate, painstakingly painted tiny "M's" on candy shells?* Our leaders are charlatans, business has hijacked the government, and wars spiral out of control. But we still make the Reese's Peanut Butter Cup, dammit . . . tell me that doesn't stir the red, white, and blue in your soul. What do they have in China, the People's Nutritious Breadwafer?

But I do fear for my kids.

This generation is more sedate than we were, growing up: more computer and videogames, less running around the neighborhood until dark. At the same time, candy technologists are still feverishly working round the clock, high on atomized sugar in the air, dreaming up new concoctions for the innocent. Gone are the simple ribbon candy and horehound of yesteryear; hello, Bertie Bott's Every Flavor Beans, in seven trillion flavors. (Try the earwax.) Every year the candy marketing machine gets bigger, slicker, more effective; it chugs along 24/7 now, and resistance is nearly impossible.

My wife thinks I am overthinking this. But what does she know? She hasn't got a sweet tooth in her head. Leslie is a passionate amateur nutritionist, a swami of soy, railing against trans fats and the evils of partial hydrogenation. Thankfully, she's also an incredibly creative cook who can transform a dirty heap of root vegetables and a pinch of oregano into a balm to melt your soul. She's not against candy per se, but it has no hold over her; she is immune to the sugar rush. She doesn't taste the danger like I do.

With her dietary sensibility and my fear, together we monitor our kids' candy consumption. We restrict the flow but don't choke it off. Keep it rare—a "treat"—and you keep it special, goes the theory, without going so far as to trigger gluttonous rebellion. I'll go further: Candy tastes better in small doses. Asceticism makes you strong; we're using this as a first lesson in the value of moderation, and it seems to be working. *When you can snatch the Milk Dud from my hand, it will be time for you to go.*

But we are the exception, it seems. Most parents seem to be of the "Ah, what harm can it do?" school. Everywhere we go, if there are kids in a house, there is a bowl of peanut M&M's on the piano. There are "goody bags" after every party now, a bucket of mints at every cash register. You can't get a damn ice cream now without them blending fifty kinds of candy into it. Bankers and dry cleaners rain lollipops into the open beaks of our chirping children.

Don't blame the drug . . . blame the pushers. Candy itself is innocent and pure of motive: a colorful array of small, prepackaged reward modules, available everywhere for self-administration. It's not good for you, but it damn sure makes you feel good, and that'll do just fine, thanks. For all its proud frivolity, candy has attained a sacramental value. To partake of it, as an adult, is to say, "I worked my butt off in that cubicle all day and I have *earned* this; NOBODY comes between me and my Jujubes."

And despite the peril, to restrict that reward to children seems wrong. Adult self-indulgence is usually an order of magnitude more dangerous than this, after all. When the alternative is a drunken road trip for unprotected sex, surely 'tis better to risk drowning in nostalgia and buttercream. Maybe candy is an important release valve for society, the cadmium rod that keeps the nuclear core from overheating, reminding the stressed and the overworked and the waiting-on-a-gun-permit that there is still good in the world. If a candy bar can bring a few moments of joy, what is the accumulation of that joy in a lifetime?

Maybe America's national good nature, second only to Canada's, is due in part to the ocean of candy we devour every year.

Or maybe my wife is right. I'm overthinking it. And maybe a mouthful of cavities is just a smile laced with silver and gold.

FRENCH TOAST SANDWICHES WITH TOFFEE-CHOCOLATE CRUMBLE

SERVES 2, OR 1 IF EXTREMELY HUNGOVER
(BUT YOU WILL REGRET IT LATER)

2 large eggs
2 tablespoons milk
1/4 teaspoon ground cinnamon
1 teaspoon sugar
1 tablespoon butter
4 slices day-old bread
1 toffee-chocolate bar (such as Heath Bar), chopped into small pieces
Maple syrup
Powdered sugar

Whisk the eggs and milk together in a pie plate or wide bowl.

In a separate small bowl, mix cinnamon and sugar, then add to egg mixture.

Melt the butter in a flat skillet over medium heat. Coat both sides of the bread with the egg mixture. Add the bread to the skillet. After 2 minutes or so, flip the bread to brown on the other side. Place one slice on each plate. Sprinkle toffee-chocolate crumbles evenly on each toast. Place the remaining slices on top and press down to slightly melt the chocolate. Add maple syrup and dust on powdered sugar. Enjoy!

Note: Resist the temptation to put the toffee-chocolate pieces on the French toast while it's still cooking; they melt and get too gooey (and could possibly form a space-age adhesive that will yank all your fillings out—trust me on this one).

RECIPE

PHYLLIS GRANT

Works best if your husband is out of town on business, your life feels barely manageable, a tenth load of barfy laundry is in the machine, and the escapist dreams are coming fast and furious about walking the streets of New York City by yourself with a camera, a sexy sundress, and kick-ass wedge sandals.

Note: Whatever you do, don't sit down. Just keep moving. Make some coffee. Perhaps eat some salty caramels. Remember the salve of cooking. And motherfucking get on it.

1. Fill a large pot with cold water. Add a handful of salt. Use your hand to swirl the water and dilute the salt. Lick your fingers. Keep adding salt until you taste the ocean.
2. Plug your kids into the television.
3. Lean over the sink to peel potatoes. Say fuck fuck fuck fuck over and over again. Try to untangle depression from fatigue from clumsiness from failure. Remind yourself that sleep deprivation is a form of torture. Stand up straight. Splash potatoes one at a time into the salty water. Slide pot onto the stove and crank the flame.
4. Bring your kids some ginger ale. Comment on how it's their fourth day missing school and of pouring rain. Decide it's very boring to talk about the weather. Try to make the conversation have more depth. Mention how hard it would be to be homeless in all this rain.

5. Feel tremendous relief that no one in your house has vomited within the past twelve hours. Knock on wood. Knock on your head.

6. Drain the potatoes. Splash boiling water on your hand. Acknowledge that until you get some sleep you should stay away from the garbage disposal and the car.

7. Press replay on your favorite One Eskimo song. Feel the guitar and the drums thud bounce fly all around your heart. Wonder who the lead singer is talking about when he sings *you've been my queen for longer than you know*. Slide down to the dirty floor. Blow away some onion skins and dog hair. Feel bummed that you've never climbed onto the back of a motorcycle or a horse and taken off into the sunset, arms wrapped around a body, ear pressed up to the back of a heart.

8. Jump to your feet as your son flies into the kitchen and asks *Mama so why is it that the homeless don't have money and they don't have food and they don't have a house and I don't understand why they can't just get some money but I do understand that they're lost I really do get that I do.* Explain as best you can with words like society and mental illness and drugs and addiction and responsibility and neglect. Remember that your son is only four.

9. Simmer asparagus tips in chicken stock. Announce to the empty kitchen that you plan to make a soup of the remaining asparagus stalks once everyone in the house is well. Strain liquid into a mug and hand it to your daughter. Tell her to *plug your nose and just get it down or I will have to take you to the hospital where they will probably stick you with a huge needle in order to feed you intravenously.*

10. Wash your favorite plate. Slice, spread out, and salt potatoes. Drop cooked asparagus tips onto the potatoes as if you're releasing Pick Up Stix. Add heaping spoonfuls of shallot vinaigrette. Blop crème fraîche down all over everything. Wipe some off your chest, your eyelid, your cheek.

11. Look at the plate and know that something is missing. Wonder if anyone is still reading your neglected food blog. Chop spring onions. Curse your dull knife. Drizzle some olive oil. Remember that everything is better topped with a poached egg.

12. Pick up the camera with your right hand. Ignore the ringing phone until you realize it's your husband. Secure the phone between your

left ear and shoulder. Embarrass your husband with a vivid description of what you're going to do to him in bed that night *if you ever get your ass home from Los Angeles because oh my god I'm drowning here my love I am I really am.*

13. Stop talking. Look through the viewfinder and focus on the front of the poached egg. Listen to your husband talk about his studio meeting. Note that the more activities you do at once, the more awake you feel. Trip out on your contentment.

14. Consider including wine in the photo. Admit how staged it always looks even though it's oh so real.

15. Tell your husband to pause his story and yell down the hall to Bella that *Dash is four and he needs to be allowed to be four and he still believes in magic and don't ruin it for him just like we didn't ruin it for you please Bella.*

16. Puncture the egg with your fork. Watch the yolk slide down all over the potatoes. Take a photo. Think about how much you'd like to throw your husband against the wall and kiss him. Almost drop the camera. Notice your heart is racing. Take more photos. Take a bite. And another. Eat everything. Lick the plate.

POTATO AND ASPARAGUS SALAD WITH CRÈME FRAÎCHE AND POACHED EGGS

Sᴇʀᴠᴇꜱ 4 ᴏʀ ꜱᴏ

Lots of kosher salt

12 Yukon gold or German butterball potatoes

2 shallots, diced

1 clove garlic, bashed, Microplaned, or finely diced

1 tablespoon lemon juice

1 tablespoon champagne vinegar or white wine vinegar

2 teaspoons Dijon mustard

4 to 6 tablespoons olive oil

2 cups chicken stock

10 asparagus spears, trimmed and cut into 4 pieces each, or 40 asparagus
    tips (save the stalks for asparagus stock or soup)

6 eggs

2 teaspoons any kind of white vinegar

¾ cup crème fraîche

3 spring onion stems (or chives), thinly sliced

Fill a large pot three-quarters of the way up with cold water. Add several tablespoons salt. Peel the potatoes and slide them into the water right away. Place over high heat and bring to a boil. Once the water boils, turn down to a simmer. The potatoes are done when a paring knife slides in easily. If you're not sure, just cut one open and taste. Drain the potatoes in a colander. If they're falling apart a bit, remove them one at a time with a slotted spoon. Set aside to cool.

In a bowl, combine the shallots and garlic. Cover with the lemon juice and champagne vinegar and let sit for a few minutes. Whisk in the mustard, then slowly whisk in half the olive oil. Taste. This salad is best with a very tangy dressing. Add more olive oil if it's too strong.

Bring the chicken stock to a boil in a medium saucepan. Turn down to a simmer and add the asparagus tips. Cook very briefly (1 to 2 minutes, depending on size). Taste one. Make sure there's still some crunch left. Remove with a slotted spoon and place on a kitchen towel. Save the broth for soup or lunch or sick kids.

Fill a large wide pot of water for the eggs and bring to a boil. Once boiling, turn the heat so low that there are no bubbles on the surface of the water. Add the white vinegar and a pinch of salt. Stir. Crack 1 egg into a bowl. Slide the egg into the water. Repeat with remaining eggs. I like the yolks very runny, but I hate it when the white is still raw on top. The only way I know to test for doneness is to use a slotted spoon to pull an egg out of the water and touch the top to make sure it's completely cooked. Slide an egg onto a clean kitchen towel or paper towel. Remove all the eggs the same way. It's OK for them to sit for a few minutes. If you want, you can reheat the eggs in the hot water right before serving.

Slice the potatoes and spread them out in a single layer on a big plate or platter. Salt each slice. Spoon on the shallot dressing. Scatter the asparagus tips all over the potatoes. Carefully (or not) blop crème fraîche all over the potatoes and asparagus. Add more salad dressing. Place the eggs on top. Add a few sloshes of olive oil and sprinkle the spring onion slices all over. Serve (and eat) right away.

PART TWO

FAMILY

FROM THE LAND

MAX BROOKS

I garden to get fresh air. I garden to be physically productive. I garden to feed my family by means other than a paycheck spent at the grocery store. Most important, I garden to remember.

My mother always spent some part of her life laboring in the earth. No matter where my family lived, no matter what was happening with my mother's busy, glamorous, Hollywood career, she never strayed too far from some patch of dirt. I remember her citrus orchard in our secluded, half-acre Beverly Hills home, and how as a little boy I used to snack on the French sorrel from the patch next to our front door, and how she would raise holy hell if I tramped through her rows of lettuce or string beans in the back of the house.

That was when I first learned the joys of watching plants grow, when I brought home a germinating pea in a plastic cup of dirt. It was part of a school project, the third grade's attempt to introduce us to agriculture. That little pea went into our garden, along with a few beans and corn kernels. It taught me about the value of patience, and the anticipation of seeing how much progress each morning would bring. I remember nothing tasting as sweet as the corn that I planted myself.

I remember summers on Fire Island, where my mother and her sisters fenced off a tiny plot of salt-soaked sand between our families' two beach shacks, and how they worked all summer with sprinkler hoses, sacks of soil, and seed packets, all so that for the last few weeks in August we could enjoy fresh greens with the fish my cousins and I caught for dinner. She taught me the importance of fish as fertilizer; how her friend Dom DeLuise christened her strawberry guava tree with a wheelbarrow full of fish heads.

She had grand plans for our new house in Santa Monica, which was finished in 1984, when I started the seventh grade. The sloping backyard would be terraced, irrigated, and lit for a day/night gardening experience. Every night dinner included at least one item "from the land." I'm not sure if that line came from Dom DeLuise or Pearl S. Buck's *The Good Earth*. Either way, the phrase was as much a staple in our house as the chard and kale and radicchio served at our table every night. And after dinner my mother would lead us in ritual mass slaughter of our enemy, the nefarious cut worm. Flashlights in hand, we'd descend onto the hillside. My mother was an expert in counterinsurgency as well as hand-to-hand combat. Gleefully she picked off each squirming pest and, with her trademark theatrical "HHAA!" crushed them beneath her heel.

My mother didn't believe in pesticides, or even chemical fertilizers. She liked to say that she invented the word "organic" long before anyone had even heard of it. She was the first mother among my friends' families to pay attention to ingredients on food labels and to question what industrial farms were spraying on our store-bought produce. She always insisted that gardening was the only way to ensure what we were putting into our bodies.

My father had other ideas. While careful never to say this to her face, he made sure I knew that her ties to the land went back to her "Italian peasant heritage." Maybe he was right. As far back as I can remember, my grandma kept a small plot of tomatoes and basil next to her little house in Yonkers. Her father had been a grocer during the Great Depression, and as a result, my mom bragged, they never went hungry. My mother used to talk about visiting her grandparents and the smell of basil heavy in the air. She once took a cooking class in which the scent of chopped basil— and the sense memories it conjured up—made her break down and cry.

Maybe it was nostalgia, maybe it was her heritage, maybe it was her way of counteracting an increasingly toxic society, maybe it was all these, but that hillside micro-farm in Santa Monica was her masterpiece. She was just as proud of it as of any of the little golden statues she'd won for pretending to be other people. By this point, however, I was quickly losing interest in the kind of growing associated with plants. I was moving into adolescence, and, in my mind, basil had been replaced by boobs.

For twenty years, I lived as an urban hunter-gatherer. Food was just something to keep me going during the day, and plants were just something old people cared about. Any interest in agriculture came from my general curiosity about survivalist culture (which I translated into my first book). Any connection to my Italian heritage came from learning how to make a decent marinara sauce (from canned ingredients), and that was only to impress the girl who would one day become my wife.

Then my mom got sick. A lifetime of label reading and organic food turned out to be useless in the face of uterine cancer. We were all living in New York at the time: my parents, me, my wife, Michelle, and our newborn son, who was lucky enough to spend a few precious hours with his grandmother. It was an artificial existence, and apart from nuclear subs or the international space station, I'll be damned if any life is more removed from nature. The only places I ever saw trees were in the cramped, over-manicured, urine-soaked corrals that passed for parks. The only time I ever planted anything was in Valhalla cemetery in Yonkers.

A few years later we moved back to California, and while I waited for my new home office to be finished, I set up a temporary work space in my parents'—my father's—house. I figured it was a way to save the money I would have thrown away on renting an office. It was also a way of staying physically close to an eighty-year-old man who was alone for the first time in his life. From the attic window I could look down on the garden, overgrown now, neglected and brown. I'm not sure exactly when I picked up the mattock and got to work. I'm not sure when a one-time visit to Armstrong garden center became a weekly (sometimes daily) habit. I'm not sure when I started permanently wearing a Leatherman multi-tool on my belt or when I set up pots and plastic sheeting and grow lights in a corner of my father's attic. Those three years are still very much a blur.

Gardening is now an integral part of my life, as much as it ever was to my mom. Tomato plants are growing again on her hillside, as well as basil and potatoes and sometimes a few more exotic crops like cotton, tobacco, and a lot of sugar cane. I also have a few coffee plants, one of which started as a houseplant I gave my dad for his bathroom window.

It's taken a few years, but we're just getting our first big crop of beautiful purple berries.

As supportive as he was of my mother's hobby, he simply tolerated it. But my dad now takes an active role in mine. Together we go through the tomato plants, picking the best for sandwiches and sauce. This season we've made sixty-two jars of marinara, more than enough for an entire year. My father has also invested in several fruit trees; last June we were drowning in peaches.

Neither one of us is particularly religious, so keeping my mother's garden alive seems the best way to honor her memory. "She'd be real proud of you," my dad says over a bucket of harvested Brandywines. "She would," I respond, "but she'd be pissed about the mess."

I won't say I feel her presence when I'm working in the soil, but memories of her are never far when I'm digging a hole for fish guts, or tasting this season's strawberry guava (we still have that tree!), or killing slugs in the small plot of my own house. Like her, I don't use pesticides, and like her, every kill is personal. Sometimes on weekends my son helps me defend our crops. I explain to him, like "Grandma Annie" explained to me, that while it's never good to kill, sometimes it's necessary when protecting our food. Most of the time I go out alone at night, flashlight in hand, with the reverence of a religious ritual. I'd like to believe that there is such a thing as an afterlife, that a part of my mom still exists somewhere. I hope, as my dad says, that she'd be proud of me for continuing her tradition, and that maybe, just maybe, she watches over my nightly pest hunts, smiling at each theatrical "HHAA!"

HOMEMADE YONKERS, NEW YORK, ITALIAN TOMATO SAUCE

Only the salt and olive oil are store-bought; all other ingredients are homegrown. Portions tend to be rough and peasanty and depend on the number of people eating.

MAKES ABOUT 1 QUART

Roma tomatoes, roughly 4 blenders full (I also like to mix in a few homegrown Brandywine and cherry tomatoes for flavor)

Basil, 1 fistful per quart of blended tomatoes

Garlic, 1 half clove per quart of blended tomatoes

Salt

Olive oil, 1 tablespoon per quart of tomatoes

Puree the tomatoes, basil, and garlic in a mixer with as much water as needed to allow for blending.

Add salt as needed for taste. Add olive oil.

Bring to a boil and boil for 5 minutes. Reduce the heat and cook, stirring, all day (yes, all day), until the liquid has reduced to a sauce.

Either serve immediately or pour into jars and freeze.

RACHAEL RAY SAVED MY LIFE

MELISSA CLARK

I don't hold a grudge against my mother, a self-taught gourmet, for not teaching me how to cook. No, I wouldn't have been ready. A late bloomer, I came to appreciate food only recently. I never understood why my mom salivated at hearing a story of a good meal or why she stocked her pantry with ingredients I couldn't pronounce, or ripped out restaurant reviews and recipes from newspapers and magazines, stacking them in her bedroom, her office, the kitchen. My mother became a foodie at the tender age of sixteen when, on a family trip to New York, she went out for her first Indian meal. She was so enthralled with the spices, the textures, the tastes—a far cry from the noodle kugel, gefilte fish, and boiled chicken she ate at home in Montreal. On that trip she became obsessed with ethnic foods, and it ignited a lifelong relationship with food in general. When I was a child, the most memorable thing about our family kitchen was vases blooming with cooking utensils: confetti-colored spatulas, potato mashers, zesters, graters, wooden spoons—small, medium, and large—nutcrackers, wine openers. These were just the items I recognized. Others were nameless, functionless, foreign, and just plain weird. (I once used a large, wide metal spoon to scoop up my fish, Paul Simon, while changing the water in his bowl.)

I was a skinny kid, verging on scrawny. My priorities were as follows: friends, swimming, tetherball, volleyball, handball, tennis, roller-skating, and bike riding. Food didn't even make the list. Despite all my activities, dinner usually found me taking a few bites and then cutting the remaining chicken/hamburger/turkey/brisket into unrecognizable bits and either depositing them into a napkin or slipping them to Peanut, the dog. My mom reminds me that the only culinary activity that held my interest was decorating holiday cookies. I globbed on frosting, sprinkled on jimmies, but even then, after only a few, I grew bored and fled outside to play some more. Sure, I knew a good meal when I had one, but my general attitude toward food was apathy.

My mom, however, is known for bringing together friends and family over thoughtful brunches and adventurous dinners. One memorable dinner involved a French chicken stew with lots of herbs made in a heavy pot. My mom sealed it with a paste of flour and water, then baked it all day in the oven. Once guests arrived, she brought it to the table with a sharp knife, which she used to cut dramatically through the crust, revealing not only the perfectly baked chicken but the herb-infused aroma that enveloped the room. I believe she received a standing ovation.

My parties were quite different. I relied on the power of the potluck. I'd provide, say, couscous, and encourage my friends to fill in the blanks. And there were many blanks. I invited my parents to one of these parties. They arrived early and were appalled by my bowl of chips on the table. "What are people going to eat?" my mom said, eyeing the chips nervously.

"Everyone's bringing something," I assured her.

"To the party *you're* hosting?"

She moved quickly to the kitchen to, I don't know, whip up more food? But the cupboards were bare. There wasn't even a box of couscous.

They say the teacher appears when the student is ready. I suppose I was ready that Tuesday evening when I'd just returned to my home in Los Angeles from a trip to Toronto where my television show, *Braceface*, was being produced. I was cranky from travel, and too hungry to eat. I used what little energy I had to click on the television. I'll never forget what was on. The woman was wearing a brown leotard, the absolute wrong top for her diminutive breasts. Her voice was piercing, grating, rough around the edges. I'd heard about her, but had never seen her show. "I'm Rachael Ray," she bellowed, "and I make thirty-minute meals." I liked the concept instantly. I was a girl-on-the-go with frequent trips to Canada, production meetings, screenings, lectures, dates, Bollywood dance classes. I was willing to learn a quick recipe or two to squeeze into my day. I dropped onto the couch; my cat followed.

Rachael looked into the camera and squawked, "You know how to chop an onion, right?"

"Duh!" I called back.

Wait—did I? I had adopted my grandmother's method of cutting erratic, choppy bits. So I wasn't neat, I reasoned, but it all winds up in my stomach anyway. I watched, intrigued, as Rachael sliced off the two ends of the onion, cut through the middle, peeled off the skin, and ran her knife through the halves, producing a perfect dice. On a commercial break, with renewed energy, I moved the cat aside and dashed into my own kitchen, got a decades-old steak knife and sawed through an onion, imitating her moves. It was like magic.

A second show followed. "You again?" I hollered at the TV, but I couldn't seem to change the channel. She was now making a "Stoup," her invented name, I learned, for a cross between a stew and a soup. I soon realized, like any neophyte, that I had to learn her language before I could proceed. "G.B." was the garbage bowl she kept on the counter to discard peels and cellophane wrappings. "E.V.O.O." was extra-virgin olive oil. A sandwich was a "Sammie," and if something tasted delicious it was "Yum-o!" If a piece of penne didn't make it into the boiling water, she'd declare, "Man overboard!" or "Oh, my gravy!" And she didn't *mix* ingredients, she gave them a "shughe." Like a teenager shirking from an embarrassing parent, I cringed. My shoulders were up against my ears and I could barely look at her. But I kept listening because deep down, I knew I was learning.

Did I know, upon coming home from the market, to wash and store my herbs *immediately* in zip-top bags? No! Before discovering Rachael Ray I didn't even *shop* for herbs. Did I salt my pasta water before meeting Rachael? Never! Did I make my own salad dressing? Absolutely not! Before tuning in, I was the couscous queen. A typical dinner was couscous and black beans, or couscous and white beans, or couscous and a jar of tomato sauce—you get the idea. Now it was couscous and white beans and chopped flat-leaf parsley, or couscous and black beans with chili powder, cumin, and coriander. Baby steps.

Rachael gave each meal a cutesey name that she repeated incessantly over the course of an episode. "I'm working on a Mexican Meat-zza. Get it? It's kind of like a pizza, but it's made with meat!" or, "Today I'm making pasta and peasto. It's a pesto made with peas—pretty clever, right?" I wasn't sure if she was being condescending or truly thought her audience didn't get it.

One evening while procrastinating on the Internet I discovered the "Rachael Ray Sucks" community where her critics gathered and flooded the site with vicious comments like "She looks like the Joker from Batman!" or "Today's recipe was straight out of the G.B." I laughed at the snarkiness but felt a pang of heartbreak. I'd made strides because of this woman. I'd acquired at least a dozen recipes—By Gosh It's Goulash, Fast, Fake-Baked Ziti, Mac and Jack Salad, Funky Fries, Clam Bake Stoup—and my culinary confidence was starting to soar. Before Rachael, my kitchen had been a mishmash of hand-me-downs, but she taught me the importance of a good knife, and so I bought one. Since so many of her recipes called for citrus zest, I bought a zester, and soon my kitchen resembled my mom's—vases of candy-colored spatulas, soup ladles, potato mashers. My friends surprised me with a full set of Rachael Ray cookware—pots and pans with her signature orange handles.

I still had issues with my TV tutor. I winced as she butchered the English language ("Whaddaya think of them apples?") and cringed at some of her themes ("Food for People *and* Dogs"), but there was no denying the effect she was having on my culinary prowess. Finally, after eight months of cooking under my new mentor, I decided to host a party—a real party where *I* cooked the food. No chips, no couscous. I glanced at the calendar and realized Mother's Day was approaching. Did I dare prepare a meal for my foodie mother? I sent out feelers to my family. Everyone was free that afternoon. "Come over for brunch," I wrote. Game on.

A few thirty-minute meals add up to hours of prep. Friday had me at the farmers' market and a trio of local grocery stores. Saturday found me in the kitchen slicing, dicing, mincing, washing, peeling, sautéing, and Microplaning. As the Sunday brunch hour neared I was exhausted, not exhilarated the way Rachael seemed after each episode. In fact, when the doorbell rang, I wanted to dive under the covers. What if they hated it? What if it tasted horrible? Upon entering my home, guests tried to identify aromas.

"Is that rosemary?" my sister asked. "Thyme!" my mom guessed. It was both, plus oregano, dill, and chives. I'd set everything out on platters in the dining room and made little cards identifying the dishes: Stuffed Salmon in Flaky Dough, Roasted New Potatoes with Sweet Paprika Butter and Parsley, Asparagus and Caramelized Onion Salad. It was only after she started scooping food onto her plate that my mother had an epiphany. "You didn't make all this, did you?" she asked cautiously.

"Of course I did," I said.

"You *made* it?" my dad clarified, in a tone that expressed sincere doubt.

"It's Mother's Day," I said in a small voice.

My mom stood frozen, a glass of Prosecco in one hand, a plate brimming with salmon, potatoes, and asparagus in the other. She gave me a look that expressed first suspicion, then delight and pride. "Melissa," she said, "this is the best gift ever."

Better than the massage I bought her last Mother's Day? Or the bouquet of roses the year before? Or the computer I chipped in on for her sixtieth birthday? The cashmere sweater from Barneys? A simple gift of food was better than all that? I suppose it was. But I was given the gift that day—understanding in my heart that food is love, family, and community—and finally being able to create a meal that confirmed all of this, and so much more.

"I'm glad you like it," I said.

"Not like," she clarified. "Love."

Since that brunch I have hosted dinner parties both intimate and grand, contributed to potlucks, suggested recipes for other people, and have even improvised in the kitchen, for example, substituting tofu in the Chicken Greek-a-Tikka Salad with Parsley-Feta Pesto.

Rachael Ray saved my culinary life. No, Rachael Ray *gave* me a culinary life.

After the Mother's Day brunch, as we cleaned up in the kitchen I said, "Well, I finally learned."

"Did you ever," my mom said, leaning in for a hug. And then, "If it makes you feel better, your grandmother never taught me to cook, either. She could barely chop an onion."

TOFU GREEK SALAD SANDWICH
WITH PARSLEY-FETA PESTO

ADAPTED FROM RACHAEL RAY

SERVES 4

4 whole wheat pita breads
1 cup plain nonfat yogurt
1 teaspoon ground coriander
1 teaspoon ground cumin
1 teaspoon dried oregano
1 package extra-firm organic tofu, cubed into bite-size pieces
1 heart romaine lettuce, chopped
2 vine-ripened tomatoes, chopped
1/2 seedless cucumber, chopped
1/2 red onion, chopped
3 ribs celery, chopped
1/2 cup pitted kalamata olives
6 pepperoncini (hot peppers), chopped
1 lemon, juiced
Extra-virgin olive oil
Salt and freshly ground black pepper

PARSLEY-FETA PESTO

1 cup fresh flat-leaf parsley leaves
1/2 cup feta crumbles
1 clove garlic
1 teaspoon coarsely ground black pepper
3 tablespoons chopped pine nuts
1/4 cup extra-virgin olive oil

Before you begin the salad, wrap the breads in foil and place in a 300°F oven to warm.

To make the salad, in a medium bowl, combine the yogurt, coriander, cumin, and oregano; add the tofu and let sit for a few minutes.

Combine the chopped lettuce, tomatoes, cucumber, onion, celery, olives, and pepperoncini on a serving platter.

Whisk together the lemon juice and extra-virgin olive oil to taste in a small bowl. Dress the salad and season with salt and pepper.

Drain the tofu cubes and heat a large skillet over medium-high heat. Add the tofu and cook for about 5 minutes, stirring, until lightly browned. Remove from the heat and let cool for a few minutes before adding it to the salad platter.

Remove the bread from the oven and cut each in half.

To make the pesto, combine all the pesto ingredients in a food processor, adding the oil through the tube at the top as you blend.

Spoon the salad ingredients into the pita bread and top each sandwich with generous helpings of pesto.

PIE-EYED

LISA McNAMARA

My mother came from a family of diabetic Sephardic Jews, all danger-
ously underskilled in the culinary arts and, it seemed, devoid of a sweet
tooth (diabetes notwithstanding). In our house, desserts were scarce,
only making an appearance on special occasions: honey cake for Rosh
Hashanah, *hamantaschen* for Purim, macaroons or sponge cake for Passover. They were better than nothing, and I was lucky to have them, my
mother, who had grown up in the Depression, would remind me, but
as a small child it was difficult to muster much excitement for coconut,
prunes, and nuts. What I craved were the kinds of confections I had seen
on television: old-fashioned sweets like fudgy brownies and chewy chocolate chip cookies and lattice-topped pies bursting with ripe fruit. How I
ached to come home from school to be greeted by a plate of warm cookies,
a big slice of layer cake, or a wedge of pie topped with a scoop of rich ice
cream. Instead, my mother, neither cut from TV-mom cloth nor from the
"Eat, dahlink" breed of Jewish mother, would give me a bowl of cereal or
a plate of crackers with a little saccharine-sweetened apple jelly for my
afternoon snack.

That's why the happiest outings were when she took me with her to
buy bread, which in those days meant a trip to a real bakery. I wished I
could live there, among the thrilling aromas of cinnamon and chocolate, instead of at our house, which smelled of boiled chicken and tomato
sauce. The plump, white-haired women, their ample bosoms straining

the buttons of their pastel uniforms, always looked so cheerful. And who wouldn't, surrounded by cakes adorned with roses sculpted from royal icing, fat éclairs filled with golden custard, and hundreds of cookies? I would stare longingly at the glass case of cookies—thumbprints with dollops of chocolate or raspberry jam in the center, sandwich cookies with creamy fillings, butter cookies coated with colorful sprinkles—until one of the nice ladies asked my favorite question: "Would the little girl like a cookie?" Then the bakery lady would wink at me as she tucked it into my hand, urging me to taste it just to make sure the rest of them were good enough to sell to the other customers. It was as though she knew my stern, slim mother would tell me that I had to save it for after dinner.

My much-older brother—playmate, best friend, and protector—was pained by my mother's strict rules about giving me sweets and made it his mission to rescue me from dessert purgatory. On the rare occasions when my parents went out, he would drive us to the store to buy a cake mix and at home, using a cracked rubber spatula and a pair of round cake pans warped from years of disuse, we would make cake together. He'd lift me onto the kitchen counter and let me stir the ingredients until my arm got tired and always made sure I could lick some of the bowl. Thanks to him and Betty Crocker, baking began to seem less like pure magic and more like the kind of magic I could learn.

My brother left for college when I was six, halting my education in the kitchen, but those early lessons had started me on my way. In those days the cake itself was always the goal—we frosted it while it was still warm so we could gorge ourselves before my mother came home and stopped us. ("You'll make your sister sick!" she would say, scowling as she put the remainder on a plate on top of the refrigerator, well out of my reach.) But even then I sensed there was something more to baking. It was a way my brother showed his affection for me, and a way he could provide me with something I was missing. Those lopsided cakes were small acts of love.

By the time I was ten, my mother had fallen seriously ill with uterine cancer. One of our housekeepers, a tall, gentle woman named Hazel, shared my passion for baking. When my mother was in the hospital, we would bake something special for home. She, too, used mixes, but she did so with finesse, turning out cakes with even layers that didn't bulge on top, were never burnt on the edges, and were always evenly frosted.

Guiding my hand as I held the spatula, she showed me how to make frosting swirls like those pictured on the cake mix box. When my father came home from visiting my mother, Hazel told him that I had made the cake by myself and cut him a thick slice. My father, who had a peculiar habit of frowning when eating something he liked, frowned a lot over those cakes.

As the years went by and I was often left to care for my mother, baking was one of my comforts, reminding me of my brother and Hazel, even though I now (truly) baked alone. I had mastered the mix cake and was venturing into a new world of scratch cakes and cookies, muffins, and quick breads. I followed recipes in the 1950s cookbooks in our kitchen, which were notorious for rarely giving detailed instructions. Nevertheless, I learned how to add beaten egg whites to lighten a cake and how to sift and measure flour properly. I discovered that when the recipe said to use butter it meant sweet, not salted, and I practiced rolling cookie dough into neat little balls so that they would be nearly identical in size and shape when baked. A shy, awkward teenager with frizzy hair and a thick unibrow, I had grown into a high school misfit who never dated or attended a dance. Only in the kitchen did I feel exceptional.

Then, after my mother died when I was in eleventh grade, things began to change. The kitchen became my exclusive domain and, free to make whatever I wanted whenever I wanted, I baked with abandon, eradicating the odor of boiled chicken from our house once and for all. Both my father and I ate my creations greedily, but even so I baked more than we could consume. I began to bring cakes and cookies to school as gifts to the teachers who had been so kind during the long months my mother spent dying. It was the only way I knew how to give something back to them. My teachers, in turn, shared these gifts with other students and word of my baking abilities spread. Before long, my house became a destination for after-school or late-night snacks. In my kitchen, the popular girls and the boys who would never have given me a second glance before saw me in a different light. There, the summer after I graduated from high school, my wish for a boyfriend came true. The president of the drama club, on whom I'd had an unrequited crush for two years, developed a passion for my poppy seed Bundt cake and, along with it, for me.

By my late teens, my repertoire had grown—my German chocolate cake and Boston cream pie outshone those from any bakery, my banana cake was dense and moist, my angel food cake light and airy.

It occurred to me that baking was perhaps one of those talents that had made less-than-attractive women seem more attractive to men for hundreds of years. I imagined that if I had been born a century earlier in my paternal grandparents' native Kiev, before electrolysis and orthodontics, I would have been the village *mieskeit*, a Yiddish word meaning homely. Despite my substantial dowry, I am certain my father would have had difficulty marrying me off. "Wait," he would say, as the potential suitor turned away, unwilling to take me, even in exchange for three donkeys and a good milk cow. "She may not look like much, but her strudel is to die for." And years later, my fat husband would tell that story to our unibrowed daughter as I attempted to impart my skills to her, sparing her the lonely life of a spinster.

For my first live-in boyfriend I learned to make sour cream *kolaches*; for my first husband—whose startling increase in girth during our three-year marriage was an unfortunate side effect—Key lime pie with a real graham cracker crust.

In my mid-twenties, after my first marriage ended, I met the man who would become my second husband. He cared nothing for cakes or cookies, eschewing dessert—unless it was pie. But he scoffed at my Key lime pie and dismissed cookie-crusted cream-filled pies as pretenders. For it to truly qualify, pie had to be handmade, with a butter or lard crust, and filled, ideally, with Maine blueberries or crisp sweet and sour apples.

In short, he wanted something I had never made.

Where I grew up, in Miami Beach, pies were either behemoths that sat in delicatessen dessert carousels, better to look at than to eat, or cryogenically preserved in the supermarket freezer case. There was, however, one pie that held a hallowed place in my childhood memory. I can still picture it standing tall on the round kitchen table at my aunt's house, its brown crust glistening with sugar, steam curling out of its tidy vents, infusing the house with the smell of cinnamon and apples.

My aunt fancied herself a Jewish Jacqueline Kennedy (someone had once told her that she bore a resemblance to the then-First Lady) and refused to do her own cooking. Luckily for all of us, she hired a cook, Cora: a large, clubfooted woman with a wide smile full of gold teeth and a hairnet knot on her forehead. Cora was my hero.

Cora had my three cousins to care for and a five-bedroom house to clean in addition to her cooking responsibilities, so she baked pies only occasionally, usually for Hanukkah. As my mother and aunts marveled over the tenderness of the brisket and the juiciness of the roasted chicken, my cousins and I ate just enough of our meat and vegetables to satisfy our mothers, making sure we saved plenty of room for dessert.

My father and uncles asked their wives why they couldn't learn to make pie like that. They might as well have asked a centipede why it couldn't walk on two legs. When I married my first husband, I asked Cora to teach me how to make her pie. Sadly, she died before I could collect this gift. Like many great home cooks, she baked without recipes, and the secret of the pie was lost. I missed Cora for her hearty laugh and the way she let me help her in the kitchen when I was small, but I never missed her more than when my second husband declared his love of pies.

The expression "easy as pie" is misleading—pie is only easy to make once you know how. It's simple enough to dump a can of food-colored sugar and modifiers masquerading as fruit into a frozen crust and call it pie. But to craft one by hand from butter and flour with a filling made from fresh fruit is a very different thing. And if, like me, you must learn on your own, without a patient teacher or secret family recipes, the quest for pie perfection can be long and laborious. Julia Child taught me soufflés, but with pie, I was on my own.

Unlike cakes and pastries, where following a recipe to the letter will produce relatively predictable results, pies require more from the baker. Fruits, like people, need to be respected as individuals. Certain fruits demand more sugar, or less acid, or more thickening. My early attempts produced apple pies with gummy, underbaked crusts and lumpy, mushy fillings, or blueberry pies that tasted of overly sweet pancake syrup. The shriveled berries seemed stranded on a life raft of pale crust afloat in a dark, murky sea. Yet, undaunted by my failures, I continued my experiments with thickeners and sweeteners until I was satisfied that whatever came out of the oven would taste better than what had gone in.

Unfortunately, it was around that time that we divorced. Like my pie skills, my expertise at relationships was only half-complete. My self-image as the village *mieskeit* compelled me to say yes whenever someone proposed, believing that it might be the best (or only) offer I would get. That I did not love either of these men was beside the point. Having someone to cook for was better than being alone—at least until it wasn't.

Newly single, I once again turned to baking both to keep me company and, more important, to help me find new and better company. I'd learned about a study designed to identify which scents men find sexually stimulating. It so happened that the smell of baked goods, specifically cinnamon and pumpkin pie, was judged more arousing by test subjects than the most exotic perfume. Researchers speculated that these scents might stimulate the septal nuclei, a portion of the brain that induces sexual arousal. That, or the aroma of pie, produces a nostalgic response, recalling memories of their mother's (or *someone's* mother's) kitchen.

Fascinated, I conducted my own very unscientific study, asking every man I knew what his favorite dessert was. With few exceptions, the answer was pie. Pie like their mothers or grandmothers used to bake, but that in the world of career women with scarce free time, no one seemed to make anymore. Although none of them articulated it, the implication was clear—a woman who could bake such a pie was exceptional. A twice-divorced workaholic, I yearned to be an old-fashioned girl with an old-fashioned husband for whom I could bake old-fashioned pies. Armed with the knowledge that pie was surefire man-bait, I continued my quest with renewed zeal, now focused on perfecting my crust.

I experimented with flours and fats, baking times and temperatures, metal and glass and ceramic pans, setting them on oven racks of different heights or even directly on the oven floor. I used my predominantly male coworkers and clients as my taste testers, and no matter how dissatisfied I was with a particular attempt, everything I baked was gratefully eaten to the last crumb and indeed made me very popular at the office. I even garnered several marriage proposals. Mercifully, another thing I had learned along the way was how to say no.

At last, after years of practice and hundreds of what I deemed failures, I had achieved a crust that was crisp and flaky both on the edges and on the bottom, one that held up to a juicy filling without getting soggy. It was a classic formula: plenty of cold, sweet butter, unbleached flour, salt, and ice water—minimally handled, thinly rolled. I used the slender wooden French rolling pin I bought after husband number two's departure. None of the elaborate earthenware or silicone or air-cushioned pans can top simple Pyrex for even browning.

By the time I made an apple pie that came close to Cora's, I had married again, this time to a man who could have happily gone without dessert for the rest of his life. He loved me without my baking, for which I was unspeakably grateful, if a little disappointed. And so my motivations for baking shifted yet again. My confections were no longer my weapons of mass seduction. Instead, they became a way for me to give something special to those who hadn't a mother or grandmother or wife to bake for them, or the time or ability to bake for themselves.

I've never had that unibrowed daughter to whom I could pass on my knowledge, but I happily share it with those who are interested in preserving a technique that is, in our increasingly hectic times, in danger of becoming a lost art. Thirteen years into our marriage, my husband haunts the farmers' market throughout the year, seeking out the heirloom apples called Bellflower, the rare marionberries and boysenberries, fragrant Meyer lemons, and the deep orange-red Sierra Lady peaches, presenting them to me with a victorious flourish and delighting in my happiness as I receive them. Of the many gifts that have been bestowed on me throughout my baking odyssey, my husband's gifts of beautiful fruit delivered with unconditional love are perhaps the sweetest of all.

APPLE PIE

CRUST

2½ cups unbleached all-purpose flour (King Arthur works best)

¾ teaspoon salt

½ pound sweet butter, very cold, cut into 64 pieces, ⅓- to ½-inch cubes
   (I like Plugra or Strauss brands because they contain little moisture)

7 to 10 tablespoons very cold water

FILLING

3½ pounds apples (my favorite is the Arkansas Black, but Gala and Jona-
   gold work well, too), peeled, cored, and sliced ¼ inch thick

½ cup light brown sugar

¼ cup unbleached all-purpose flour

2½ teaspoons ground cinnamon (I like Penzeys brand China Cassia best)

1 tablespoon apple cider vinegar

½ teaspoon salt

1 tablespoon granulated sugar

1 to 2 tablespoons whole milk or cream

To make the crust, spoon flour into a measuring cup and swipe off excess with the flat side of a knife. Put the flour and salt in the bowl of a food processor. Pulse for a few seconds to combine.

Sprinkle the butter cubes over the flour-salt mixture. Cut in the butter using about 13 to 15 one-second pulses. There should still be very small pieces of butter, about half the size of a pea, visible in the mixture.

Transfer the mixture to large bowl. Add 4 tablespoons cold water and mix together with a spatula. As you add the rest of the water, 1 tablespoon at a time, use your hands to mix so you can feel the dough's texture. You only want to add enough water for the dough to just hold together when you squeeze it in your palm.

Divide the dough into two pieces and shape each piece into a round, flat disk about 6 inches in diameter. Wrap the dough disks individually in plastic and refrigerate for at least 1 hour before continuing with the recipe.

Note: My favorite pie pan is a glass 9-inch, as it lets you see if the bottom crust is browning while it bakes.

Preheat the oven to 400°F and place an oven rack on the lowest rung.

To make the filling, combine the sliced apples, brown sugar, flour, 2 teaspoons of the cinnamon, the vinegar, and salt in a large bowl; toss to coat the apples well.

Roll out two pie dough disks into about 11-inch rounds so you have about a 1-inch overhang when it's in the pan. (A good way to measure is to turn the pie pan upside down on the dough round and leave an inch beyond the outer rim of the pan.)

Line the pan with the bottom crust and then pile the apple mixture on top; shape it into a mound. Lay the top crust over the apples and fold over the bottom crust—crimp and seal. Cut vents in the top crust to let steam escape.

Combine the granulated sugar and remaining ½ teaspoon cinnamon. Set aside.

Bake the pie for 45 minutes. Remove from the oven briefly to brush the top crust with milk and sprinkle with the cinnamon-sugar mixture. Return to the oven and bake until the crust is golden brown and the filling is bubbly, about 20 minutes more. If the top crust or edges appear to be getting too dark, cover loosely with aluminum foil and reduce the oven temperature to 375°F.

FOOD OF THE GODS

BETHANY SALTMAN

My dad is haunting me in the grocery store. Preparing to host my very first grown-up Thanksgiving, I have been spending a lot of time food shopping, and my dad, never one to miss a food-related outing, is along for the ride. The thing is, he died nine years ago, from complications of a stroke, when he was sixty-two and I was thirty-four. And it's awkward. With a celestial nudge, he leads me to the MSG-laced packets of gravy mix, which he used to add to pan drippings, but I want to make our favorite meal my way. I remind him that I am allergic to MSG. But even he, a dead man, knows when he's being outdone.

Pushing my cart, I stop in front of the untouched display of Wonder Bread—which he used to load with sautéed onions, butter, celery, salt, and dried sage. I feel my heart beating in my chest, and I see him, standing at the mustard-yellow stove, a short guy with a bald head and a mustache, a lit cigarette within reach. He's attentive, relaxed, sniffing every now and then. I see myself, a skinny girl of eight, standing a few feet behind her dad on the linoleum floor, wanting to love him.

My mouth was watering instead.

Experts in the field of child development use an odd phrase to describe one aspect of healthy child and parent bonding: "goodness of fit." The phrasing is weird, and the concept vaguely disturbing. It points to the cosmic chaos that every parent (especially those with more than one child) knows: some kid/parent connections are easier to forge than others. Sometimes a spastic, high-energy kid is born to an easily overwhelmed mom. Occasionally a natural-born talker is born to a silent type. Other times a super-sensitive, über-feminine girl is born to an insecure auto parts salesman who loves a good joke and all-things-food dad.

Occasionally this dad may find himself in his last weeks of life in a nursing home, unable to speak coherently, read, write, remember the names of the Beatles, or even smoke. He'll watch the young rising star Rachael Ray on his TV and say, "I like her." And his daughter, on leave from a Zen monastery to deal with this situation, will say, "Me, too."

Goodness of fit is an idea borne of a well-meaning desire to explain the shame of relationships that don't quite work, which offers some relief, especially to those of us in such relationships with our primary people. ("OK, it's not my fault!") And yet it misses the mysterious ways relationships can edge and shift and turn, moment to moment, through space and time.

The father-daughter bond I see developing between my husband and our five-year-old Azalea is the kind that is reported to lead to everything good, from a positive body image to a drug-free youth. And even though my relationship with my dad feels thwarted, at best, it did offer me something deep and lasting. Mainly, my dad taught me that you don't have to be a professional aesthete to be passionate about culinary adventure or some kind of fancy "artiste" to devote oneself to one's own creativity. Though at the time it was annoying and even embarrassing, I now appreciate my dad's relentless pursuit of his own vision, such as asking the waitress for a bowl of lemons so he could fix the hollandaise for his eggs Benedict. There was something old-school sweet, quiet, and personal about my dad's passions—and risky.

By the time I was twelve, my dad's auto parts business had failed, and he declared bankruptcy. He'd survived his first heart attack but had done little to change his ill-advised habits. We lost our house and his beloved Jaguar, and we were living in a small duplex in a new town. My parents filed for divorce.

Going through the business of separating was a particularly ugly time in my family's life. I was the new kid in eighth grade, about to lose the father I had barely wanted in the first place. My older brothers fought like pheromone-soaked animals. The whole scene was pretty gross, and my dad was seriously getting on my nerves. But I remember coming home from school once and watching him cook in our dim, rented kitchen. It was annoying to have him there at that time of day, jobless and restless, as that was the time I usually found respite from my brothers and the world at large in the solitude of cooking after school. I made dishes like sautéed chicken breasts with mushrooms, or homemade mac and cheese, discovering myself, and the way my body got quiet and knew what to do next. I had gotten tips from TV chefs like the Frugal Gourmet and Julia Child, and from cooking segments on *Regis and Kathie Lee*. I had learned about real garlic, how to peel it, crush it, cook it. I used to go to the store with my mom and ask if she could buy, say, boneless chicken breasts (a staple in the eighties gourmet explosion). When she said they were too expensive, I learned how to debone the whole breast myself—on the sly, so as not to raise eyebrows about my uppity tastes.

But that afternoon, my dad was home, cooking canned potatoes, which he had sliced. He added Italian bread crumbs, canola oil, and dried tarragon—one of his signature flavors—and fried the heck out of those little water-logged, potato-flavored slices. I felt resistant to sharing anything with my dad, as a vague and persistent shame about him had begun to grow. At twelve, I was intensely needy, and obsessed with looking cool. It was dawning on me that my dad's grease-scented hands, his El Camino half-car/half-truck, and his lame attempts to seem lighthearted in the midst of such obvious failure all painted a portrait of a pathetic blue-collar dude. So against my better judgment, I sat down at the round table in the corner of the kitchen and let my dad plate me up some spuds. They were soft and sweet on the inside, crunchy and salty on the outside. Those potatoes were profound.

––––––––––

The truth is, I haven't cooked gravy that often. I have stock-based sauces and stews (a roux is one of my favorites picked up from cooking shows), but only a handful of real, live Thanksgiving gravies. Even so, after all those years of watching my dad let it rip with his gravy—ingredients aside—I learned, in my body, what this gravy is and what makes it good, allowing me to be uncharacteristically fearless about it. Good thing: In just a week, I will be sitting down with friends and family to a meal I will have made almost singlehandedly. I have been shopping for a couple weeks, and I have already started cooking.

My dad didn't have a sweet tooth, nor do I. As much as I like baking (not to mention the homemade confections around the house) I always need to follow a recipe, and even still, I can't seem to get it right. Or maybe it's *because* I have to follow a recipe—baking is, after all, much more of a science than cooking—that I am not very good at it. Yesterday, Azalea and I made a delicious chocolate shortbread cookie dough with *fleur de sel* to put in the freezer; but we made a pie dough that tasted gross, like shortening instead of butter, so we threw it out. The way I learned to cook from my dad—starting with pure instinct and raw desire, then developing just enough skills to conjure food on a plate, or steaming in a bowl—does not work with baking. What I learned from my dad is more like a sleight of hand, a mystical experience.

It was only in that arena of my dad's otherworldly food life that I felt even a little bit comfortable around him. When he moved out West, I visited him a couple of times, and I remember how jazzed he was to take me to his new supermarket and introduce me to the gals bagging his glass bottles of Coke and garlic salt. They called him "Jeffy." At his favorite egg joint, the waitress brought his ramekin of extras before he could even light a butt, and they had such banter going I wondered if they were sleeping together. He invited fellow Michigan expatriates in the apartment complex to a poolside shindig and served his favorite new dish, a barbecued masterpiece of secret ingredients and jarred sauces he called Ass-Kickin'-Chicken. He was tan, happy, popular, feeding the masses, and they loved him for it. I had to admit, it was like tasting the food of the gods.

———————

Call it lack of goodness of fit, or just bad luck, I still never really liked my dad. I realize now what a bummer that is. Sure, he was a little goofy and awkward with me, and he made some bad calls over the years, such as thinking I, a five-year-old, would enjoy driving 100 miles per hour in his sports car, but he was also pretty sweet. The way he just *loved* food opened me, if not to him, directly, at least to my own love of food. Ultimately, his devotion to food warmed my own little frozen-pea heart and prepared me for a life of spiritual practice, one in which I can embody my dad's passion while steering my ship through clearer waters.

The Buddha taught that karma moves in every direction, including backward, a pinwheel of cause and effect, tumbling through the universe. In other words, my desire to put my maple-buttery hands all over my farm-raised turkey, roast it, and offer it to the people I love *is* my dad's delight in sensory pleasure and the meals he magically invoked. By preparing a meal in my own way, alone in my tiny kitchen, I am feeding the connection between my dad and me, even beyond life and death. It sounds crazy, and it is: the way love casts a spell over a dead bird, transforming it into a bond that never existed.

The rest, as they say, is gravy.

MYSTICAL GRAVY

Any kind of mindful practice will do—a few minutes of yoga, meditation, or taking a walk and feeling your feet against the earth will ground you in your body, a must for making Mystical Gravy.

Read as many recipes as you can.

Taste some gravies before tackling your own. Notice what you love. Do you like it thick, thin, greasy, or clean? Chunks or no chunks? Light or dark? Buttery or acidic? Or both? Try to open your mouth-heart to gravy.

IN THE KITCHEN

Just for kicks, try cooking in silence. Flavor your bird well, rubbing it with herbs, oranges, butter, whatever you like. Don't skimp on salt. Stuff it with something delicious. Cook it according to whatever recipe you have chosen.

When it is cooked, remove your bird from the pan.

Look at your drippings. Taste them. Relax your body, taste again, taking note of the flavor. Do you notice a deep richness or a plain oiliness? This will help direct you in the next steps. If you want, you can skim some of the fat at this point. But save the schmaltz!

Put a quarter cup (or so) of drippings into a large jar. Add about the same amount of plain white flour, and whisk it all together. Add 4 or 5 cups of cold water if you have a lot of drippings, or of chicken stock (from a box or otherwise) if not. Trust yourself to make the right choice. Put the lid on the jar and shake.

Either put the remaining pan drippings in a large saucepan or, better yet, place the roasting pan across two burners. Turn the heat up to medium-high. Slowly add some of the flour mix from the jar. Let it boil, whisking the whole time.

Stay focused and relaxed. Don't talk to anyone, if possible.

As your gravy thickens, add a little more of the flour mix, lightly boil, whisk, and then taste. Make more flour and water mix if you need to.

Do you need to add salt? Pepper is important. More salt. Don't be shy. It's a once a year thing.

Keep adding the flour mix, whisking and tasting.

If it's too flat, add some wine or cider vinegar.

If it is too weak, add some butter, one tablespoon or five. And/or more stock.

Imagine someone you love eating your gravy.

Salt. Pepper.

Relax. Stay quiet.

Whisk the gravy and keep on keeping on until you are happy.

FOOD HATER

JEN LARSEN

I was the astonishing age of twelve before I learned that pork chops were not naturally coated with crispy, delicious, partially hydrogenated soybean oil breading. When my friend's mother set the plate in front of me, the leathery thing served with a side of broccoli did not look edible. It didn't even look real. I was suspicious.

"What is this?" I said, and was astonished by her answer. "No," I replied. I pushed the plate away. "That is not a real pork chop. It is not crunchy." I refused to eat, and I ended up going home early that night.

In the car, I told my mother about how they tried to poison me there at the Mazzenga house, and that I didn't understand how the world could be full of such cruelty and carelessness.

"Some people cook differently," my mother said.

"Some people cook food" is what my mother should have said, followed by, "instead of shaking and baking, or hamburger helping, or cranking open a tin can of carrots and boiling the stuff inside until it can be used as spackle for the cracks in your heart."

My mother is a saint. No, my mother is not a saint—but she is a delightful woman, and I love her very much. I feel that I should say that up front. She has many good qualities, and many friends, all of whom can attest to those good qualities. My mother can bowl, crochet, run a religious education program one-handed, type over a hundred words a minute and never break a single one of her faux nail tips with their tiny, impeccably painted seasonal designs. My mother can do so many things, and you should know that before I tell you that my mother murdered food. She boiled things and microwaved them and fried them to death. Her spice cabinet consisted of salt, plus cinnamon for eggnog. Her famous dish, the one that I still crave thirty years later, is tuna noodle salad, and here is the recipe:

1 can of tuna, drained
1 box of noodles (elbow-shaped), cooked and cooled
1 tomato, chopped
All the mayonnaise in all the world
Salt

Mix. Serve out of giant yellow Tupperware bowl with two spoons, one for you and one for your little brother.

In my darkest hours, at my highest weight—three hundred pounds!—I blamed my mother. Every last pound, every last craving for the monosodium glutamate that finally replaced my blood at about age eight, my inability to understand food that wasn't breaded. My brother eating instant oatmeal out of a packet when we were left on our own for lunch; me thinking two boiled hot dogs stirred into a box of macaroni and cheese was a fancy gourmet treat. All of it my mother's fault.

I thought, in those darkest hours, at my highest weight, things that still make me feel guilty, like: Why wasn't my mother charged with child endangerment? Why weren't we taken away to farms where they force-feed you green beans and teach you of curry and coriander and dill and soy and balsamic things? Why was I left to muddle through a childhood of boxed foods and sent off into the world genuinely afraid of freshly ground black pepper?

I developed an acrimonious relationship with food, and I blamed it on her. I resented that I had to keep eating. I resented the fact that if I wanted to stay alive, I needed to put calories in my body, over and over. The demand never stopped. There was no point at which you could sit back, satisfied that you had done your job and you were done with that chore for the rest of time and could go take a nice bath. Your stomach would be there, telling you to eat Chinese takeout in the tub.

As a marginal adult, my fridge became a living monument to the graceful lines of the to-go container: Styrofoam, cardboard, paper, foil. I was generally able to pay the rent and hold down a job and attend college and then grad school, but I subsisted on cheap restaurant foods (what was the point of spending a lot on food?) and candy bars to fill in the cracks between unsatisfying meals. My evening routine rotated between the dive restaurants and convenience stores in various neighborhoods, because I didn't want any one proprietor to become suspicious. I was afraid of being monitored. I knew that the way I ate wasn't the way other people ate. I ate all the wrong things. I was always hungry, and I was always looking for a way to not be hungry anymore. I was always looking for something I never quite found. I didn't understand the satisfaction other people took in food; I could recognize that things tasted good, but I didn't understand how food could be *important,* how it could be anything but a nuisance. Eventually it became the enemy. In concert with genetics and restaurant portions, I weighed over three hundred pounds by the time I was thirty-something.

And oh, did I resent the fact that I could not cold-turkey quit eating like other addicts could quit shooting heroin into the tiny veins of their eyeballs or kidnapping children. So when I found the closest alternative to quitting food, I jumped on it like it was tuna noodle salad: weight loss surgery. Weight loss surgery is where they take your body and they take food and then they separate you surgically so that the two will never play nice ever again. Your stomach is sliced into a shadow of itself so you can't really fit food into it, and your intestines are rerouted so you don't get a whole lot from the food that you do manage to fit inside. It's a food-hater's surgery; it's a drastic move.

In the first months after surgery, food disappeared from my life entirely and was replaced by shakes that tasted like someone had ground up hatred and war and was feeding it to me through a straw. But I could only take small sips, and the idea of putting anything else in my body was the most wonderful, nauseated feeling in the world. It was a relief.

But unfortunately, eventually I recovered from the dramatic after-effects of the major surgery. And somehow I was startled, disappointed, and deeply unhappy to find that I still needed food to live. That maybe I should have been listening to my doctors, who talked a lot about the need for post-surgery patients to cook small portions of healthy things and put them in their faces. Making friends with the delivery kid from the Chinese place around the corner wasn't one of the best-practice recommendations in the post-surgery instruction manual.

In less than a year I lost 180 pounds, yet somehow I managed to keep all the dysfunction.

Obviously all of it was still my mother's fault.

I mean, my mother taught my brother and me—or we learned, in the face of the food she prepared, or didn't, and the care she took, or didn't, or couldn't—that food wasn't important. While I embraced this lesson, my brother beat the odds. Ken broke free, ran wild, and discovered that *good* food is important. Cooking is important. My brother is a graduate of culinary school, a pastry chef, and a marathon runner.

He is someone who spends a fortune on olive oil—*good* olive oil, he tells me (and I like to think that somewhere, evil olive oil is plotting the destruction of upscale food shops everywhere). He is someone who takes pleasure in selecting bright, fresh produce and clean, well-marbled cuts of meat that look like photos from glossy magazines. He understands the double meaning of *nourish*, the real meaning of *diet*, and I don't know how he did it. He has never been able to offer me a reasonable explanation. He shrugs. "I like food," he says.

When he came to visit me once, he said, "Let's cook." He turned down all my fancy restaurant suggestions. I offered to pay, and he still said no. I called him crazy, and he shook his head at me.

We went to the market—not just the local supermarket, but the upscale grocery store where grapes that look like regular grapes to me cost as much as gold-covered grapes in a diamond reduction sauce. He selected cuts of chicken and organic greens that were a green so vivid they didn't look real to me. He selected fresh herbs, even when I protested that we had some dried herbs somewhere in the cabinet. "How can you waste your money?" I said.

As we cooked at home, I tried to just observe in a scientific manner, but he pressed a knife and a tomato into my hands. I made a mess of it trying to chop it, but I quickly discovered a remarkable focus. Everything depended on my hand holding the knife, my fingers steadying the tomato, my entire body straining not to cut off one of my thumbs. I became so small and at peace with my single focus: knife, tomato, driving need to avoid pain and blood.

The kitchen was bright but poorly laid out; all the equipment belonged to my roommate and the stove was kind of wobbly, but my brother acted like none of it mattered. He poured each of us a glass of champagne and he slid the chicken breasts across dishes set out in a row: beaten eggs, flour, breadcrumbs, and then settled them in a hot pan full of golden oil. There was sizzling, and the smell was rich and real. I was fascinated by him doing this so quickly and simply, every movement deft and sure. He did not set himself on fire, not even once.

"This is simple," Ken said. "See how this took just a few minutes?" He let the chicken brown while he tore up the greens into a bowl. The green against the white porcelain, the golden rich smell of the chicken, the regular, dull *chunk* of the knife on the cutting board. Maybe cooking was immersive and sensory; maybe it could be an experience, in the essence of the word, instead of a chore.

You have to understand: to me, this was a revelation. A revolution, even.

Ken swept my smashed tomato bits and some purple onion on top of the lovely fluffy pile of greens and whisked a dressing together—emulsion is science, but it's also a kind of magic. He tossed everything. A rhythm emerged: Flip the chicken, take a sip of champagne. Try to remember the lyrics to the song we wrote about how we deserved more Christmas presents than anyone in the world. Get plates (my roommate's plates) out of the cabinets and pile everything together: perfectly golden chicken breasts, greens on top.

"Chicken Milanese," he said.

"It has a name," I said. "I totally just cooked something with a name."

He patted me gently on the head, and we sat down together at the table to take the first bites. We smiled at each other with full mouths, and I had a full heart. We had just spent a bright, slightly terrifying (to me) evening together, working side by side instead of shouting across a table in a restaurant full of strangers.

I must have cooked before. I must have made food, sometime, somewhere in one of the kitchens in one of the apartments I had lived in. I
must have made a meal for myself. I *had* chopped, measured, mixed,
sautéed, made food. But that memory had been buried under piles
of takeout boxes and the conviction that it wasn't worth it and that I
couldn't do it.

After this epiphany, my brother left and I went back to eating takeout.
It is hard to shake a lifetime of conviction.

———————

Months later, I stopped at a California Pizza Kitchen for lunch. I was between appointments, feeling rushed, and threw myself headlong into
the first open place. When I saw chicken Milanese on the menu, I felt
my entire body untense. I realized that I was evoking that night with my
brother, the smell of the oil in the pan and the green of the salad, and I
realized how much I missed him, each of us on a different coast. While I
was waiting for my food, I texted him—*hey I miss you*.

I stopped typing after *hey I miss you*, and I picked up my fork even before the waiter settled my plate down on the table. It looked good, but not
as good as it was supposed to. It tasted good—but not as good as it was supposed to. It made me think of my brother (*hey, did you know we make better
chicken Milanese than California Pizza Kitchen?*) and it made me want to go
home and make it the right way.

I couldn't fit everything I wanted to say in my tiny screen.

*Hey, food is a kind of magic. You take ingredients and put them together,
and you make something that's more than ingredients. You've made
something with a name, as if you were a biblical god calling forth the
heavens and the firmament and the carbs. You've made something even
more important—and if you'll forgive me for being cheesy, what you've
made is a memory. I will not ever forget hanging out with you that night
and the taste of champagne and the pleasure in teamwork and how I did
not stab myself in the eye with a paring knife and kept all my thumbs and
realized I was lucky to have the brother I do. The best of all possible brothers; the best of all possible chicken Milanese.*

I thought about texting my mother—*I'm sorry, Mom*—but then she'd ask why and then I'd have to confess, and the idea made me not want to finish my lunch. The waiter said, "How's your meal?" and I smiled and said, "Fine, thank you." When my phone chimed I lifted it to look at the screen. My brother had texted back: *Next I have a recipe for spaghetti Bolognese for you.*

CHEF KEN'S CHICKEN MILANESE

RECIPE PROVIDED BY CARRIE ELLMAN-LARSEN

SERVES 4

4 skinless, boneless chicken breasts

3 tablespoons vegetable oil

½ cup all-purpose flour

1 egg, whisked

½ cup bread crumbs

3 tomatoes

1 or 2 cloves garlic

12 ounces arugula

3 tablespoons extra virgin olive oil

Squeeze or two of lemon

Salt and freshly ground black pepper

Rinse and pat dry the chicken breasts. If possible, buy thin-sliced chicken breasts or pound the breasts thin to make sure the chicken cooks quickly and evenly.

Heat the vegetable oil in a large skillet over medium-high heat. Fill one shallow plate with the flour, one with a whisked egg, and one with bread crumbs. Lightly coat the chicken with flour, then coat the chicken completely in egg. Coat the chicken generously in bread crumbs. (Sometimes I use packaged Italian-style bread crumbs for more flavor, or you can make fresh or use panko and add seasoning.) Place the chicken in the skillet and fry until golden brown on both sides. If the chicken is thin, this should be only a few minutes per side.

While the chicken is frying, chop or slice the tomatoes, then dice the garlic. In a large bowl, toss the tomatoes and garlic with the arugula. Drizzle the salad with the olive oil and lemon juice and season with salt and pepper to taste.

When the chicken is done cooking, place each piece on top of a paper towel for a minute to drain the excess oil. Plate the chicken and top with the salad. Add an extra squeeze of lemon if you like.

THE CASSOULET SAVED OUR MARRIAGE

DEBORAH COPAKEN KOGAN AND PAUL KOGAN

Dear Paul,

I am laughing at the fact that we have to write this essay in the eye of this new marital storm. If you put it in a sitcom—middle-aged, married parents of three, in their twenty-second year of sharing a home, consent to writing a joint essay called "The Cassoulet Saved Our Marriage" as they battle it out, once again, in couples therapy—the executive in charge of the project would say no, sorry, that's over the top. But this is our life, not a sitcom, and I'm thinking that if we can write this essay together under these conditions, not only will it remind us of how we maneuvered around our last marital roadblock by tackling something as crazy as making a cassoulet, it might help us around this one.

It's hard to believe that this winter, assuming we have it in us to come together again, we will host our eleventh annual Cassoulet Day, that daylight bacchanal to which we invite twenty or thirty friends to warm their bellies with a meal we've spent three days cooking. Or rather, to be fair, you're really the chef on those days. I just chop stuff, roll the forks and knives into fraying white napkins, and put out the plates and wineglasses either the night before (if I'm on top of things) or five minutes prior to the guests' arrival.

That all-day feast *is* us, more than anything else we do as a couple or family. It's who we are, what we believe in, the values we want to impart to our kids: slowing it down; taking the necessary care to do a task well; creating something where there was nothing; celebrating for the sake of celebrating; nourishing both friends and their friendship. Remember how much we laughed when Sasha, who was then seven or eight years old, said, "Mom, Dad, what do other families do for Cassoulet Day?" as if it were Thanksgiving? The yearly ritual, which you launched back in that cold February of 2000, had become so ingrained in our daughter's calendar, it had never occurred to her that Cassoulet Day was invented by her daddy.

I'm sure part of you, whether consciously or not, chose a French dish for our yearly tradition, just as the cracks were starting to show in our foundation, as a reminder of the young lovers we once were, trading life histories for the first time on the banks of the Seine. Paris is also where we first learned how to cook by cooking for our hungry friends—who couldn't afford to go out, either—in our kitchen on the rue St. Joseph, with its view straight into that garment factory that must be long gone by now. Twenty-four years old when we moved into that apartment: What could we have known then about how our needs and hungers might change come middle age?

When I pause to take stock of all the many blessings I have to lose through the possible loss of you—two decades of shared history, an intact family, a whole life sautéed over the pilot light of our love—the rending of our yearly Cassoulet Day from the calendar cuts deep. That tradition symbolizes what we can do when we're at our best. I'm crying as I type these words, feeling the difficulty of this moment in time, imagining the loss of that day like the loss of a limb, or my heart.

How heartbreaking, how absurd to be in this place of marital limbo. And so we tackle our uncertainty about our future the way we tackle everything together, which is the same way you, over the course of three days, tackle our cassoulet: step by step, ingredient by ingredient, day by day.

It's funny. All these years, I've never once asked you what your impetus was to start the tradition.

Love,
Deb

Dear Deb,

It's a good question. Why *did* we start this? The way I remember it, we met one spring in Paris and fell in love. When you got back from Romania, or Russia, or some other far-flung reportage trip, we moved in together on the rue St. Joseph. We then abandoned Paris for Moscow, and then Moscow for New York, got married, had our first two kids. All in the span of a few years. And then came Cassoulet Day!

Why? I think you are right, part of it was to carry a tinder of our Parisian love back to New York. And part of it was my love of hosting the crowd, building the ultimate dinner party. Maybe it was also a reminder of my childhood evenings growing up in Russia, when fellow writers, academics, and friends would crowd into my mother's small Moscow apartment, talking and drinking late into the night. A *tusovka*, we called it, a word that has no equivalent in the English language.

The one thing you and I have always agreed upon, through good times and bad, is that the dinner party is the finest achievement of civilization. Getting a crowd around your table, seeing the chemistry swirl, the stories and egos bursting forth, new bonds being formed, old friendships getting stronger. We loved it, and we loved making it happen together.

Cassoulet Day, then, embodied the ultimate dinner party on steroids. It was a social festival in our tiny New York apartment, a chance to squeeze in an oversized crowd—a pageant we can bring together, entertain, and make merry. And it was the chance to create a tradition: the yearly celebration of you, me, our friends, and food.

The other part of it for me was the history. That first year, 2000, I researched the history of the dish back to its origins. I loved that cassoulet came from the peasants, from the earth. They had all this duck left over from making foie gras for the nobles. So they made confit, and they threw in pork sausages, mutton bones, whatever they had, along with the beans to make this incredible, heavenly, gut-busting dish. It was not fancy food.

I read that in the town of Castelnaudary, a siege took place in the 1300s or around then, and the only way they survived the siege was by gathering whatever food they had inside the walls and making a huge dish, keeping everyone fed while the siege went on, and defeating their enemies . . . with cooking!

And then competing schools of cassoulet arose: one in Toulouse, the other in Carcassonne, and each one claimed to be the "true" cassoulet, the right way to make cassoulet. The differences were minimal, like whether it's right to add tomatoes, or sausage, but these differences were discussed passionately, were fought over with real ardor. That's what I fell in love with: the passion, the history.

And the part I loved sharing with you was that we could make our own court around it. We could gather our friends from various walks of life, create a "salon" as they came together, took pleasure from meeting each other, got drunk together, all participating in this theater, on a stage we created.

———————

Remember that one year we invited a couple of chefs, two men who owned great restaurants in New York, Dan Barber of Blue Hill and Peter Hoffman of Savoy? We also invited a friend who at the time was the lead restaurant critic for *The New York Times*. As they were sitting there, loving the cassoulet and drinking wine, I introduced them casually, not thinking anything of it. The next day, I got a scathing e-mail from the restaurant critic, saying he was incredibly upset that I would openly introduce him to the restaurant owners.

Turns out that as a critic, he had to protect his identity. No one on the restaurant side could know what he actually looked like, so he could eat in their restaurants without special treatment: the only way to write an objective review. And this was an ongoing game the restaurants played with the critics, trying to guess what they looked like. And at our Cassoulet Day, we messed with the game.

It made me realize: Often, even when we have the best intentions, we mess with the game.

Cassoulet Day, on the other hand, is the one thing we always get right: It is us, as you say, at our best. When I think back on our twenty-one-and-a-half years together, I remember much good, and very little bad. Maybe I hold on to the kitchen smells, the garlic sautéing, the duck fat sizzling, you chopping carrots, me chopping onions, both of us crying. Maybe it's selective memory.

So I beg of you: Help me keep Cassoulet Day going. Stay as my co-chef and co-host.

I cannot imagine making cassoulet alone any more than I can imagine life without you. Please don't let a great tradition die.

I love you,
Mr. Cassoulet

―――――――――

Oh, Mr. Cassoulet,

You know I love you. That's never been an issue. What is at issue is nobody's business but ours, but since we've been asked to share this publicly, I will interject a simple note here to say that what we're going through is its own particular beast: no more or less frightening, no more or less painful than the beasts of any long-term marriage, except in our case it keeps rearing its head in a way that feels, at least for now, intractable. That being said, I want to believe that even if we find ourselves at that nebulous fork in the road, where we choose Irreconcilable Differences Drive over Lovers Lane, we might continue cooking our yearly cassoulet for so many reasons, not the least of which would be our children's sense of continuity and tradition in the midst of the inevitable chaos of a rupture.

I sometimes wish I'd been forced to take a class on marriage: to really study the institution; to understand its inner workings and pitfalls; to remove the rose-colored glasses that romantic comedies and advertisers and the wedding industry stick on our noses, over and over and over again. Then again, maybe marriage is one of those things, like cooking cassoulet, that can't be taught. You just have to *do* it, getting your hands dirty, your apron splattered with fat, year after year after year, making tweaks and improvements along the way, just like when you figured out that cannellini beans held up better than great northern or navy, or that it was better to buy a whole duck and have the butcher cut it into eight pieces rather than to buy separate limbs.

Not that I'm comparing our marriage to a dismembered duck, but you know what I mean.

Let me end with this thought: No matter what happens to us in the future, you have made so much of our life thus far a celebration, and for this I will always be grateful. Will cassoulet save this marriage? I hope so.

Love,
Your humble sous chef

———————

Hello, Sous Chef,

It's crazy how much effort it takes to make this one dish. I was just looking through my notes (I wrote it all down a few years ago), and it took us thirteen hours to cook: four hours the Friday night before, and then eight hours nonstop on Saturday, then another hour to do the sausages on Sunday morning before the guests arrived.

- Skinning two whole fresh ducks, rendering fat from that skin, marinating them in spices, and then confiting them slowly in their own fat: four hours.
- Picking out stones and dirt from four pounds of dried cannellini beans, one batch at a time.
- Chopping mountains of onions, carrots, thyme. (I always admire how handy you are with a knife.)
- Cutting, trimming, and then browning eight pounds of lamb shoulder: also four hours.

And so on and so on.

By the end, I am teetering on my tired feet, covered in grease, and your hand is numb from chopping.

Is it hard? Yes. But so is making a relationship work, which is why we did this year after year, I think. Not for our friends, but for us. It was just something no one else did, our own crazy thing that set us apart. And once we did it for a few years, it just felt right to keep going.

It was us. It is us. And what I thought, without saying or admitting it, is that you and I were a unique couple, special and different from the others we know. Every couple thinks this, of course, but I really believed it. Maybe it was our origin story, our quirky backgrounds: Who would have expected a Russian émigré, via New York and Princeton, working for the Russian mob, and a suburban Harvard graduate working as a war photographer would meet in Paris? Or for them to move to Moscow together only to survive the 1991 coup? Maybe it was our backgrounds, or the dramatic international backdrop, but our beginning felt auspicious. It fed our conviction: We would do something world-changing with our lives.

So Cassoulet Day happened by chance but came to epitomize this special thing we could accomplish through our joint efforts. The only year we didn't do it, if you'll recall, was that February right after your dad died, and we had more pressing concerns, like just making it through each day. But for ten nearly uninterrupted years it brought us together in a common goal, like a marathon, only stationary, and covered in grease.

Where did it bring us? I think to a good place.

Love,
Paul

THE REAL CASSOULET GUIDE

I've compiled my notes made over the years into a kind of mixed recipe and general guide to making the cassoulet. Having done this eleven times, I've learned that the times and process will depend on things like the oven, the particular pots and pans, and the ingredients you are able to source locally.

So you should expect to make the cassoulet a few times before you get it "right." Experimenting and trying different approaches is a large part of the enjoyment. By the second or third time, you will have calibrated your own process so the cassoulet coming out of the oven will be uniquely your own, which is the real treat for you, your friends, and family.

THURSDAY

PART 1—PREP THE DUCK

Time: 15 minutes

½ cup coriander seeds

½ cup cumin seeds

1 whole duck, quartered

8 duck legs, halved

Salt

2 heads of garlic, peeled

Note: Ask for duck breast and duck legs with the skin already removed and saved for rendering. Otherwise, allow 3 hours to take the skin and fat off the duck and render about 5 cups of duck fat.

Crush the coriander and cumin seeds. Pat dry the duck meat and rub salt and the spices on both sides. Place the duck in a large zip-top bag. Crush half the garlic. Add both the crushed and whole garlic to the duck meat, seal the bag, and shake it up. Marinate in the refrigerator overnight.

FRIDAY

8 pounds lamb shoulder, trimmed of fat and cut up

10 carrots

10 medium tomatoes

2 quarts beef stock

4 Spanish onions

2 bunches thyme

1 pound Applegate Farms bacon (no nitrates)

3 7-ounce packages D'Artagnan duck fat

2½ to 3 pounds dried cannellini beans

2 bay leaves

1 head of garlic

Note: Consider buying salad, parsley, flowers, and sausage on Sunday (or on Cassoulet Day), so as to maximize freshness.

PART 3—COOK THE BEANS

Time: 2½ to 3 hours

   11 A.M. Friday

Set two large pasta pots, about three-quarters filled with water, over high heat. Do this first, as it will take them a long time to come to boil. You'll be putting about 1½ pounds beans in each pot.

Rinse and sort through the beans in a strainer, pulling out the odd bits of rock and dirt.

When the water comes to a boil, add the beans, turn off heat, and let soak for 1 hour.

While the beans are soaking, chop and add to each pot of water:

½ pound bacon, chopped small

Onions—1 per pot

Bay leaf—1 per pot

1 bunch of thyme per pot

1 to 3 unpeeled garlic cloves per pot

4 handfuls of salt per pot

After the beans have soaked for an hour, return the water to a boil and simmer the beans for 1 hour.

Pour the beans through a large colander held over a plastic lidded container, so you can reserve the bean juice. The beans then go into one of two Dutch oven casseroles, covered with a little cooking liquid so they don't dry out while preparing other ingredients.

Where to put all these partially prepared batches of ingredients?! In a small kitchen, it may be hard to find room for everything. Consider making space in the dining room to put containers of ingredients awaiting the next step—assembly.

PART 4—CONFIT THE DUCK (WHILE THE BEANS ARE SOAKING)

Time: 3 hours

Preheat the oven to 275°F.

Pull the duck fat out of the refrigerator and let it come to room temperature. Pat down and dry the duck. Lay the duck out in the roasting pans and cover the duck with the solid fat. (Keep the cooked garlic pieces in.) Place the pans containing the duck and fat on the stovetop, and over very low heat, melt the duck fat. If necessary, add more duck fat so that the fat covers the meat. When the duck is fully submerged in bubbling fat, place the pan in the oven and roast for 2 hours.

This is an assembly line of multiple batches because of how much duck there is. Prepping this took 45 minutes. I used all 3 duck fat packages.

While it's cooking, return to chopping the bacon and onions for the beans.

Strain all the duck out and put it in a plastic lidded container. Save about 1 to 2 cups of the strained duck fat, chuck the rest.

PART 5—PREPARE THE LAMB

Time: 2 to 3 hours

Put away the duck and beans and take out the 8 pounds lamb. Pat the lamb dry, then trim and brown in duck fat. Set aside.

Then brown the 10 carrots in the same duck fat.

Chop and add to an empty casserole dish:

About 6 medium tomatoes

Beef stock

Red wine (Syrah), or you can use a more traditional white

Some bean juice

Lots of thyme

Add the lamb to the casserole dish and let the lamb simmer on the stovetop for 30 minutes.

Part 6—Do the Layering

Layer the beans, lamb, and the juices, then duck, more beans, and so on. If you'd like, add pieces of whole baked garlic for flavor. When both casseroles are full, you can add bean stock to keep everything moist, saving the remaining liquid. It should all fit, like magic (or 1970s college kids in a VW) in the two casserole dishes!

After eight hours of nonstop cooking today (Friday), and three hours Thursday night, it proves well worthwhile to prepare it two days in advance. This way you can have Saturday "off." (Usually I am completely wiped out.)

SATURDAY (CASSOULET DAY EVE): DAY OFF.

SUNDAY (CASSOULET DAY)

Part 7—Cook the Sausage

Time: 1 hour plus time for shopping

17 fresh sweet sausages (ideally, find some fresh ones that are made daily)

Salad

Parsley

Flowers

5 excellent fresh baguettes

Clementines, 2 boxes

Brown the sausages, then cut each into 4 to 5 pieces. Brown the slices, too. Grilling takes about 45 minutes.

PART 8—THE FINAL ASSEMBLY

Timing: To plan your Cassoulet Day timing, start prepping about one hour before your guests arrive. So with people coming at 1 o'clock, you want the first cassoulet to be out at 1:30. You'd plan to have it baking in the oven at 12:30. Start prep at noon.

The cassoulets come out of the refrigerator several hours before your guests arrive so they can start coming up slowly to room temperature.

Bury two layers of sausages in each casserole, one layer deep down, the second just under the surface. (I dig holes in the casserole, then push 3 or 4 sausage pieces into the beans in each hole.)

Preheat the oven to 450°F.

Final preparation:

Spread a thin layer of reserved duck fat on top of the cassoulet.

Add extra bean liquid if either casserole seems dry.

Cover the top of each casserole with bread crumbs (I use regular Italian bread crumbs. You don't want to go overboard with bread crumbs.)

Slice 6 ripe tomatoes and layer slices on top.

I also chop a bunch of parsley and set it in a bowl to be added when the cassoulet comes out of the oven.

Put one casserole over high heat on the stovetop and bring to a boil. Place the boiling casserole into the oven. After 30 minutes, check the casseroles to see if they're boiling over. Drain small amounts of liquid if necessary. Then turn the heat down to 300°F and bake for another 30 minutes.

PART 9—THE EATING OF THE CASSOULET

Consider serving salad at 1:30 to guests, depending on how hungry they are.

Casserole 1 is ready, gets a sprinkling of parsley, and is served at 1:45.

Casserole 2 goes in the oven for final cooking.

Verdict: It's really good, not undersalted (surprise!). Amanda calls it "brothy." She is right. Everyone is complimentary. Then again, they've been drinking red wine all day.

THE HUNGER SHAMES

KAREN VALBY

They say the kitchen holds the heart and soul of a home. Growing up, my family kitchen was large, spotless, and quiet—always enveloped in that same shock of silence that follows after a train roars by. I remember coming home one afternoon in the seventh grade and calling upstairs to my mother to ask if I could have a snack. She was locked inside her bathroom, smoking cigarettes and running the tub with the drain unplugged. "You could always make yourself some rice," she weakly suggested through the door. If my mother could just pull it together already and make a pan of brownies, maybe I could forgive her screaming about a mafia conspiracy as I shut the car door on her that morning in front of school.

I grew up starving for the family harmony advertised in instant waffle commercials. Life in the suburbs was one overstuffed pantry after another, stocked by lipsticked, well-moisturized mothers who bought their families juice boxes and snack packs and zip-top bags in bulk. Kids whose kitchens have snack cabinets teeming with brand-name chips and cookies don't go home and stare hard at a cup of white rice while their mother carries on conversations with herself in the mirror.

Though my mother forbade junk food in the house, she eventually grew tired of looking at the wad of coupons I stuck to the fridge. She agreed to buy me one box of sugary cereal a year. That first time, I lingered long in the supermarket, dazzled by the offerings, before making my careful selection. At home, I laid out spoon and bowl with great tenderness. But af-

128

ter pouring a bowl of my first sweet cereal, instead of tasting freshly baked chocolate cookies in cold milk, I got a mouthful of aerated, polka-dotted pellets. I'd fantasized about this moment for a year, only to dump the traitorous bowl down the garbage disposal after three bites. I couldn't blame the cereal, though. It was the fault of our poisonous kitchen, where no one ever seemed to find any comfort or sustenance.

That spring I invited friends to my last birthday party—or rather the last party I would risk having at home. I planned the whole menu. We needed hamburgers and hot dogs, pickles, fudge swirl ice cream, pudding pops, fat bags of chips, and just this once, please, please, please, soda. I was a wreck in the grocery store, panicked that if I didn't offer the right spread the kids would smell the misery soaked into the family room floorboards. Exhausted by my anxious nagging, my mother snapped and started screaming in the middle of the aisle before running out of the store, leaving me alone in the frozen foods section with a shopping cart full of food I could not pay for. I started to replace each item on their shelves, as if somehow they had failed to impress after all.

By high school, my mother's manic depression was building from the occasional gust to a months-long squall, and she was finding it harder and harder to leave the bathroom. My father sought refuge at his office late into the evening and my older brother dove deep into a Dungeons and Dragons–induced fog. Disgusted by our dreary lot, I started eating dinner at my best friends' house. They were twins, blond varsity athletes, with a lithe, intimidating older sister and a sunny younger brother. They were adorable, and they had adorable twin sheep dogs and they drove a sky-blue Volvo to their various varsity team practices. Their family portrait showed everyone in front of the fire in matching sweaters in different colors of sherbet ice cream. The photographer even hung it in the mall outside his shop to lure in customers as if to say, *This is what a family should look like*.

Every night, I convinced my mother there was another pressing group homework assignment and she'd drop me off at the twins' house. I'd flop on one of their double beds until their mother called us downstairs to eat. Their dad ate at the head of the table in sweatpants and his Marines sweatshirt while their mother presented not just platters of beef Stroganoff or spaghetti and meatballs but also her special garlic bread and iceberg lettuce salads in little wooden bowls. There were different kinds of salad dressing on a lazy Susan on the table, and you could drink milk or soda or Tang in frosted plastic glasses.

Nobody smashed their plate, nobody threatened divorce. They just gathered together effortlessly after the sun went down, to laugh loudly and speak over one another. I tried to sit quietly and keep up with their inside jokes, staring slack-jawed when the older sister was in a mood. Once she declared to her mother that she had become a vegetarian that afternoon and so wouldn't be eating the meatballs. Another time she said she planned on wearing red to her first wedding and black to her second. Occasionally she took her plate upstairs to her room in protest of all the good humor. I liked it better whenever she left the table early, so I didn't have to worry that there wouldn't be enough dessert for the guest.

Some nights I had no choice but to eat at home. My mother, in one of her fits of energy, would announce she was making her trademark eleven-vegetable soup. She'd maroon herself around the kitchen island, extolling the importance of sound nutrition, surrounded by raw leeks and spinach and carrots, shoving all the vegetables into an old-fashioned strainer that she cranked awkwardly by hand. Nothing good ever came from that junkyard-colored soup, including an edible dinner. A week later I'd find half a pot of congealed, putrefying vegetables shoved to the back of the fridge, and my mother would have again retreated to her bedroom with the shades drawn.

In my own room, after the eleven-vegetable episode, I'd take the phone into the closet to call the twins. At some point in the conversation they'd have to go because their dad had just returned home with pizza. "Save me a piece of pepperoni!" I'd sing into the phone brightly, as if I had any claim to their food. The next night I'd be back at the twins' house, embarrassed by my own hunger and the near tearful gratitude I felt about being invited to sit down at another family's table.

———— • ————

A high school cafeteria is a vulnerable place, a cruelly lit room where teenagers take daily stock of their peers' outfits and alliances. But I was obsessed with my friends' lunches, and how I might deflect attention away from what I wasn't bringing from home. My mom left me some wadded-up dollar bills on the kitchen counter each morning and, rather than stand in the cafeteria line for Tater Tots or a chicken patty sandwich, every day I'd buy a granola bar and a pack of hard candy at the school store. I thought it better to affect disinterest in food, and hoped that by relying on a static menu of junk I conveyed a cool obliviousness to the meal.

At lunch I was surrounded by friends who slowly worked their way through brown bag lunches, licking processed cheese stains off their fingers and draining juice boxes. My friend Lorena usually sat across from me and every day she'd reach into her sack and reveal lovingly prepared turkey and avocado or sopressata and cheddar sandwiches. Her mother bought fresh baguettes and thick, flavorful slabs of rye, and the slices of plum tomato never bled the bread red and wet. Those sandwiches became the crush I could not stop thinking about during class. At lunch, I'd thumb a Mento to the top of the roll, sucking each candy rather than chewing it to buy more time.

Cruelly, Lorena sometimes would engage in conversation and ignore her half-eaten sandwich. I'd start nosing around for food, asking Lorena for a piece of salami or a taste of brownie, thinking this was the highest compliment to pay another person. If I want your food, I want more than your lunch. I want your life.

But it's tiring sitting next to somebody who is always sniffing for scraps. Lorena eventually snapped at me to get my own lunch already and leave hers alone. Mortified, I moved to the other end of the table and brought a hand to my mouth, shocked, any time I saw her throw out the remains of her food on her way out of the cafeteria. How could anyone turn their back on half a slice of pound cake or the crust of a homemade quiche? But my friends seemed convinced of the promise of another adorable meal, so much so that they would risk abandoning some of this one. Such confidence struck me as both foolish and formidable.

During senior year we were allowed to leave campus during lunch, so I was liberated from cataloging my friends' various homemade offerings each day. Shortly into the semester I followed the migration to a trendy health food store with an outdoor patio. A number of my friends had grown obsessed with their weight and worried calories and fat grams while poking at their dry salads or scooping out the bread of their bagels. Suddenly one or two were experimenting with genuine deprivation, bragging about how little each had eaten the previous evening and talking about their scales like they were undependable boyfriends, giving one night, cruel the next. I'd try to nod along, mystified by their blooming anorexia. I never could understand how going hungry could fill one up with pride and accomplishment. If you're ever offered something beautiful and delicious, you finish the whole thing. Cram it in gratefully, and hope someone offers you more.

At home, I'd been left alone with my mother. My brother had escaped to college. My father had finally agreed to a separation and moved into a small apartment twenty minutes away. When my mother was institutionalized after her first suicide attempt, my dad moved back into the house for two weeks. One night, he came home early and the two of us went to the grocery store. We took our time picking out that evening's meal, and at home I sat at the table and watched him prepare a simple dinner of chicken and rice. It horrified me to imagine my mother sitting down to her own dinner at a nearby hospital. Even the food—I pictured drab, soft green beans and too thick puddings—would taste crazy on the top floor reserved for the mentally ill, or the unmentionables as I began to think of my mother. I bucked the subject when my dad proposed that we visit the hospital that weekend. Please, not now, not while the food is cooking. I wanted to eat this calmly prepared dinner in peace, and not wonder if my mother had tried to kill herself by eating pills.

My dad returned home again on Christmas Eve, the first holiday my brother and I spent with separated parents. We ate in the formal dining room, on the good china, as if there was something to celebrate. My mother tried hard to smile while my dad made lunch, a casserole dish of shepherd's pie. It was sublime—neat layers of seasoned ground beef, mixed frozen vegetables, mashed potatoes, and a top layer of melted cheddar cheese. I later found out that a new girlfriend had given him the recipe. No matter how many times I've eaten the dish since, it's always left a disappointing taste in my mouth.

At my graduation banquet that year, the restaurant offered chicken Marsala and eggplant parmigiana. I dug happily into my meal as the social chair rattled off the names of classmates who had been voted Most Likely to Succeed and Best Total Package. I thought I had a chance at Best Party Attitude. Hadn't I thrown all those great parties when my mother was "away"? I hadn't served food, but there was always a keg and a lack of supervision. Instead, I heard my name announced as "Biggest Mooch." It took me a second to get to my feet and make my way to the center of the dining room, horrified, to accept the certificate while the social chair shrugged her shoulders. I squeezed my nails into my palms the rest of the ceremony, trying to keep my eyes from watering. There was no way to spin this. I wasn't a clown or a flirt or a kid going places. I was needy, and everyone apparently knew it. No, I didn't want dessert, I told the kind waiter standing over my shoulder, thank you. I was full.

Five months after my high school graduation, my mother was dead. She overdosed on pills after gnawing at her wrists with a kitchen knife. Lorena's mother sent me a box of homemade lemon bars in the mail, a gesture of kindness that knocked me to my knees. That Thanksgiving, my brother, father, and I gathered around my grandmother's gleaming cherry wood dining room table. My grandmother, who'd found her daughter dead in her guest room just one month before, had redirected all of her pain and energy into creating the perfect meal, and the conversation lurched uncomfortably from the tenderness of the meat to the smoothness of the potatoes. My mother's absence hung around the table like an uninvited guest everyone had agreed not to acknowledge. The adored family cat had run away not long after my mother died. Cleaning up that night, I noticed a glistening pile of turkey scraps in the trash can that ordinarily would have been presented to the cat as a holiday treat. Somewhere, she, too, was lost and hungry.

When I moved to New York City after college, I fell into my first great love affair with food. I lived next door to a Mexican restaurant and passed twenty more delis and diners and trattorias and Chinese takeout joints on my walk to the subway. Food was everywhere, and all I had to do was go deep into debt enjoying it. All my friends, shedding their own suburban or small-town histories, lived purposefully far from their families in cramped apartments without counter space or a four-burner stove, or even room for a dining table. This was a city where people went out to eat in loud, clattery restaurants with specials on chalkboards and waiters desperate to turn over tables to more paying customers. There was always a new place to try, and always a reason to celebrate or commiserate. On the rare night at home, I relied on a greasy pack of takeout menus and beached myself on the sofa in front of the TV, my legs draped over my roommate's lap.

A friend invited me to her apartment once, both of us blue and bored, and we decided to see how many hours we could lounge around watching bad television. Every so often she'd pop up from the couch and promise to return with snacks. All she was able to procure from her little galley kitchen seemed like magic. In the course of a long, lazy day, she'd poke her head from around the corner with offers of salmon salad sandwiches, pasta with kale and cannellini beans, a bowl of freshly washed red grapes, a raspberry and mango smoothie, and finally some leftover butternut squash soup with crushed cherry tomatoes and sharp Parmesan cheese floating gloriously on top. With every dish my friend seemed to reiterate that she was glad for my company and wanted me to stay. After working our way through each treat, I would look up and marvel that my friend simply must open a restaurant and there had never been soup served as perfectly as hers and who else but a woman as wonderful as she kept salmon salad on hand. Laughing at my panting enthusiasm, she told me that there was no one else in her life who was more fun to feed. I'd never felt so well taken care of in my life, even as I was struck by the knowledge that I would never know how to open my home to another as she had done. I'd spent so long taking care of myself that a life in which I gracefully welcomed and nurtured another had never occurred to me.

After ten years in New York, my husband and I moved into a stone cottage with a dishwasher and a dining room in Austin, Texas. We unpacked all the boxes that had been stacked up on our six-person dining room table, a gift from my grandmother, who had died a few years before. I hated sitting around that table after my mother died, but in this new house the wood gleamed differently, as if eager for company instead of rebuffing it.

I'm not sure when luck reappeared in my life, but my husband cooks dinner every night. I walk home in the evenings and see the kitchen light on in the back of the house and know that comfort waits for me within those walls. He listens to loud music and drinks beer while he cooks, and when he frets about dull knives or missing ingredients, he still sounds like he's enjoying himself. He likes food, calmly approaching each new recipe as if it were a story that promised a happy ending. Most of all, he seems to enjoy cooking for me. Each evening, after I hear one last mad dash of preparation, ice clinking in a glass, the final twist of a pepper grinder, he lays food out in front of me and waits to see my reaction before he digs in himself. It's as if my happiness, my oohing and beaming over a particularly good tomato sauce or stir-fry, kick-starts his own hunger.

Two years ago my daughter came into my world, hungry. We adopted Ava Bekelech when she was eleven months old. She had a worrisome pooch of a belly and birdlike arms and teeny ankles that buckled under her weight as she tried to heave herself upright. On the morning we met in Addis Ababa she regarded her new parents with understandable wariness as the two of us fumbled like ninnies, arms entangled, both trying and failing to put her in a diaper. Smelling our fear, she let loose a hot stream of urine and broke into sobs. "Get the bottle!" I cried. She chugged her formula down, cried some more, then fell asleep, a line of drying milk sealing her to my husband's shoulder.

For the next week she refused all my prodding spoonfuls of organic baby food and looked always on the verge of wailing. Finally, one of the exceptionally kind Ethiopian women working at the guesthouse where we were staying told me that my daughter was hungry. "She won't eat!" I cried. The woman mashed some biscuits into a bowl of porridge, took my new child in her arms, and spoon-fed her two heaping bowls. My joy at seeing my baby girl finally sated outweighed my own sense of ineptitude until I rocked her to sleep that night. What a gross failure of a new mother was I that it took another woman to step in and nourish this vulnerable child?

When we returned home to Austin our lives were instantly built around our now insatiable daughter's eating schedule. She graduated quickly from baby food to lumberjack breakfasts. "She eats like you!" my husband cried in delight. Which meant she ate everything and did so with gusto. No finicky child, mine. I watched every bite of beans and vegetables and noodles and eggs go into her mouth with extraordinary pleasure. *"She's here! She's gaining weight! She's happy!"* every meal seemed to announce. On the rare night she left some food in her bowl I found myself pleading in a tense sing-song voice for her to eat the last few bites. My husband told me to let her be, but I worried over the lost nutrition or whether she'd wake up in the middle of the night hungry. And so I coaxed, I needled, I bribed with the promise of dessert. She was a good girl if she ate everything.

One night my husband winced and shook his head sternly at me after I told our daughter she couldn't get up from the table until she'd finished her last bite of supper. "You need to relax with the food," he told me later, after she'd fallen asleep. "That child needs to start deciding for herself when she is full. I don't want eating to be such a loaded undertaking in her life as she grows up. She's healthy and happy, Karen. She's already as big as a basketball and she is never, ever going to go hungry again."

And so, two years later, I try to praise this perfect child of mine not for her empty bowl at the end of a meal but for bringing it to the sink without having to be asked. Both of us seem to have learned—me at thirty-seven, she at three—to approach a dinner table with less rabid energy, which means family meals are longer and more relaxed. I try to model for her an eating life of deliberate gusto rather than anxious stuffing. We eat well. We linger at the table. We savor. "Mmmn, mmmn, mmmh!" she and I moan when a particular bite pleases and we turn in unison to gaze adoringly at our trusted chef.

My daughter has recently decided that she'd like her agnostic family to start saying grace before every meal. So at night we wait patiently for my husband to lay our plates before us. The food waits while we grasp hands and give thanks for our many blessings. Usually Ava thanks the world for Buzz Lightyear, and for our dog, and for the Dumbo ride we went on months ago at Disney World. But the other night she surprised us by straying from her usual litany of gifts.

"Thank you for dinner," she said, squeezing both of our hands. "Thank you for us. Thank you for myself." She stopped then and looked up at me with a child's breathtaking sense of wonder. "Can I say that?" she asked me very seriously. "Can I say thank you for me?" I nodded *of course* while blinking back tears. "Thank you for myself," she said with more certainty. "I love myself. Your turn, Mommy. You say that, too. Say thank you for Mommy."

"Thank you for myself," I said, my voice wobbly but determined. "And thank you for you. And thank you for this dinner." And then mother and child together let out a happy cry of delight over the still-warm plates of food before us. "Let's eat, Mommy!" And so we did.

MY HUSBAND'S DORO WAT
(TRADITIONAL ETHIOPIAN CHICKEN STEW)

Traditional doro wat is made by adding 3 or 4 hard-boiled eggs about 10 minutes before it's ready to serve. The first time my husband made this he forgot the eggs, and it tasted so good he never bothered adding them.

SERVES 4

2 pounds skinless chicken legs and thighs
Juice of 1 lemon
2 teaspoons salt
2 onions, chopped
3 cloves garlic, crushed
1 tablespoon peeled and chopped fresh ginger
4 tablespoons (½ stick) butter
2 tablespoons paprika
¼ cup *berberé* spice (found in specialty shops or sold at Ethiopian restaurants)
¾ cup chicken stock
¼ cup red wine
Salt and freshly ground pepper

Mix together the chicken pieces, lemon juice, and salt in a large bowl and set aside to marinate for about 30 minutes.

While the chicken is marinating, puree the onions, garlic, and ginger in a food processor or blender. Add a little water if necessary.

Heat the butter in a large saucepan over medium heat. Add the paprika and stir to color the oil and cook the spice through, about 1 minute. Do not burn. Stir in the *berberé* and cook for another 2 to 3 minutes.

Add the onion-garlic-ginger puree and sauté until most of the moisture evaporates and the onion cooks down and loses its raw aroma, 5 to 10 minutes. Do not allow the mixture to burn.

Pour in the stock and wine and stir in the chicken pieces; season with salt and pepper. Bring to a boil, then reduce heat to low, cover, and simmer for about 1 hour, adding water as necessary to maintain a sauce-like consistency, until the chicken is cooked through and very tender.

Adjust the seasoning and serve hot with *injera* (a traditional Ethiopian flatbread) or rice.

MAY IT NEVER BE THE LAST BRISKET

STACIE STUKIN

My collection of Jewish cookbooks is well worn with food-stained pages. Some belonged to my Great Aunt Hattie and others were purchased at dusty thrift stores along Fairfax Avenue in the Jewish neighborhood of Los Angeles. They are published by local Hadassah chapters and contain personal recipes for individual potato kugels and carrot tzimmes and have titles like *Love and Knishes* and spout wisdom such as "from hunger you will not starve," and ultimately they advise: "in the Jewish kitchen, don't look for fancy-schmancy; don't look for nouvelle anything and don't look for gourmet."

My mother owned only one Jewish cookbook, and she called it "Jennie." With a cracked spine held together by red electrician's tape, *Jennie Grossinger: The Art of Jewish Cooking* was her tome. Grossinger was the doyenne of the legendary Catskills resort my mother visited as a child in the 1940s and 1950s. There she heard Borscht Belt shtick from comedians like Shecky Green and Jackie Mason and ate exotic starters like Chilled Cantaloupe from California and entrees like Chicken Paprika with Spaetzle and Boiled Young Fowl in Pot with Matzo Ball. When she prepared Jewish meals for the holidays, she gave Jennie a quick peruse because like any art, Jewish cooking is an inexact, improvisational science, and she had absorbed her cooking knowledge through that inexplicable Jewish mother osmosis that flows from generation to generation. Then she promptly put it back on the shelf in its place next to Craig Claiborne's *The*

New York Times Cookbook. Her everyday cooking was equally nourishing. On weeknights she would sweep into the kitchen after a day shuttling me around to various extracurricular activities and without even taking off her coat, she began to prepare dinner.

Her techniques were idiosyncratic. Why should cooking screw up a perfectly good manicure? She accommodated her 1970s long red nails (acrylics were verboten) by never, for example, scalloping potatoes au gratin. Instead she stabbed the tubers with a fork before putting them in the oven. Meatloaf, made with matzo meal rather than breadcrumbs, was never mixed by hand, though a pinch of raw meat—one for her and one for me—was our secret pre-dinner snack. She mixed the ingredients with a fork in a shallow round stainless steel bowl so she could pat down the meat, turn the bowl over, and tap out a perfectly molded loaf straight onto the foil-lined baking sheet. And as she lived in California (like "Jennie") she often served sliced cantaloupe as a starter, as it required just a few whacks of the knife and a quick scrape of seeds to get gorgeous results: fresh orange flesh that was both succulent and sweet. My brother, my father, and I could just scoop out the juicy fruit with a spoon.

Her not touching food also precluded baking, since it required kneading and rolling dough. Baking also requires following precise directions, and this was not a strength of hers: No one ever had much success telling Hermine Salzhauer Stukin what to do.

Her stubborn character was developed in Brooklyn and her trajectory from east to west followed her beloved, underdog Dodgers. She was Yeshiva educated; "I could *daven* [pray in Hebrew] faster than the boys," she told me. But that Jewish education was tainted by the ire she and my grandmother incited when they suggested to the rabbis that my mother become a Bat Mitzvah. "Sacrilege, that's what they called it, and we walked away humiliated and ashamed," my mother recalled with disgust and a little sadness that the male rabbis of the time did not think her worthy of this religious rite of passage solely because she was a young woman. I never did get a formal Jewish education because my mother claimed she did not want to subject me to the same sexism, so my religious education took place in the kitchen and at the holiday table. I have since learned that biblical commentary equates the Jewish dining table to an altar, a domestic spiritual epicenter that is a place for blessings and worship and where sacred relationships are built that lead us in to our private and public lives. This is especially poignant during Friday night Shabbat dinner, a ritual we casually observed growing up. These dinners were Kosher style. That meant we never had a glass of milk with my mother's very rare roast beef and asking to butter the challah was met with a grimace. Saying prayers over the candles and the bread and wine (or Concord grape juice) was a comforting ritual that kicked off the family weekend. On Saturdays, my mother taught me her stellar shopping skills. On Sundays, my father and I went to hardware stores. When he took on a household project, I assisted and learned to wield tools with skill, and when things didn't go so smoothly, I learned a few amusing profanities, too.

When we got older, the ritual evolved into Sunday night dinners at the newest restaurant. While my mother was not interested in creating gourmet extravaganzas at home, her love of foie gras, escargot, osso buco, and charcuterie, coupled with my father's knack for picking wine, turned my brother and me into the kind of people who muse about lunch while eating breakfast and then contemplate dinner during lunch.

The allure of that Friday night ritual seduced my husband and me when we married and made a home together. We began hosting our own, unorthodox versions of Shabbat. We served odd cuts of grass-fed braised beef, vegan coconut vegetable curry, or not-so-kosher foods like shrimp this or bacon-wrapped that. We choose not to concentrate on the Jewish-correctness of the menu but rather to celebrate the time with friends. This *mitzvah* (commandment or good deed) of hospitality increases both the joy and the glasses of wine served. Inviting people into the home on Friday night is one of Judaism's foremost commandments, and it's one we happily obey.

A recent Friday night between Rosh Hashanah and Yom Kippur, as I prepare dinner for my husband and friends, I stand over the sink cleaning jasmine brown rice. I slowly swish my hand round and round, stirring the grains rhythmically clockwise, then counterclockwise, rinsing off water clouded with talc. Then I do it again—swishing, rinsing, swishing, and rinsing—until the water runs clear. This mindful act of cleansing feels auspicious, a perfect ritual for this week following the Jewish New Year, a time when we take a hard look at ourselves, our relationships, our sins; we forgive and we celebrate that we are blessed with the opportunity to cleanse and start anew.

As I rinse the rice and ponder my atonement checklist, sadness washes over me. I take a long, slow breath and recognize grief. My mother died almost four years ago, and one of my last memories of her took place this time of year, in the kitchen.

I see my frail mother, wasting away from leukemia, as she plans to prepare a brisket in her beloved Chinese red kitchen. Her insistence that she leave her deathbed to make Rosh Hashanah dinner is not about the food.

"Don't worry about it, I'll make the brisket," I say.

"No," she insists. She is visibly agitated, and it doesn't help that she has refused pain medication. She is lying in bed propped up by pillows, a small plate with sliced avocados, tomatoes, and duck pâté on her nightstand. She has not touched the food. She lost her appetite long ago and we're lucky if she drinks milk or eats Jell-O.

"Why not?" I ask.

"Because," she says. Because. That is it. She is adamant and strong and I know to take heed. We negotiate. I will make the matzo ball soup, a honey cake, and all the sides. But the brisket, that is hers. She further commands that I invite guests.

This determination comes from the Jewish domestic responsibilities that pass from mother to daughter, the sacred religious tradition that passes from generation to generation and the spiritual and healing power of a dining table seated with friends and family. It is also a last stab at normalcy, a fleeting moment when her paprika-red gravy seasoned with coarsely chopped white onion melds with the fluffy white of peeled, boiled potatoes.

In spite of her weakness, she swiftly makes her way around the kitchen, and although she's emaciated, she looks remarkably normal. Her short hair is coiffed. She wears a blue hooded sweatshirt (tailored, of course) over a classic French blue-and-white striped sailor T-shirt, matching pants, and blue slippers. Her nails are manicured, though she abandoned the long red variety for shorter ones painted a sheer cream. I watch her trim the brisket—she grabs a chunk of fat with just the forefinger and thumb of her left hand, her pinkie extended almost like she's drinking a cup of tea. She trims with the knife in her right hand. There is no handling of the meat, and no other fingers touch it. She separates the fat from the muscle in precise and swift cuts, making her away across the flank of beef. Even in her terminal state she is still the fussy master of *mise en place*, and we joke that if necessary she could make a brisket with one hand tied behind her back and blindfolded, too.

———

Her kitchen habits reveal our differences. I like chaos when I cook; she was very neat. I love to read cookbooks for leisure, I own way too many, and I consult recipes obsessively. She had just a handful of cookbooks and rarely referred to them. Guests were never permitted in her kitchen; I like communal cooking. While she had impeccable timing, with every last detail and dish prepared in advance so she could fully enjoy the dinner banter, I relish escaping into my kitchen to cook last-minute dishes. And the idea of brown rice rinsing and swishing as a mindfulness practice was certainly not in her repertoire.

I, the daughter of Brooklyn Jews who lament the dearth of bialys in the world and love herring in sour cream, went a bit rogue. Perhaps it was the California sunshine, the hippie Jewish camp in Malibu, the yoga, and all that cognitive behavioral therapy (hugely distasteful to my matter-of-fact, suck-it-up mother). Then there was the meditation, the flirtation with vegetarianism, the six years of abstaining from alcohol, the not getting married until I was forty. And where were the grandchildren? My mother would never ask aloud, but my failure to procreate was disappointing ultimately to both of us—especially as I insisted on flitting between New York and Los Angeles without any sort of plan for settling down.

I never think of these differences between my mother and me as rebellion, more as a kind of filling in of the holes. There were spaces that she didn't fill, so I did. We worked together to create a narrative of our lives as mother and daughter. She did this part. I did that part. And in the end we had a complete picture of our life together. She may not have agreed with my choices, but she did not judge them, either. And in that space between her opinion and my actions, I was able to develop that Jewish-mother-instilled confidence to follow my own twisted path and make lots of mistakes, bolstered by her unconditional support and love.

This also meant I became an accomplished baker. Why should we not have a great, made-with-love-by-hand flourless cake on Passover with Valrhona chocolate, orange zest, and brandy? Unlike my mother, I want to touch my food and have tactile experiments in my kitchen lab, like rugelach with sour cream dough and gluten-free mandelbrot. I will happily fight tough, uncooperative dough until I perfect a Hanukkah Meyer lemon tart using lemons from my mother's tree. I still use a recipe for lemonade from my mother's 1958 edition of the *Betty Crocker Cookbook*—which she fondly called Betty Crapowitz—and have updated it with lavender from my garden and vodka, too (the abstention from alcohol thing has abated).

Yet, for all the ways we are different, there are just as many similarities: an appreciation for an impeccably set table with cloth napkins, good china, and sterling flatware, keen attention to detail and aesthetics, and pride in being a hostess who never lets a guest clear a plate or wash a dish. These likenesses help me channel her when I long for her presence, beyond just passing memories. Invoking her memory through a concrete experience—like making a meal for those I love on a Friday night—proves to me that I understand where she came from and that I am part of that continuum. In fact, my husband says he knew he could marry me when he tasted my brisket. And like my mother, in spite of my growing collection of Jewish cookbooks, when I make Jewish food, I rarely consult them. Yes, I have her copy of "Jennie" and I read it like one would a novel, to find a compelling narrative that is at once universal and highly specific, but ultimately I have discovered that osmosis applies to me, too. Jewish mother or not, I have absorbed the knowledge about how to cook holiday meals. On Rosh Hashanah, I will serve sliced apples to dip in honey, I may even make challah, and I will infuse my brisket with something a little fancy like chanterelle mushrooms and Bordeaux. I will open my home to friends and family and bless the wine, the candles, the bread, the food, and be grateful that this does not have to be the last brisket.

HANUKKAH MEYER LEMON TART

Hanukkah is traditionally all about fried food—hence the latkes. Instead of frying dessert, I like to end the heavy meal (in our family we serve stuffed cabbage) with this delicate tart. I've tried it with flaky crusts, but I've come to prefer this more substantial shortbread shell, which isn't too sweet and never disappoints. The sour-sweet Meyer lemon curd is bursting with flavor, and it's a great reminder that winter is citrus season.

MAKES ONE 9-INCH TART

1 cup all-purpose flour
1 tablespoon sugar
¼ teaspoon salt
½ cup (1 stick) unsalted butter, not too cold
1 tablespoon water
½ teaspoon vanilla extract

In a large bowl, combine the flour, sugar, and salt.

Cut the butter into small pieces and work it into the flour with your fingers until the mixture forms small crumbly pieces and begins to hold together.

In a small bowl, combine the vanilla and water and stir the liquid into the flour mixture with a fork until just blended. To avoid tough dough, don't handle the dough more than necessary; work it only until it holds together when you press it between your fingers.

Form the dough into a flattened disk, wrap it in plastic, and let it sit for 30 minutes on the counter (not in the refrigerator).

Preheat the oven to 375°F.

Press and mold the dough into a 9-inch tart pan with a removable bottom using your fingers, making sure it is even along the bottom and sides.

Bake for about 25 minutes, until golden brown. Remove to a wire rack and cool to room temperature.

MEYER LEMON CURD

2 large eggs
2 large egg yolks
¼ teaspoon salt
½ cup sugar
½ cup Meyer lemon juice
Zest of 1 Meyer lemon
6 tablespoons (¾ stick) cold unsalted butter, cut into pieces
Zest of 1 lemon

Put a medium bowl in the refrigerator (this will help chill the hot lemon curd when it comes off the heat).

In a heavy-bottomed pan, beat the eggs, yolks, salt, and sugar until well blended.

Turn the heat to medium, add the lemon juice, lemon zests, and butter, and whisk constantly for a few minutes until well blended. To prevent curdling, from this point forward, do not stop moving the whisk.

Reduce the heat to medium-low and continue whisking until the curd thickens. This can take as long as 10 minutes (I move the whisk from my right hand to my left to reduce fatigue). Keep whisking, and at some point you will notice the swirls from the whisk stay visible in the curd, indicating it is thickening. The curd is done when it resembles thin sour cream.

Remove the chilled bowl from the refrigerator. Push the curd through a fine strainer with a spatula into the chilled bowl. Let the curd sit about 1 hour until it reaches room temperature.

Pour the curd into the tart shell and spread it out evenly.

If you like, refrigerate the tart to set the curd, or serve it at room temperature. I prefer the latter, as I feel it better showcases the unique Meyer lemon flavor.

IT TAKES A MARKET

ELIZABETH CRANE

When I was a new mom, the "it takes a village to raise a child" meme was in its infancy. I embraced it at once. *A village!* I thought. *I'd love a village.* My village would include friends and family, old and young, and we would all cook and eat together and involve our kids in everything. Food is love, after all, as it was in my childhood of chicken soup, gut-busting Thanksgivings, and chocolate ice cream. My personal equation, therefore, was village + food = loved child. I imagined couples laughing around a dinner table sharing coping strategies over polenta and cannellini beans and roasted chicken, and small children crawling about eating peas and bread crusts. This was ideal. However, with grandparents far away, family scattered across the state, and no close friends nearby, my sleep-deprived self had no time for real meals and even less time for pundits preaching some nonexistent utopia. My village refused to materialize. Isolated with my child in an apartment in the middle of the city, I took to muttering, "Where's my f%&#ing village?"

The year my first son was born, 1993, a new farmers' market opened in San Francisco, and I desperately wanted to go. I had worked in kitchens for years and considered myself an informed consumer, but pregnancy changed my perspective on food. Like many pregnant women, I had been reading about harmful pesticide residues on fruits and vegetables. Suddenly, it wasn't just my health I was risking every time I ate a conventionally grown apple. The lure of a largely organic market was strong. So what if I had delivered only three days before? I promised my mother, scandalized that I was even out of bed much less taking the baby outside, that I would be very careful, and set off, carrying baby Philip in his sling.

The Ferry Plaza Farmers Market offered a dazzling array of greens, vegetables, and fruits. I was distracted in one direction by samples of locally made cheese, in another by the offer of strawberries so ripe they almost fell from their stems. A tall man approached me and said, "Here." I looked up into his twinkling blue eyes shaded by a pith helmet perched on his head and smiled, unsure how to respond. He smiled and gestured with hands that held a huge peach and a knife; he said again, "Here," adding, "you need this."

He twirled the peach one way and the knife the other, deftly dropping a slice of the fruit into my outstretched hand. I'd be lying if I told you I remember the exact way that peach tasted; I've tasted so many since, its flavor is lost in the larger memory of *peach*. What I remember are the man's hands, large and gnarled and a little grubby, the sunshine that warmed the top of my head, the air, and the peach: a sweetness, softness, and tang like nothing I'd ever tasted before.

I smiled. "You're right," I said. "I need some of that." He directed me to his stand, the Aerie, and to the box that particular peach had come from. His name was Fitz Kelly, and I learned that he had driven two hundred miles—from Reedley in the center of California's Central Valley—in the dark hours of the morning, to bring peaches to San Francisco. I introduced him to Philip, and we made a show of weighing the baby in the scales. By the time I left the Aerie, I had obtained several pounds of the most expensive, most delicious peaches I had ever eaten, and I had made a friend.

That summer, I made the Saturday trip as often as I could to the foot of Market Street and into the exaggerated "island" in the traffic where the farmers' market set up and broke down every week. Back before the world knew the Ferry Plaza Farmers Market as the upscale year-round destination it has become, it was a Saturdays-only, slightly funky assembly of small growers with a commitment to heirloom varieties, sustainable growing practices, and nurturing San Francisco's food-loving community. Many of the faces behind the makeshift tables were the people who worked on the farms and grew what they were selling. They set up their stands in a tight, intimate racetrack oval in what was, on other days, a parking lot in the middle of the wide Embarcadero. Every Saturday, the market created a leafy green oasis on top of the gray and cracking blacktop.

That first summer, Fitz and I tracked Philip's weight in his scales, bandied recipe advice, chaffed the other customers, and created a miniature community within the larger world of the market. I ate peaches and nectarines, apricots and plums, and learned more than I ever thought I'd know about the difference between "sustainable" and "organic." Fitz, opinionated Irishman to the core, would happily pull on his mental sparring gloves whenever anyone tried to argue that organic certification was the best measure of a food's purity. He stood firmly in the sustainable camp. "I live on the farm," he would say. "And I expect to die on the farm. D'you think I would do anything to hasten my own end?" Organic certification meant nothing, as far as he was concerned, and he would confound customers by declaring, "I'm not organic, I'm better than organic." His conviction that his fruit was raised in the most responsible, cleanest manner with the least environmental impact—conveyed one customer at a time—was his modus operandi, and it worked for him. It certainly convinced me. That and the fact that every piece of fruit that summer was sweet, tart, and plentiful in a way that I felt was entirely for the benefit of me and my baby.

When that season was over, all too soon, Fitz asked whether I would be interested in working at the peach stand the following spring. Despite the obstacles—what would I do with Philip?—I accepted. I was going to get as close to those peaches as possible.

That's how the Aerie became "the stand with the baby." I wore Philip in the backpack that first year; I changed diapers in the back of the van, sat in the passenger seat to nurse, and handed peeled slivers of fruit over my shoulder and into his greedy maw. We enjoyed the fruit, but even more, I found that chatting with strangers was a marked improvement on my isolated days as a new mom and as a writer. Suddenly I had hundreds of people to talk to every Saturday, most of whom were not shy about sharing their enthusiasm for my newfound commitment to local produce. Philip had dozens of unofficial aunts, uncles, and grandparents who took a keen interest in his development, pinched his cheeks, and exclaimed over his appetite for peaches. Entirely by accident, I was growing the village that my young family lacked.

As Philip expanded his meal choices from breast milk and peaches, he ate nothing but what passed my fairly rigid standards: fresh, unsprayed, locally grown produce. Even though I continued to work at the market, this little nutritional idyll was not destined to last. First, Philip became an active and vocal toddler with preschool friends who shared their neon-orange goldfish crackers and yogurt squeezies. By the time my son Michael was born, three-and-a-half-year-old Philip had no patience with my choices of cereal, my insistence on whole grains, and my refusal to serve hot dogs at every meal. As they grew, it became clear that they had their own ideas about what to eat, and they had the power to sidestep my best intentions. One day I put down two identical plates, each with a bun containing a hot dog and a squirt of ketchup, one in front of Philip and one in front of Michael. Then I turned my back on the table and started wiping up the counter. When I turned back around, Philip had eaten the hot dog and left the bun, while Michael had licked the ketchup off the hot dog and left it on the plate, eating only the ketchup-y bread. Both were clamoring for more. This became my best reminder that no matter what I did, the boys were going to assert their individual preferences about food. I could bring the boys to the table, but I could not make them eat.

I found myself at the supermarket more often, abandoning the farmers' market for the sake of expedience, shopping at odd hours, racing to get the week's groceries purchased in the time I could carve out between Philip's school, Michael's nap, my work hours, and mealtime.

The boys often accompanied me grocery shopping, so where we shopped and what we bought became contentious. There were "treats" everywhere. My progress was slowed by my dueling need to read every label on every can, box, or bag before it went in my cart—or back on the shelf. Once Philip could read, it was his job to survey the labels. A typical conversation would go something like this:

Philip: Mom, can we get this?

Me: Well, what's in it?

Philip: Water, high-fructose corn syrup—

Me: No.

Michael: Want this! (handing it to his brother)

Philip (reading): Monosodi—

Me: No.

It wore me down. I didn't want to be saying "No" to everything they imagined would taste delicious, but I couldn't bring myself to say "Yes" to the kinds of crap they wanted. Instead of being the Benevolent Earth Mother, I was the Mean Food Cop. Unless I wanted them to subsist on junk food, I simply had to get back into a farmers' market routine. And I needed to bring the boys.

———————

It wasn't hard to convince Philip and Michael that a Saturday morning at the Ferry Plaza was better than any cartoon show. The fresh cinnamon doughnut muffins and the bountiful strawberries lured them in. I had almost forgotten that the farmers at the market knew me, knew my kids, and loved us all, even if we had been a little neglectful. I'm sure the boys got tired of all the exclamations over how they'd grown, but I basked in it. *I grew these kids*, I wanted to say, *just like you grew those vegetables, and here we are again, helping each other grow further. Thank you, and you're welcome.*

The boys quickly discovered that vendors almost always provided samples, and that if you smiled and asked nicely, you could often get even more free food. They discovered spring asparagus—which they ate raw, looking like country bumpkins chewing grass stems—summer stone fruit, and winter squash and greens. It was easy to say yes to the treats my boys begged for at the farmers' market. Extra raspberries? More mandarins? My pleasure.

When a small Saturday farmers' market started up in my neighborhood, I was hired as the onsite manager. And my children, too, became part of the deal. Philip, now eleven, was old enough to walk or bike to the market by himself, so it became his job to bring our produce home—if he wanted a big, heavy watermelon, he had to carry it himself. Soon Michael, now eight, established himself as the juice boy at the stand that sold fresh veggie juices and vegetarian wraps. As his competence and confidence grew, he worked behind the counter prepping fruits and vegetables, eventually making custom juices for "his" customers. He kept track of what his customers liked, including the extra knob of ginger that I pre-ferred in my beet-carrot-apple juice. The vendor paid him three dollars and all the food and drink he could consume, which, considering his ap-petite, was a pretty good deal for Mike. Plus, his loyal customers stuffed tips in his apron, or left him cookies "for later." The village was watching out for him.

Philip's first real work-for-money job came when one of the vendors couldn't get his own sons to help him at the market, so he hired Philip to unload the produce, work all morning selling it, and load up whatever was left at the end of the day. I couldn't tell which made him happier: the growth in his biceps or the growth in his bank account. Phil, Cole, and Sam—sons of other market vendors and shoppers—quickly established a bond that involved daring each other to eat unusual produce. Somehow, foods I introduced were nowhere near as interesting to Philip as foods he discovered on his own. "Why didn't you tell me that Yellow Finn potatoes are great mashed?" he'd ask, or "Romaine lettuce is much better in salad than [insert whatever green I was prepping]." It bugged me at first, but then I decided I didn't mind. I felt fortunate that he cared about food, and that he could take in what vendors and customers recommended and use that in his own menus. The village was watching out for both my boys.

And that should be the happy ending to this tale, that we all work at a farm-ers' market and that my kids eat nothing but ridiculously healthy food. The truth is that my children continue to confound me simply by being themselves. Both eat a sizable portion of fruits and vegetables, true, but they have completely different appetites and wildly divergent body types. Plus, Philip is a carnivore and Michael is a committed vegetarian (that hot dog lunch was prophetic). I maintain the illusion that I influence the food they eat—after all, I still do the majority of the shopping—but it's just that, an illusion. One Saturday, I came home from the market to find both kids slumped on the couch and the evidence of their "breakfast" on the coffee table in front of them: an empty bag of pretzels and an empty jar of homemade chocolate cream cheese frosting. I understood in that mo-ment that when they went to college I would no longer have any say at all in what they ate. Sometimes that thought wakes me up at night.

Philip is now a freshman in college, and Michael is a freshman in high school. As they grow up and away, I just have to trust that their food habits, over time, will nourish their bodies and keep them healthy. In his first weeks of college life, Philip complained that, while the dining hall food was for the most part just fine, the fruit was "lousy." When I reminded him of the world-class farmers' market only a mile or so from campus, his voice brightened and he said, "Oh yeah, I'll get some people together and go this weekend. D'you think they'll still have decent grapes?" He's got his priorities straight: seasonal produce from a local source—and his new extended family to share it with.

BEST-EVER PEACH CRISP

WITH DEEP APPRECIATION TO FITZGERALD'S PREMIUM TREE FRUIT,
FORMERLY THE AERIE, IN REEDLEY, CALIFORNIA

SERVES ABOUT 6 (BUT YOU'LL WANT TO HAVE
SOME LEFTOVER FOR BREAKFAST)

Preheat the oven to 375°F.
In a medium bowl, stir together:

½ cup all-purpose flour
½ cup whole wheat flour
¾ cup sugar
1 teaspoon baking powder
½ teaspoon salt

Set aside.
    In a separate bowl, stir together:

¼ cup sugar
2 tablespoons all-purpose flour

Add and fold in gently:

4 to 5 cups peeled and sliced yellow peaches

Pour the fruit mixture into a 9-inch pie plate (see Note) and scrape
in all the juices.
    Into the dry ingredients, stir with a fork:

1 beaten egg

The mixture should be crumbly. Spread it over the top of the fruit
mixture.
    Drizzle over all:

½ cup (1 stick) melted unsalted butter (or use as little as half a stick of but-
    ter if you like)

Bake for 45 minutes, or until the top is crusty and browned. Serve
warm with vanilla ice cream on top.
    Note: Place a foil-covered baking sheet under the pie plate. This
recipe has been known to boil over!

TALK WITH YOUR MOUTH FULL

CATHERINE NEWMAN

What with the flickering candlelight, the gentle clinking of silverware, and the rapt philosophical talking about personhood, it's like the best dinner date of my life. John Coltrane is playing moodily from the stereo, and I experience that simultaneous full-hearted calm and spicy-minded excitement of falling in love. Even though where I am is at home, and who I'm eating with is my kids.

"If you got a brain transplant," Ben, eleven, is saying, shoveling lentil soup into his mouth with a biscuit, "I mean, if they could do that—give you someone else's brain—you'd pretty much *be* that person, right? I mean, you'd have their memories and thoughts."

I picture it—looking down into my lap as though through somebody else's vision—and it makes me shudder. If Ben goes on to rewrite *Frankenstein* or direct horror movies, I won't be surprised.

"Don't," Birdy says. She's eight and using her fingers to pull arugula out of the salad bowl and stuff it into her mouth. "Don't. That gives me such a weird feeling. Like, *your brain wouldn't even recognize you.* Ach! Don't!" She grimaces: balsamic vinegar, spicy leaves, existential angst.

The candles burn down, plates are shoved aside, the cat is nudged off the table for the umpteenth time—and now we're onto a kind of Orwellian scenario of human memory gone virtual: "What if there was a kind of flash drive," Ben is musing, "and everybody could—pfft!—download your thoughts and memories? That would be really cool. And really terrible."

"Mostly terrible," Birdy says. "I mean, the inside of your own mind is your only real privacy." I look at her eyes glittering almost black, and understand that what's behind them is hers alone. I want to know more, always.

Which makes this experience—dinner with my children—different in every way, then, from a *bad* date—the kind of date where there is nothing left to wonder after your companion talks and talks while pages fly from the calendar of your numbered days, before he finally concludes, "I had a great time. When can I see you again?" without noticing that you've already chewed off your own foot to crawl away from the table so you can douse yourself in gasoline and light a match.

It's funny, because when the babies are small, every meal is like the worst date of all, dining with the most selfish and boring person who wouldn't know a good schnitzel if it bit him in the kneecap. When Ben was newly born, I looked at our dinner table and only saw a good place to store diapers and butt ointment and the remaining fragments of my sanity. Who needs a dinner table when you can stand over the changing table with a piece of cold pizza in your hand, cranking and re-cranking Brahms's "Lullaby" to keep the baby distracted for the one minute it takes to chew and swallow?

Then there were the years of eating dinner while I bounced on an exercise ball with a baby in my arms; while somebody gulped noisily from the spigots formerly known as my own personal body; while crumbs sprayed around the high chair like there might be hungry pigeons to feed; while a diapered somebody stood next to me, held onto my thigh, looked up into my face, and said, straining and tragic, "I pooping, Mama." "Yes, you are, sweetie!" And I'm *eating eggplant Parmesan.*

Back then I imagined that, at best, we would one day return to some approximation of the life we'd had before: dinnertime that involved some eating, some chatting, something more than five unbroken minutes at the table. I love to eat, and so I craved the old luxuriously relaxed meals—meals that weren't dominated by my vigilance and anxiety as somebody toddled away from the table to go choke on a Tinkertoy and fall down the stairs, or by my irritation as somebody rubbed sweet potato into her own head and then cried about it, accusatory, "Hair yucky!"

Ten minutes was all I wanted. I wanted only not to be the person walking the baby up and down the clam shack parking lot while my scallop roll arrived, cooled, and congealed. And I had no idea what I was in for because it's so much better than that now. It's even better than it was before we had kids. I'm not saying the kids are better conversationalists than their father. I'm just saying he wasn't raised in a household saturated with my exact range of interests. And the kids were.

It's not that we never bore each other. A friend's Wii game that's a computerized simulation of *Star Wars* as represented by animated LEGOs? Let me tell you how many minutes I can stand to talk about that for: zero minutes. OK, one minute. Long enough to say, "But why don't they make it like you're flying the real *Millennium Falcon*, since you could pretend to fly the LEGO one with just the LEGOs themselves?" Only upon asking do I realize that, despite its rhetorical nature, the question is, paradoxically, going to generate a long answer. But I should talk, given my tendency to wax poetic about plates of humble food. "I'm sorry," Ben says politely one evening. "I think I interrupted you. Did you want to say more about the quinoa?"

"Just that it's really good," I say again, sheepish. "I know I'm the one who made it, but it's just so good." Their father and I can get into a conversation so boring that if we had wallpaper it would be peeling off the walls and rolling itself up tight. "So you're saying that if we got the algaecide for the roof shingles, it could double as a mold barrier in the basement?" The kids glaze over over their plates of glazed sweet potatoes, and you really can't blame them.

But how it mostly is is natural selection and neuroscience and the big bang and if you could only eat one thing for the rest of your life what would it be? (The lobster roll in Kennebunkport.) And would you go to the moon right this second, if they showed up at our door with your space suit all ready and everything but you'd be gone for a whole year? (I would not.)

I'm a journalist, so I am often, by necessity, thinking about interesting things, and the kids are naturally curious. After I explained to them how dopamine works, Birdy said, "Do you think I like Laffy Taffy because it's good? Or do you think it's releasing dopamine and so my brain craves more of it?" (I always worry that people overhear us and think we're chatting about heroin.) And natural selection is endlessly fascinating: people with a keen eye for mushrooms, for example, surviving to reproduce while the idiot mycologists die out. On deadline, I can tell I've been talking too much about the antisocial behavior piece I've been working on when Birdy blurts out, about a SpongeBob SquarePants character, "Oh, Ben, I disagree. Squidward may be an introvert, but he's totally not shy."

Conversation is the family ethos, and when a bunch of kids from the local college come to dinner one night (we're part of a dinner-hosting program), the kids revive an old gimmick of ours: the Question Jar. Everybody writes down a question, and then we take turns pulling them out and reading them, and then everybody shares their answers. It's a great icebreaker, and the children are sweetly encouraging of the young people, who hesitate.

"Gosh," one of them says, after Ben has described a home built around a cylindrical crystal elevator and Birdy has described one papered in hundred-dollar bills.

"What would my dream house be like? I guess it would have one of those things in it. You know those things? They're towel racks, but heated? So your towels are warm when you get out of the shower? One of those."

"Nice," Birdy says, supportive. "That would be way cozy."

Once, after a year or so of the question jar, Ben said, at a restaurant, "I know we don't have the Question Jar with us, but does anybody want to do a jarless question?" Michael and I laughed about that one.

"Otherwise known as *have a conversation*?" I said, but the kids didn't get what was funny.

But how did it happen, this inclination to conversation? It's not like one day a good dinner was when someone in a battery-operated seat stared vibratingly at the ceiling fan long enough for his parents to gobble their meal, and the next was when that person opined on Darwin or the death penalty over squash soup. It's gradual, of course, and there are years when all somebody does is hum while somebody else talks about farts. But curiosity about the world is contagious, and it penetrates eventually, as long as we remember to share it. So we talk. We start sentences with "I wonder why . . ." and "What if. . . ." We get the *paper* paper delivered, even though we could read it free online, because I want it to be like my own childhood, with everybody grunting and groaning aloud over the inky woes of the world instead of ruing privately over a screen. We talk to each other in the car instead of on our cell phones. The kids climb into bed with us on the weekends and we talk then, too. We make time and space for talking—dishes pushed aside, computers shut down for the night, homework allowed to remain unfinished for just a few more minutes. We talk about issues of consequence, where the stakes are high and there is practically a moral imperative to have an opinion and voice it ("I think the whole idea of a last meal before execution is wrong," Ben suggested once. "It's like, *We're killing you, sure, but enjoy your steak!*). We talk. And when our mouths are too full of soup, we listen.

There are doubtless measurable benefits to dinner-table conversation. It's a natural check on overeating, for example. Even if you're talking and eating at the same time, you simply can't generate the same food-shoveling velocity that you could if you were eating silently. Plus, I'm sure it's good for mental health, for social health, for learning how to become a good date—although, my god, I'll miss them when there's someone they're dating besides us. But mostly the benefits are immeasurable. What dinner-table conversation gives us is time to stop and appreciate how much we have, right now, even as we imagine, deliriously, that it could go on forever.

LENTIL SOUP WITH VINAIGRETTE

SᴇʀVᴇS 6

Active time: 15 minutes; total time: 1 hour (conventional) or 3 to 6 hours (slow cooker)

This is a forgiving recipe, with respect to both ingredients and method. If you don't have broth, use all water. If you're dying to get this into your slow cooker in the morning and are already in your work clothes and you simply can't sauté the veggies first, then dump them all in raw. But do make the vinaigrette, because it's that one detail that raises this from the depths of humdrum to the heights of moderately exciting.

2 tablespoons olive oil

1 onion, chopped

2 stalks celery, diced

2 carrots, diced

2 cloves garlic, finely chopped

2 teaspoons kosher salt (or 1 teaspoon table salt)

¾ cup tomato sauce, crushed tomatoes, or tomato puree

2 cups lentils, rinsed and drained (I like to use the tiny green *lentilles du Puy* for this, but regular brown lentils are just fine, too)

4 cups chicken broth (or vegetable broth or more water)

2 cups water

1 bay leaf

1 sprig fresh thyme, or 1/2 teaspoon dried thyme

1 teaspoon balsamic or sherry vinegar

VINAIGRETTE

¼ cup olive oil

2 tablespoons balsamic or sherry vinegar

1 clove garlic, pressed

½ teaspoon salt

Heat the olive oil in a wide pan over medium heat. Add the onion, celery, carrot, garlic, and salt and sauté until the vegetables are limp and browning, about 10 minutes. Transfer to a slow cooker with the remaining ingredients and cook on high for 3 hours or on low for 6 hours. Meanwhile, whisk together the vinaigrette ingredients. Taste the soup for salt, then spoon into bowls and serve with a drizzle of vinaigrette over each bowl.

STOVETOP METHOD

Place the lentils in a soup pot with the broth, water, bay leaf, and thyme, and bring to a boil over high heat. Lower the heat, cover the pot, and simmer while you prepare the rest of the ingredients.

Heat the olive oil in a wide pan over medium heat. Add the onion, celery, carrot, garlic, and salt and sauté until the vegetables are limp and browning, about 10 minutes, then add the tomato sauce and vinegar. Scrape the mixture into the cooking lentils, stir, and simmer the soup over very low heat, partially covered, for 1 hour, stirring every now and again to keep it from sticking, and adding water if it looks like it's drying out. Meanwhile, whisk together the vinaigrette ingredients. When the lentils are nice and creamy, taste the soup for salt, then serve with a drizzle of vinaigrette over each bowl.

PART THREE

LEARNING TO EAT

A WHITE FOOD DISORDER

DANI KLEIN MODISETT

Before I divulge the not-very-deep-dark secrets of my children's relationship with food, I feel the need to confess something about myself.
There is never a time I don't want to be eating. Even right now, I'm typing, but what I'm thinking is,

> When is lunch? What is lunch? How about some egg salad with dill?
> Nah, too mushy. Hand-cut turkey on a crusty baguette with red leaf
> lettuce, sliced Roma tomatoes, and grainy mustard? Nice, but a little
> Martha Stewart-esque and labor intensive. How about what you really
> want? A soup-bowl-sized latte with a softball-sized blueberry-oat
> muffin top? Just the top, the top won't kill me. OK, write one more
> page, paragraph, no two, two more paragraphs, or how about finish
> a thought? Better yet, start a cohesive thought, a thesis, the point,
> write the point of this piece and then you can eat . . . I promise.

Eating is one of the driving forces of my life. When I was fifteen I read the
autobiography of esteemed playwright and director Moss Hart, *Act One*,
with his extensive descriptions of the food he either ate or planned to eat
while he was writing and I knew I'd found my soul mate. Hart was laugh-
out-loud funny, George S. Kaufman's collaborator and co-creator of such
classics as *You Can't Take It with You* and *The Man Who Came to Dinner*, but
like me all he really wanted to do was eat. He was the first man, other than

my father, I loved. If only he hadn't died of heart attack two years before I was born.

Sometimes when I am trapped in a dull conversation my mind wanders and I think about designing a T-shirt or a belt buckle that says, "I'd Rather Be Eating." Although partial to sugary, creamy treats, I've also been known to absentmindedly plow through a sixteen-ounce container of imported shaved Parmesan cheese even if it's not imported. I can eat a pound of Costco Parmesan in under an hour.

Given my appetite, I should be a very large woman. But I am also very vain. I come by it organically having been raised by a former model and a man who, once diagnosed with cancer, refused any kind of chemo treatment that would make his hair fall out. These are my people. To state that I have an internal, relentless, draining, sometimes paralyzing struggle between feeling like life is not worth living without excess food while simultaneously believing that I am only a valuable woman if I am the size of a movie star's leg is like saying there's some fighting in Israel that may never end.

Did I just compare my disordered eating to the problems in the Middle East? Yes, I did. But only to the extent that I am certain both are conflicts that will not see resolution in my lifetime. Does my preoccupation with food and my body size—what I believe to be a decidedly female preoccupation, at that—render me shallow, callow, and self-involved? Yes, dear readers, some days it does.

So imagine my joy when I found out my first child was going to be a boy and then the second one, too. Thank you, God, for sparing the next generation of women in my family from my heinous food-body issues. Boys will be easy, I thought! They run around a lot and stuff themselves and go run some more. They wear sports jerseys like they're Versace separates and don't start obsessing about their bodies until they're at least forty and it's likely I'll be dead by then or at least too feeble to feel guilty about their physical dissatisfaction. Hello, boys! YIPPEE!

Three years have passed since the birth of my *second* boy and dinner is over. I'm flipping through a magazine, *L.A. Parent*, which my mother generously, OK, pointedly, bought me to provide suggestions about how to better feed my children. Not that they're undernourished or gaunt or full of rickets or listless, tired, cranky, moody, or coming to blows every day like she would have you believe. At least not because of malnutrition. But it is true that my oldest son, Gabriel, has never tasted meat, and the only green foods he's eaten are Christmas M&M's. The younger one, Gideon, simply will not eat anything that isn't white. Think for a second about what this means to only eat white food: cheese, bread, noodles, *vanilla* yogurt, milk (thank God), butter, cream cheese, and French fries. Fries do fall largely into the golden yellow hue, but before you deep-fry them in oil they are white, so they are safe.

In the interest of full disclosure I will acknowledge that the boys will sometimes eat a red hot dog, if the weather outside is a balmy sixty-three degrees and the planets have aligned and they're really hungry and know they will not get anything white if they don't at least eat a hot dog for "protein." Skimming through the pages of my magazine I feel sick over this; all the ads of happy children eating broccoli stalks, dancing in fields of grass eating organic turkey sandwiches on whole grain bread, laughing with their perfectly groomed parents, make me want to gag. Until I hear the sound of my son actually gagging from the bathroom. It sounds disturbingly like a cat with a hairball, particularly unnerving since we have no pets, so it must be my son. My husband, Tod, speaks over him.

"Gabriel, I am not kidding, I want you to eat this carrot!"

"No, Dad, no! I can't. I hate them. I hate carrots. I tried. I tried," he says, and then he starts to cry. I had no idea my then-six-year-old, my husband, and a carrot had even gone into the bathroom.

"What's going on?" I yell from the kitchen.

"Nothing," my husband barks back. "He has to eat one carrot!" My husband is not one to yell. His initial reaction to any kind of news primarily dances between "Cool," or "That's not good." But my son's refusal to eat any vegetables since we stopped spooning pureed mush down his throat at two and a half has taken him over the edge.

I walk quickly to the bathroom.

"Honey," I say, pulling Tod into the hallway, "I'm not a nutritionist, but I don't think forcing a carrot down Gabriel's throat in the bathtub is the way to go. He'll end up hating carrots *and* bathing. Let's dry him off and we'll figure out something else. I'll go talk to Dr. Bess." Dr. Bess is our pediatrician, whom I like very much. Besides being highly qualified, she also always lends the right perspective to parental concerns. We're pretty sure she had a hearing problem as a child because there are endearing remnants of it in her speech. English is not her second language and yet she has trouble pronouncing her R's, and her face is always completely turned to yours for any responses to questions so she can read your lips simultaneously. Additionally, she volunteers at Children's Hospital in East Los Angeles several mornings a week before coming to work in Beverly Hills, where, by the way, they have excellent croissants. The whole city of Beverly Hills is chock-full of Parisian pastries of the finest quality, which, given what the women look like there, clearly very few of them enjoy. Anyway, Dr. Bess is a great doctor for our family because when I need her to step up with real concern, like when my younger boy was in the NICU after he was born with breathing problems, she was there, fully focused every morning at 6 A.M. But, for the run-of-the-mill mommy concerns that we privileged parents find catastrophic, her response can't help but include, "Your kid's not deaf, right? I think you need to relax." I appreciate her nonalarmist style. Particularly with a dear husband who, God bless him, runs to extremes where the boys' health is concerned.

"He's going to have terrible vision if he doesn't eat carrots!" Tod says, walking past me, the reviled orange stub in his hand. Oh, right, it's going to be the lack of carrots that screws up his vision, I think defensively. Not the fact that both of us have worn glasses since the third grade.

"I'm not sure that's true," I say instead, choosing a more compassionate tone than I want to, the one that has enabled me to stay married for ten years. "I mean, that there is a direct correlation between carrot eating and eyesight."

"Yes, there is. And even if maybe there isn't, something has to change here, he's a growing boy, he needs to eat vegetables." Or at least I think that's what he said, because all I heard was, "You have failed my sons as a mother."

I can't believe how wrong I was about boys and food! Gabriel and Gideon actually have a disorder all their own. It's what I've come to call a "white food" disorder. Not that I don't enjoy a good mac and cheese binge now and then, but at least I balance it with a green salad and a glass of wine, or three, made from unsulfured grapes. Thank God for fruit smoothies or I don't know how I'd get any color into their bodies at all. I've tried the "hiding-the-good-stuff" technique that Jessica Seinfeld popularized a few years ago. It's a little tough to pull off without a kitchen staff, particularly when you are trying to camouflage the nutrient-rich food into a white background. Or candy.

"Why are my chocolate chip cookies orange, Mom?" Gabriel asked when I tried to slip sweet potatoes in them.

"Tastes like dooty," Gideon said of the carob chips I used instead of real chocolate, while spitting them onto the table.

Spitting was one thing, but choking and gagging in the bathtub crossed a line. It felt like the domestic equivalent of water boarding to get Gabriel to eat healthy. I was eager to consult a professional.

Two days after the projectile carrot dinner, we're in Dr. Bess's reception area waiting to be called. I'm thumbing through another parenting magazine when I hear my name. "Dani?" I look up. "How *are* you?" asks Pamela, one of the Perfect Moms from Gabriel's preschool. Her hair has that stick-straight look of a chemical job, and clearly she's had her face detailed like a luxury car, lips inflated like tires and the scratches of age buffed out of her skin, but she's still Pamela. Why is it that almost four million people live in L.A. and yet there are times when it feels no bigger than Mayberry?

"Oh, hi, how are you?" I ask.

"Good, good. Just here for Chloe's checkup. Chloe, you remember Gabriel!" Chloe looks at Gabriel.

"Sure, hi."

"Hi," Gabriel says. "Want to play Scribblenauts on my mom's phone?" Chloe looks to her mom before answering.

"It's fine, dear, go ahead." She leans in and whispers to me, "Normally, I don't let her play with screens during the day, but I'm sure it's OK just this once."

"Yes, that's how I feel. Just this once."

"What? Mom?" Gabriel looks up. "You always let me play on your phone in waiting rooms."

"Busted," I say to Pamela, avoiding eye contact. Awkward pause. Pamela forages through her purse, pulling out a mini-bottle of hand sanitizer. She squirts some on her manicured hands.

"Here for a checkup, too?" she asks me.

"No, we're here because I only eat white food," Gabriel answers, without looking up.

"Gabriel!"

"Mom, what, you said that yourself."

"Well, yes, my husband and I are concerned that Gabriel and his brother eat very few fruits and vegetables."

"Oh, that must be tough," Pamela says, fishing in her purse for something. "Chloe loves these seaweed snacks." She pulls a lightweight, foil-wrapped cube out of her purse.

"I take these with us everywhere. Have you tried these, Gabriel? They're super-yummy." She shakes the package in her hand like it's a maraca.

"No, thanks."

"Sweet that he says 'thank you,'" Pamela says. "So polite."

"Yeah, he's great."

Pamela leans in. "I'm sorry about his food issues. Very hard. People think it's just girls that have problems with food, but it's not true."

"Really? People think that?"

"Yes. But he's lucky to have you as a mom because you know all about that subject."

"Excuse me?" I say. Our mutual friend Sarah must have told her about my eating history. The years when I lived on air-popped popcorn and frozen yogurt. Or the coffee-only year.

"I just mean . . . you know, since you have experience yourself with . . . " Pamela adds.

"Gabriel Modisett?"

A nurse with 1960's eyeliner and Betty Boop red lips saves me.

"That's us!" I jump up. "Gabriel, let's go, it's us."

"OK, Mom."

He finishes a move on his game.

"Gabriel, please!" I say sharply. Please help me get away from yet another woman who feasts on the dark pasts of others while keeping the truth of her life sealed tighter than a container at a Tupperware party.

"Good luck, Gabriel," Pamela yells after us. "Call me, we'll have lunch and really catch up."

"Sure," I say, shutting the pink door to the examining room.

"Ugh."

"What, Mom?" Gabriel asks.

"Nothing."

There is a knock at the door.

"Come in," I say.

"Hello, Big Boy," Dr. Bess says, walking in and closing the door behind her.

"Hey," Gabriel says.

"Hi," I say.

"To what do I owe this honor?" Dr. Bess asks, looking in Gabriel's eyes.

"Well, Dr. Bess, Gabriel has a small problem with his eating."

"He looks good to me."

"I only like white food."

"Really?" she asks.

"Well, yes, pretty much," I answer. "The other night we tried giving him a carrot, but he gagged on it and then spit it out."

"Yeah, in the bathtub," Gabriel adds.

"Interesting place to eat a carrot," she says, turning her face toward mine, prompting me to explain further.

"I gotta pee!" Gabriel blurts. Dr. Bess turns her face to him. He jumps up and down, "I have to pee, I have to pee!"

"Go ahead, it's right outside."

"OK," he says, and runs out.

"So, how did the carrot end up in the bathroom?" she asks, pulling up a stool.

"I don't really know. I think my husband brought it in there. He was trying to get Gabriel to eat a vegetable, any vegetable, and I guess he just went too far that night and the thing is . . . he's not wrong, I mean, the kids are terrible about eating vegetables and I don't force them to because I don't want to give them food 'issues,' but then there are times when I think I really don't do enough and you know . . . I don't work. Not really, I write and produce some stuff, but I'm not, I'm not what you would really classify as a 'working mom,' I mean, I'm a mom who works, but that's different of course because I'm around all the time and I don't make much money now. I used to before I had kids but now . . . oh god . . . that's not really true, I never really made a lot of money, not like hedge fund money. I did OK for an 'artist,' whatever that is, but now, with the kids and the days, the really long days, I'm pretty distracted, you know, it's hard to focus and be really productive and, you know, produce and. . . ." Dr. Bess checks her watch. "My point is, is that if all I really do is care for my children and caring of course implies feeding them, you don't need a degree in home economics to know that the basic definition of caring for a child involves keeping them well fed, it is just so heartbreaking to me that my children refuse to eat any food that comes out of the ground, although they will drink smoothies if you put whipped cream on top but. . . ." My eyes tear up. "Clearly, I am ruining my children because there are kids out there who happily eat broccoli spears and corn and squash and . . . and . . . ocean plants. I was just in your waiting room with a little girl whose mother told me she looks forward to eating seaweed! And yet my boys are terrified of food with color, unless it's fake color, crap made with high-fructose corn syrup and Red Dye No. 2 . . . and now . . . now . . . my husband is accusing me of blinding our children by not feeding them carrots, that there is going to be some kind of irreparable damage done to Gabriel's eyesight if he doesn't eat a stupid carrot!"

I fall back into the cold steel of my chair and try to breathe.

Dr. Bess gets up, pulls a tissue from a box, and hands it to me. She kneels down to my eye level and lifts up my fallen chin with her hand.

"Does your husband really think you are blinding the children by not feeding them carrots?"

"No," I say, sniffling, "of course he doesn't." I blow my nose.

"Good," she says. "This is all going to be fine."

"Sure, sure . . . it's . . . I was just so excited to have boys so I wouldn't pass on my eating issues to them and now they have their own and. . . ." My eyes swell again.

Gabriel bounds into the room.

"Mom, what . . . ? Don't cry, Mom, it's fine," he says, giving me a hug.

"That's exactly what I just said, Gabriel," Dr. Bess says, and then looks him right in the eyes. "Let me ask you a question. Do you go to the bathroom regularly?"

"Yes."

"I don't mean pee," she adds.

Gabriel rolls his eyes. "I know what you mean. Yes, every day."

"Good for you! And your energy is good? You're happy?" He thinks for a minute.

I wait quietly for the answer.

"Well, yeah, when you guys don't make me choke on carrots."

"I'm sure that wasn't fun, Gabriel," Dr. Bess says quickly, anything to keep me from another round of mea culpa. "But you know how lucky you are that your mom loves you so much, right? And that she just wants what's best for you always, right?"

"Sure," he says. "Don't worry, Mom, I told you I'm fine. Geez." Dr. Bess looks back down at her laptop.

"His weight is normal, height normal." She looks up. "How about sleep? Do you sleep well, Gabriel?"

"That he definitely does," I answer, full of pride. As if I have anything to do with the fact that my kids sleep like dead people. Their sound sleeping makes me feel like at least my children aren't wracked with anxiety. Yet.

"He eats, poops, sleeps, and all his vital signs are normal. So where is the dire problem?" Dr. Bess asks.

"I have a white food disorder." Gabriel says.

"That's what I call it, you know, as a joke," I say, adding "Ha!"

"Uh huh. So, how about we stop saying that, Mom," Dr. Bess says, "and you and your brother try one new fruit or vegetable a week?"

"OK. I'm not sure my brother will do it, but I can do that."

"Great! Mom, you OK with that?"

"Um, sure." By this point I'll agree to anything to wrap this up. Not only am I embarrassed by my excessively revealing rant earlier, but it's way past lunch and I'm so hungry I could marinate Gabriel and spread him on a Beverly Hills baguette.

"Thank you, Dr. Bess, we'll definitely keep you posted on his progress," I say, walking toward the exit.

"Great," Dr. Bess says over her shoulder, moving on to the next kid crisis.

With time still on our parking meter, we duck in to a little Old Hollywood themed café on Beverly Drive, where I inhale a chicken Caesar

salad with freshly baked croutons, shaved Parmesan, and salty ancho-
vies "from Italy" according to our Russian supermodel/waitress. Just our
luck, Gabriel's grilled cheddar cheese on sourdough is accompanied by
a side of steamed broccoli. Vegetable of the week, locked and loaded! He
lifts the tiny green tree to his lips and reluctantly parts them. He chews
and, although clearly not happy about it, swallows. Small victory.

"Blech," he says.

"Good effort, honey," I say, picking up the check and looking at the
movie posters on the wall to avoid revealing to him the minor look of
disappointment on my face. And then I see it right in front of me, the
canary-yellow poster for Frank Capra's *You Can't Take It with You.* I smile
and wonder if my boyfriend Moss Hart ever choked on broccoli with his
mother before he became a gourmand.

"One of Mommy's favorite writers wrote the story for that movie," I
tell Gabriel.

"Oh," he says, licking the back of his spoon where vanilla bean ice
cream once sat.

"He was a great writer. But an even better eater!"

"Mom . . ."

"I'm just saying . . . keep up the good work, honey."

THREE SMOOTHIES

EACH RECIPE SERVES 2 COLOR-RESTRICTED EATERS, OR 1
EXHAUSTED ADULT WHEN THEY TURN OUT TO BE NOT IN THE MOOD

WHITE SMOOTHIE

1 frozen banana, cut into chunks

1 cup milk

½ cup vanilla yogurt

Whip up in a blender. Add nothing. Drink with a bendy straw.

BERRY SMOOTHIE

1 cup frozen raspberries/strawberries/blueberries

½ cup berry yogurt

½ frozen banana, cut into chunks

1 cup milk

Whip up in a blender. Thicken or thin to taste by adding either more milk or more fruit. Drink with a spoon. Complain that it is not sweet enough.

MOMMY SMOOTHIE

1 shot espresso

1 cup lowfat milk

Crushed ice

2 heaping tablespoons imported unsweetened cocoa

½ frozen banana, cut into chunks

Whip it up in a blender. Sit down and drink in a quiet corner of the house while the kids pretend to beat each other up until one of them starts crying. Make sure it's a real cry, not the fake kind. Resolve the fight. Continue drinking.

ONE BITE AT A TIME

ELRENA EVANS

I worry my daughter is too skinny. I've been saying this for weeks now, to anyone who will listen, but that's just the problem: no one will. "They always slim down around this age," I keep hearing. "And didn't she just start walking?"

Yes, I know they always slim down when they start walking, and yes, my seventeen-month-old daughter did just start to walk, finally. But she doesn't really eat. Not that she's picky, nor that she doesn't eat much; this is more along the lines of she doesn't eat at all. Entire days can pass without her letting a single morsel of food into her mouth, and the only reason we can measure this time in days instead of weeks is that every few days I desperately shove something in there when she's not paying attention. Just leave her be, people say; she'll eat when she gets hungry. But I'm not convinced she will: My daughter has inherited, from both her parents, a very wide stubborn streak.

That is precisely the reason, at least one reason among many, that I don't want to make food an issue with her. I really, *really* don't want to make food an issue with her. The food/weight/body image conglomerate is messy enough, with what you eat determining what you weigh determining what you think about yourself. I'd like to raise my daughter as free of this nexus as possible, given the messed-up, wacky, female-body-obsessed culture in which we live.

When she was a baby, food was a blissful nonissue. She nursed, and she gained weight, and she nursed, and she gained weight, and she kept right on gaining until her little legs were so fat she couldn't sit in her baby seat without getting stuck. I loved it. I knew, intellectually, that the fatness of the child is not necessarily correlated with the goodness of the parent, but still, I was thrilled with my secret knowledge that those lovely fat rolls came not from a bottle or a jar, but from my body. My own wonderful, marvelous, milk-making body. My daughter began her life as a petite little twenty-fifth percentile newborn, and topped off at the absolute apex of the growth chart as a fat little pumpkin six months later. She was fat, and I was loving it.

Our food issues began the day we tried to feed her something other than mama's milk. We waited the recommended six months, then waited another month just for good measure. And then, with much pageantry and excitement, we gave her a spoonful of baby cereal mixed with about nine spoonfuls of my milk. She wanted nothing to do with it. I'd been forewarned that some babies don't take to solid foods too readily, so although disappointed, I wasn't discouraged. We simply put the cereal away, and later, we tried again.

And again. And again. And again. My daughter wasn't disinterested in solids, she was militantly hostile. When it got to the point that she would turn purple from crying simply at the sight of a bib, I decided to forget the whole enterprise. We put the baby food away, and decided we'd try again in a month.

At eight months, the only change was that she was fatter and could scream harder. At nine months, she was strong enough that I was afraid she'd hurt herself—or me—throwing tantrums in her high chair. By ten months, I was desperate. I packed up my chubster and hauled her off to a La Leche League meeting, where I stayed afterward and asked the leader, fighting tears, exactly how long a baby could survive on nothing but mother's milk.

"I could give you citations on all the research that's been done on the topic," she told me, "and if you want me to, I will. But before I do that . . ." She paused, glancing significantly at my daughter.

"I want you to look at your baby," she said. "I want you to really look at her."

I did. She was sitting on the floor, "reading" a book about trains. I didn't see whatever it was I was supposed to be seeing. I looked back at the leader.

"She's the fattest baby in this entire room," the woman said.

And sure enough, she was. By a lot.

Armed with the defense of my baby's fatness, I gradually stopped worrying that she was starving to death. We quit offering her solid food. And eventually, she began to eat: a bite here, a taste there, an entire banana. She was finally putting something in her mouth other than my breast, and I was happy.

Then, about six weeks after her first birthday, I got pregnant. Almost everything I read, even lactavist literature, warned that my milk was about to suddenly wimp out on me, if not dry up completely. And I started to worry again. Every day as my daughter gleefully nursed I looked at the calendar and tallied the days until the start of my second trimester, the time that I knew was most likely to be bye-bye, milky.

The second trimester rolled around, and my daughter kept right on nursing. I hand-expressed milk to see if there was anything still there, and much to my surprise, there was—a bit thinner than usual, perhaps, but it was milk, and she drank it with gusto. I kept trying to encourage solids. By this time, she was sixteen months old, and her primary sources of sustenance were my milk and bananas. I thought about the baby due in a matter of months, and knew that something had to give.

I take my daughter, now eighteen months old and running a high fever, to the doctor. The receptionist is amazed when I mention that this is our first sick visit; what an extraordinarily healthy child you must have! Yes, I answer, adding in a voice only I can hear, extraordinarily healthy and extraordinarily skinny.

The doctor examines her, finds nothing wrong, and suggests the most likely cause is a virus. My daughter lolls against my chest, her hot little body pressed up against mine as it has been for two days. I am beginning to forget what it feels like to not be hot and sticky.

"Before I go," I say to the doctor in a would-be casual voice, "do you think we could weigh her really quick? It's just she's looking pretty skinny to me, and. . . ." My voice trails off.

The doctor sees through my feigned nonchalance.

"I'm sure she's fine," she responds. "They always slim down at this age. I wouldn't worry about your daughter at all."

"Still. . . ." I persist.

The doctor smiles and seems to conclude that nothing is going to reassure me until she plunks my daughter down on the scale. She lifts her out of my arms as my daughter begins to wail. I watch her place my baby on the scale, a pitiful sight: sick baby girl, crying desperately to be lifted back up into mama's arms. I bite my lip and wait for the scale's result.

In the nanosecond that it takes for my daughter's weight to flash in a large digital display, the doctor's entire demeanor changes.

"How much did she weigh at a year?" she queries, frowning at her clipboard. I tell her what I remember. We look at the scale. Fully clothed, my daughter weighs at eighteen months barely more than I remember her weighing, stark naked, six months ago.

Instantly I am relegated from cutely worrying mama to flat-out bad mother.

"You feed her three meals a day, correct?" the doctor says, her tone suddenly brisk, as she hands the sobbing ball of misery back to me. My daughter wraps her burning arms around my neck and clings to me. I realize I am clinging just as tightly to her.

"Three meals a day, and two solid, wholesome snacks," she continues. "Yes?"

I nod dumbly. I can't remember when my daughter last ate anything that would even closely resemble a solid meal. She eats bananas, I start to say, and stop myself.

"You give her whole milk to drink?" the doctor presses on.

"I—I try," I stammer, wondering if the watered-down substance in my breasts still counts as "whole." "She usually won't drink it."

"You need to try harder," the doctor says. "Whole milk, twelve to sixteen ounces per day."

My brain reels. I don't think my daughter's had twelve to sixteen ounces of anything other than breast milk in the past *week*, perhaps the past month. I am still nodding dumbly, I realize, my baby hiccuping into my shoulder. I need to leave before I burst into tears.

"Bring her back in a week and we'll weigh her again," the doctor finally says, making a note on her chart. "We need to see if she's actually losing weight, or just not gaining." I clutch my hot, apparently starving child to my chest, and bolt for the door.

Home again, I drape her sleeping figure over my rounded belly as I sit at the computer and e-mail my husband.

I knew she was too skinny! I type, my fingers flying over keys blurred by tears. *I knew she was too skinny and I've been saying it for weeks and nobody listened to me.*

I look up her weight on an online baby growth chart; she's hovering right around the bottom. Phrases like "failure to thrive" are popping up on my screen, along with "high-calorie formulas" and "gavage feeding." Pictures of babies with tubes running up their noses. With every press of my fingers on the keypad, every swipe of my hand over the mouse, my heart is beating a mantra through my brain: Bad mother. Bad mother. Bad mother. I've been starving my child, and I didn't even know it. Or worse, I did know it, and I didn't do anything about it. I sob into my baby's neck until my cries wake her from her fevered sleep.

That night, we order her favorite dinner: cheese pizza. I am officially abandoning all attempts at healthy food until I can put some weight on her. If she wants to eat Crisco, I'll get her a spoon.

I start keeping a food log. Every single bite that passes her lips is immediately written down, along with the time she ate it and how much. 8:00 A.M. —mama's cereal, one bite. 8:15 A.M. —baby cereal with whole milk, one bite. 10:00 A.M. —half a wheat cracker. My day slips away as I try to get these bites past her stubborn lips, and I look up calorie and fat contents when I can no longer convince her to try another nibble. We head out to the grocery store and I buy all the foods I think she might eat regardless of their nutritional value. Ice cream? Check. Goldfish crackers? Check. French fries on the way back home? Check. Once home, I run to my list that is stuck up on the side of the fridge: 3:00—French fries, five.

We open the bag of goldfish crackers. They're the little ones, the baby goldfish. I show them to her, and she grabs one and shoves it in her mouth all by herself. I hold my breath, watching her. She chews it up, swallows, grabs for another. And another. And another. Seven goldfish she eats in all, before running off to go play. I'm ecstatic. I grab the bag of crackers, flip it over to read the nutritional information. A serving of baby goldfish crackers, I soon discover, is eighty-three crackers. *Eighty-three?* I throw the bag down in disgust, my moment of euphoria short-lived. Who eats eighty-three goldfish in one sitting? I call the doctor, schedule her follow-up appointment. Can we make it for after we come back from vacation, I ask, figuring after a week at the shore, eating fries and pizza and frozen custard on the boardwalk, she'll be about as fat as I can hope. The receptionist schedules the appointment, I write it on my calendar. I offer my daughter some ice cream.

Two weeks later, we weigh in. She's gained. Not much, but enough to make the doctor cautiously happy. We agree to watch and wait, and I realize that this visit is only a baby step on a road I never wanted to walk in the first place.

My husband is making tortellini, another one of my daughter's favorite foods—"favorite" meaning she'll deign to eat it if she's in a really good mood. I'm chewing on my lip as I buckle her into her high chair. She hasn't eaten a thing besides breast milk and banana all day.

"Yum, tortellini!" I say as I set the plate down before her. "Remember? You love tortellini!" She picks up her fork, stabs a piece, considers it, and flings it to the ground. I take a deep breath.

"No, baby, you want to *eat* it," I say. "Yum!" I hold another piece to her lips. She won't open her mouth. I take a big bite, smiling as I chew, and then offer her another.

"C'mon baby," I say. "Just try. Just try a bite for Mama."

She sits there with her mouth clenched firmly shut, looking at me. I am starting to shake.

"Eat something," I say. "Just come on, eat something."

She won't. I grab her jaw with one hand, force her lips open, and shove a piece of tortellini inside.

"Eat it!" I scream, and she gags and spits the food out onto her tray.

"You have *got* to eat!" I am screaming at the top of my lungs, my lips inches from hers. She is trapped in her high chair, trying to pull back away from me, but I can't stop. I grab the fork from her hand and slam it on her high chair tray.

"*God damn you!* You have to eat! If you don't eat you're going to *die!* Do you hear me?" My voice cracks from shrieking so loud. I am sobbing, collapsing, holding onto the high chair tray for support. I look at my daughter's terrified face. I hate myself.

I whirl around and stomp out of the house, grabbing my keys as I run and breaking a baby gate on the way out, leaving my husband standing between the kitchen and the table, holding my untouched plate of tortellini.

I drive blindly, sobbing, not caring where I am going. The scene replays itself over and over in my head: her petrified face, my shrieking voice. I screamed at her. I *swore* at her. I hate myself so much I just want to die. I try to pray.

"I hate you!" I scream at the heavens. "I hate you and you're killing my baby!" I pound on the steering wheel as I pivot the car around a turn. "Why won't she eat? *Why?*" I shove my hand across my eyes, trailing snot and tears. "Is this punishment?" I cry. "Are you punishing me for what I did?"

My car has found its way to a national park, and I drive in slow circles around open fields where George Washington's men once camped. No battles were ever fought here: The place is significant simply because Washington's men survived the winter. I think about my own battles with food, and now my daughter's. I wonder if she will survive her own winter.

I'm classically trained in ballet, which means I practically grew up in a dance studio, which in turn means that I can't remember a time when I didn't loathe my body. Anorexia was not a disease in my world, it was a goal; but no matter how much I restricted my food intake, it was never enough. I was never truly skinny.

In college I tried to learn the art of purging, but I don't have much of a gag reflex, a fact I added to my list of reasons for hating my body. I danced and did aerobics and ran and did crunches, but no matter how little I ate, what I saw was fat. It was impossible, given my demanding class schedule, to find more time to exercise, and so eventually I quit eating.

The simplicity of the plan was beautiful. Breakfast: nothing. Lunch: nothing. Dinner: nothing. If I never ate again, I would never again be fat.

I looked at a picture of an emaciated woman liberated from a concentration camp at the end of World War II, and found her so entrancing I kept the picture in my backpack.

And I didn't eat until I nearly passed out in class one day, faint with hunger. At home, I realized my class notes were nonsense. I wasn't just starving my body, I was starving my brain.

I lay on the floor in my dorm room and cried. My brain was the one thing I had going for me, with a near-perfect GPA and thousands of dollars in scholarship money riding on my abilities. I couldn't afford—literally—not to feed my brain.

In the counselor's office, I wedged myself into the corner of an over-stuffed armchair while we discussed my "anorectic thinking patterns." I balked at the term.

"I'm not anorexic," I protested. "If I were anorexic, I would be skinny and beautiful."

My counselor raised an eyebrow.

"I don't want the sick, anorexic brain," I finally said. "I just want the anorexic body."

She lowered the pad she was scribbling on and looked at me.

"That is so messed up," she said, shaking her head.

It caught me off-guard, this total non-counselor thing to say, this lapse in her professional persona. And I laughed. She was right.

I didn't want to be messed up.

That night I made tomato soup, the salty smoothness in my mouth reminiscent of tears. I ate, and I cried, and I thought about how to step off this road I was on. I ate soup. And then cream of wheat. I didn't think about nutritional content, I was going for things I didn't have to chew. I drank a lot of milk. I ate applesauce, peanut butter. Eventually I made macaroni and cheese and sucked the sauce off the wooden spoon as I cooked. I threaded the noodles onto the tines of my fork, and looked at them for a while.

"You do not have power over me," I said. And then I ate them.

I'd like to say that I "got better," that once I started eating again, the struggle was over. But I was wrestling not only with food, but with my body, my self-image, an entire lifetime of warped thinking and skewed perspectives. I "got better," for a while, and then I got worse. I stopped eating again. I started back up. I hoped, in all of the cycling, that I was somehow climbing closer to the top of the spiral.

The car starts to feel confining. I find a place to park and shut off the engine, stumble outside, and sit down in the grass at the edge of the path. I look down at my pregnant body, clad in gray sweatpants and a stained, see-through undershirt that belongs to my husband.

I think about my daughter, about how the bony protrusions I so desperately longed for on my body are now carving their way out of hers. I think about her collarbones, her shoulder blades, how her skeleton is draped with so little flesh. I think and I cry until the sun sets, the night grows dark.

Eventually I have to get up. I have to decide to move on, to keep trying, to navigate this complicated world of food and bodies, sickness and health, one day, one moment, at a time.

I want to bring my daughter home a present, but I don't have any money with me. I crouch down on the gravel beside the open door of my car and dig around for loose change. I don't find much—dropped pennies, mostly—but it's enough. I will go to the store and buy her a banana.

I'm aware of the looks I get, steering my bulk through the grocery store in my sweatpants and T-shirt, my face swollen and red from crying. I opt for the self-checkout lane to avoid the embarrassment of counting my pennies into the cashier's hand.

And then I drive home. Home, where there are no easy solutions and no answers. I pull the car into the driveway and sit there for a moment, thinking. Then I get out.

The second my key clicks into the lock I hear my daughter's feet running toward me, and I swing open the door and drop to my knees.

"I'm so sorry," I say, pressing her to my chest and stroking her back, breathing into her hair. "I'm so sorry I yelled at you; I'm so sorry I swore at you. I'm really, really sorry." I take a breath. "Can you forgive me?"

I don't know if she knows, at eighteen months, what I am saying, but she says "yes" and I feel better. She twines her little arms around my neck and gives me a kiss.

"I brought you a present," I say, standing up with her in my arms. I show her the banana. "Would you like to eat it?"

She nods, and I carry her over to the couch where she snuggles into my lap. With both arms around her, I peel the banana, the firm yellow skin breaking open with a crack. Still holding the fruit, I offer it to her, and she leans forward and takes a bite. I feel something inside me releasing, and she leans forward and takes another one.

It's not going to be easy, for her or for me, navigating this complicated path. But we don't have to make the entire trip at once. We just have to keep putting one foot in front of the other, and take the struggles as they come, together, one bite at a time.

MAKING CREPES WITH A SELECTIVE EATER
(NOW AGE SIX)

1. Pick a crepe recipe—it doesn't matter which one. We like *Betty Crocker* or *The Joy of Cooking*.
2. Gather ingredients as your child reads the recipe aloud. Talk about the similarities between crepes, a new food, and pancakes, a food already approved for eating. Discipline your mind to avoid the long list of analogous comparisons—quesadillas to grilled cheese; sweet potatoes to carrots—that have failed.
3. Taste the ingredients your child will eat—milk, butter, sugar, salt. Talk about the other ingredients—flour, baking powder, vanilla, eggs. Note the importance of each in making a unified whole. Measure, break, pour, and stir; look, feel, and smell as you do.
4. Pour the batter into the pan and talk about the process of cooking—how ingredients react with each other, how heat transforms. Appeal to your child's scientific mind. When the crepe begins to pull away at the edge, flip it with your bare fingers lest the spatula leave an untoward mark or mar.
5. Serve the younger siblings—blissful omnivores—first. The potential trauma of a new food is best managed in relative peace and quiet.
6. Sit with your child as she looks at her crepe, plays with her fork, points out every anomaly. Keep your voice steady, light, and calm. Do not think about all the times, all the foods, that have started out with equal promise only to ultimately fail. Do not add up the number of meals—approximately 13,687—between now and when she leaves for college.
7. As always, she will either eat the food, or she will not. Either way, you will cry. Today is a good day. Sit with your child, and eat your crepes together.

VEGGING OUT

GREGORY DICUM

"I like fish," announced Xeno, pointing at the image in his Richard Scarry book of a halibut, dressed in a Sou'wester.

"Yes, fish are very nice animals," I said, pleased that a two-year-old could have an appreciation for such a non-anthropomorphic animal.

"No, eating them," he continued. "I like to eat them. Dead ones."

I knew it was coming. All the big things—the wheel of life, sustenance, and death—wrapped into an innocent toddler comment. I had been vegan for ten years before Xeno was born, but had been feeding him lacto-ovo. And I knew that his momma had been slipping him fish from time to time, but I was in denial about it. I didn't want to explain this complicated moral territory to my toddler because, fundamentally, I didn't understand it myself.

————

I will not belabor the obvious with statistics about the acres of cropland and tons of cereal grains wasted (millions and billions respectively) to raise animals. I won't survey the poisoning of the planet that takes place in the process, nor enumerate the human diseases these mountains of flesh will cause. I won't even plumb the boundless agony endured by billions of animals on their way to the end of a fork.

I knew the facts for many years. I had seen the films. I had seen animals die; I had killed animals. I had even visited a particularly nasty slaughter house in Bolivia. The images stand out in my mind: the cow struggling back to her feet from unconsciousness, only to be clobbered again with a sledge-hammer. Skinny dogs looked on expectantly, chest-deep in muddy offal. Only the haze of cigarette smoke (mine and all the workers, who seemed to breathe through the cigarettes as though they were gas masks) kept at bay the abattoir's stench and clouds of flies.

I bought half a cow there, wrapped her in plastic, and with some dif-ficulty (it took four of us) heaved the warm, bleeding mass onto the top of a Land Cruiser. The next day, when we got to our jungle camp (where I had been living while researching the population dynamics of mahog-any), there were already fat maggots in the blueing flesh. So we cut it into strips, salted it, and hung it to dry. It was stringy, tough, and a little ran-cid, and we ate it all over the course of a month.

The facts of the abattoir did not bother me, at least not enough to put me off my meat. I believed then, and still do, that anyone who eats beef must be prepared to bring a hammer down between those big eyes, and to slip and slide across the killing floor. Not that I ever did the former.

A few years after visiting the slaughterhouse, I was working as a pro-fessional environmentalist, and a different aspect of the facts of the meat industry troubled me. I had long known about the environmental degra-dation caused by meat production, but now I was troubled to find myself living in bald hypocrisy. I would not use wood from old growth forests, or countenance plutonium in my electricity. I chose organic cotton clothes and preferred not to drive when I could bike or walk. You would never catch me littering, or burning trash, or dumping motor oil in the sewer. Yet with every meal I was doing worse, bringing into my body the prod-ucts of a wantonly destructive, flagrantly unsustainable industry. I used my mouth to decry environmental destruction and to consume the fruits of that devastation.

And on top of it all, it was something my body did not need: for most Americans, it's far more practical to give up meat than to give up driving. I came to see that anyone who knows the facts, and pretends to live a life at all guided by moral considerations, has to consider a plant-based diet.

So I did.

I weaned myself over several years. First from land animals, telling myself that fish were somehow more sustainable, though most fisheries are about as sustainable as coal mines. Then I became vegetarian, accepting only dairy and eggs into my diet. In 1999 I went all the way and became a vegan.

I loved it.

Besides the freedom from hypocrisy—and the unfamiliar feeling of living up to my self-image—I felt physically great. My body lost some flab, reordering itself around a new stable weight. Various annoying health quirks completely vanished.

It was not too hard to give up cheese, which I had loved, but soon got over. If I quavered at all it was over sushi, but I enjoyed the chance to apply culinary creativity in a whole new way and, after years of moral angst, the comforting certainties of being an absolutist.

PRACTICAL MORALITY

The next time I found myself in a situation anywhere near as gruesome as that slaughterhouse was as I watched, agog, as Xeno was extracted through the front of his momma's belly. I was surprised by the resistance the umbilical cord offered to the surgical scissors.

Among the many benefits of extended breast-feeding is the fact that parents don't have to make any food decisions for months. Even so, from the start I had no intention of enforcing a strict vegan diet for Xeno. This was mostly a choice of convenience: It's possible to raise a healthy vegan baby, but it's a gigantic hassle. Those little guys need a lot more fat than we do; their brains are using it to myelinate—a physical aspect of learning with lifelong implications. Piling dairy and eggs into his diet meant that I could be sure he was getting enough fat and protein, without having to worry amid all the other chaos in a household with a young kid.

But it did put me in some uncomfortable spots. The first time I bought eggs for Xeno, I stood for half an hour in my local organic co-op considering the chart next to the fridge: which producers cut the chicks' beaks off; which hens had access to the outside; which had vegetarian diets; which were pastured. This was exactly the kind of karmic equivocation (including the highly divergent prices of these eggs) that I had put behind me by becoming vegan. I had to decide how much the karmic pollution of making the boy an omelet was worth.

Having a kid forces you to examine what you mean by how you live—at least it ought to. In my case, I thought I knew what I was doing in my life before having Xeno. But suddenly I was in over my head, constantly compromising my morals for the smoother operations of the narrow time and space around me. It was—it is—precisely the kind of behavior I had never intended to model for my child.

Having Xeno had ironically led me to grow more abstractly compassionate even as I became more practical in my day-to-day life. Suddenly, I was the kind of person who is moved to tears by photos of little children in refugee camps, yet I was simultaneously turning my back on a decade of rigidly compassionate food choices in order to privilege my child's development over all the creatures in the sea.

I'm sure a large part of my dilemma is due to the fact that my choices—including the choice to have a child in the first place—are not made by my rational intellect, but rather are the result of momentum of evolution in my DNA. For four billon years, every one of our ancestors successfully acquired the atoms it needed to thrive, explicitly at the expense of other creatures.

OFF THE WAGON

I had been growing more selfish anyway. I have traveled all over the world as a vegan and I know that, if one is willing to work at it, it is possible nearly everywhere. It is often painfully difficult, requiring the fortitude to forgo a meal or two, or to console oneself with dry rusks at the banquet table. But such is the moral life.

In the few years leading up to Xeno's birth, I'd allowed myself to bend my self-imposed rules. First in Rio de Janeiro, on a rainy day in Santa Teresa, with thick chunks of fish in a heavy *moqueca*, orange with *dendê* oil. Then in Barcelona, with a small plate of octopus—*pop* in Catalán—their arms locked in an oiled death embrace. Then a *matjes* herring from a street stall in Amsterdam: tender and raw, like bait on a bun.

It was both better and more quotidian than I remembered. Minus all the tortured knowledge, that salted anchovy is just a morsel of protein. Yet after ten years away, my fish was spiced with frisson. I knew I was morally wrong, even as I savored its umami. It brought the excitement of a secret liaison; one need not be proud of something to enjoy it deeply.

I savored my fish in secret shame. As other travelers throw their daily habits out the window in foreign lands—taking up cigarettes in Paris, say, or casual sex at Club Med—I adopted a new, and frankly hypocritical, policy: I'll eat fish when I'm traveling, particularly in countries where they prepare it well.

(I can't wait to get back to Thailand.)

MY MORAL CRISIS

All this has given me a keener appreciation for the difficulty of living a moral life—for reconciling intellect and desire. For me, this is what moral crisis looks like:

I am home alone for lunch. Standing in front of the fridge. Inside is a jar of pickled herring, unopened. My wife bought it a month ago, and does not want it. She wants me to eat it. On the counter is a fresh loaf of the sort of heavy, chewy rye bread that has gone so perfectly with pickled herring for hundreds, probably thousands of years.

I take a long knife, with a slender, straight edge, and shave a few slices from the dense loaf. They curl down to the cutting board like slices of cheese. My fingers are cold. I spread vegan margarine on one slice, and eat it.

It is chewy and satisfying. The margarine tastes just like what I imagine butter tastes like. I have another, standing in front of the fridge, with my back to it. I look out the window, but think of the herring.

I imagine them swimming in the North Atlantic: cold, blue-green water, and a silver flash. That flash is now waiting to be my lunch. It seems ridiculous, like going out into the garden and braining the hummingbird that lives there, and laying its little iridescent corpse, still at last, on a slice of rye. I eat another piece.

And then I snap. I am no longer myself, but am watching myself with the utmost fascination: I see myself open the fridge and take out the jar. I feel it frigid in my grip, and the tight snap as I open the lid, twisting as though I am breaking a small neck. I fork a little pile of glistening herring slabs onto my plate of bread and take it into the dining room. Might as well make this a little more dignified. Should I pour a glass of wine?

I am surprised by how tender and soft the flesh is. It yields with a simplicity that belies the complexity crowding in my head. It is, of course, delicious, shrouded in pickled onions and soaking the bread with its limpid fluid. I eat it all, images of a trawler on heaving gray seas grinding in a heavy net of squirming silver prey. I don't feel remorse, but absurdity.

Only when I am done do the qualms arise. I come out of my fugue to taste dead fish on my breath. "Seagull breath," I mutter, and return to the kitchen to gnaw on a sprig of parsley. It has no effect. I try an orange. Nothing. Soy ice cream? No, I still reek of wrack. Chocolate? Now I realize my cold fingers, too, smell of the dead.

By the standards of moral crisis, it's rather pissant. I haven't killed a man, or gone off on a home-wrecking tryst. But it's *my* moral crisis, and it's fascinating: a schism between self-image and impulse; incontrovertible evidence that "I" am much more—and much less—than a rational being, or any kind of unitary being at all. Actions, as we all know, speak louder than words. But just exactly who is speaking? And to whom?

And who am I cheating? Myself? My morals? The herring? I know that eating an anchovy is not going to destroy the world. The lost life, which meant the universe to that small fish, was lamentable and inexcusable, but small. I'm just narcissistically embarrassed not to be living up to my self-image as a moral person.

Either way it's a slippery slope. If nothing matters—or if all subjectivity is lesser than, and indeed subservient to my own, then why let morals guide actions at all? Why not eat tuna until the magnificent creatures are gone from the sea? Why not eat beef? Why not eat dogs? Why not eat people?

NOT QUITE CREATING THE WORLD

My daily life is now an exercise in contradictions—maybe even hypocrisy. I revel in making a quiche with Xeno, enjoying layering the Gruyère and the eggs with him, and I take pleasure in his pleasure at eating it. The next day I'm at the taqueria insisting that my burrito come without a morsel of cheese. I feel as though the fish—especially the fish oil—his momma slips Xeno is good for him, and I'm glad he has those molecules in his system, yet I also fret about the killing.

He has no problem with it: It's just me.

Eating has forever been the most intimate locus of our relationship with the physical world: It is bringing the universe into our bodies, and collaborating with it in the making of our bodies. The fact of nutrition renders the interconnectedness of all things obvious. What one eats lies at the very heart of how one chooses to be in the world: We create the world, and our selves in it, a forkful at a time.

Veganism, for me, lays bare the gulf between what I believe and how I act. In this, I've rejoined the territory of most concerned eaters—neither ignorant, nor living my beliefs. My plate has become a place of ambiguity. I can't in good conscience call myself a vegan anymore, as much as I want to.

And this ambiguity—the gap between self-image and self—is at the heart of what it is to be human, at the point of duality between our animal self of glorious appetite and our higher self of noble purpose. We are suspended in moral space, between animals and gods. We struggle from moment to moment knowing only our own—my own—actions make a material difference, much as I wish hoping and believing might have the same effect.

But how can I raise a kid like that? At least in the younger years they require some certainty. What do I tell him about the fish?

We've been ruled by our appetites for all our history. As much as our inventions are brilliant and unprecedented, they've done little more than magnify the desires of six billion hungry animals. But, perhaps uniquely, we can see why this might be a problem. We can, by now, see it quite clearly.

Living by hunting, or killing, was the best option for generations of our ancestors. Modern civilization has removed the constraints we once suffered. It has, in effect, provided us with the means to transcend biology—to choose how we want to *be* in the world. And more urgently, the side effects of heedless abundance will soon force us to choose: If we're all chewing our way through rainforest burgers, then we won't have rainforest for long.

The next step, the step we have yet to take for all our high-mindedness, is to do something about it. To prove that reason and feeling can come together to attenuate our base nature. And the place to start is the plate.

Except I, for one, can't quite do it. Over to you, kid.

COLD VEGAN BORSCHT

SERVES 4

Time: 30 minutes active cooking time, plus time to chill. Ideally, you make it the night before so the flavors meld.

All family recipes are inexact and morph with the generations, so in veganizing my Lithuanian mother's cold borscht—transmitted to me on a note card, perhaps the first time it had ever been written down—I am making it my own before I hand it on to my descendants. It's a pretty simple recipe that, with its striking fuchsia color and refreshing seasonal flavors, always gets stunning results at a summer luncheon. It loses nothing without cold borscht's usual buttermilk.

3 to 4 beets
1 bunch of radishes (8 to 12, depending on their size)
½ English cucumber, peeled and seeded
3 to 4 scallions
1 small clove garlic, crushed
1 quart unsweetened nondairy milk, such as hemp, almond, or soy milk
3 to 4 tablespoons apple cider vinegar
Boiled new potatoes, 3 to 4 per serving, sliced
Salt and freshly ground black pepper
Chopped fresh dill for garnish

Cook the beets in their jackets until tender when pierced with a knife (about 20 minutes, depending on the method; you can use a microwave or pressure cooker), then cool, peel, and grate them. Place the beets in a large bowl.

Trim and dice the radishes and cucumber. Add them to the beets.

Thinly slice the scallions, and add them, too, along with the crushed garlic.

Add the nondairy milk and vinegar (together these simulate the tangy buttermilk tradition calls for). Stir gently and season with salt and pepper and more vinegar to taste.

Put the soup in the fridge for a few hours or overnight to ripen the flavor and color.

When it's time to eat, stir the soup again and ladle it into bowls. Top each bowl with the potatoes and a generous sprinkling of chopped fresh dill.

LUNCH LADY

CAROLINE M. GRANT

Some people say that breakfast is the most important meal of the day, and others claim family dinner will keep our teenagers off the streets, but lunch is my meal. By lunchtime, you're awake enough to think about the food, but not so worn out by a long day to appreciate it. It might look like breakfast, with some eggs and toast, or its pasta and salad might look more like dinner; it can be hot or cold, eaten with a fork or spoon. Most of us don't even eat it at home. Whether we brown bag a sandwich, Tupperware our leftovers, or pick something up at the local café, cafeteria, or food truck, we eat lunch, typically, away from our families. And because it's often the first meal our children learn to assemble and eat independently, their school lunch trays and brown bags can carry weighty parental expectations and anxieties.

Like many kids, my sons took their first steps away from home foods at preschool. Ben toted cups of yogurt, sun-dried tomatoes, cheese slices, or crackers. He ate what he pulled out of his bag and listened quietly to the story being read, but he was not immune to the social influences at his little round table. One day, he came home with a note, written by his teacher. It read, "Mommy and Daddy, I want fruit leather in my lunch. Love, Ben." But when I asked my pre-literate child what the note said, he took it out of my hands, studied it closely, and pronounced, "Dear Mommy and Daddy, I hate my lunch! Give me fruit leather in my lunch! Love, Ben." It was only snack, it was only preschool, but the school lunch gauntlet had been thrown.

His note made me realize the extent of the food bubble my husband and I had unconsciously established around our children. By some measures, our sons' food options are broad. We cook a wide variety of foods at home and take full advantage of the restaurants in our neighborhood, from Thai to taqueria. Even so, whether at home or out, we still present the menu (a vegetarian menu) every day. I wondered what would happen in elementary school, where Ben would face a buffet of choices—hot food line plus sandwich and salad bars—for the first time. In the days leading up to his first day of kindergarten, I was consumed with unreasonable anticipation and concern. Would the cafeteria be too noisy for him to focus on the food? Would the staff help him find vegetarian options? Would the capricious breezes of peer pressure ("Eww, you eat tofu?") limit his choices? What would he eat? Would he eat? *My baby bird!*

Ben just wondered if he'd be made to eat a turkey sandwich.

I made a point of "discussing" nutrition. Really, I was just brainwashing. He was interested in cooking, a sponge for facts and statistics, so we'd always had these conversations, but now as I scooped up his yogurt I pointed out the nutrition information on the label. He worked out how many grams of protein were in his serving, added a sprinkle of wheat germ ("For iron, right, Mama?") and a handful of berries—all of which, I casually remarked, he could find at the school cafeteria. We talked about quick energy foods versus sustained energy foods, we talked about iron and calcium. If chips and chocolate milk were on his daily lunch menu, I knew he'd know exactly what he was getting out of them.

Instead of asking Ben what he learned in kindergarten every day, or whom he'd played with, I greeted him each afternoon with the same questions: "How was school today? Did you have a good lunch?" And every day, he gave me the same answer: "School was great! My lunch was lettuce, baby corn, olives, and celery. My dressing was balsamic vinaigrette." Or red wine vinaigrette. Or apple cider vinaigrette. He was the only kindergartener eating salad—no bowing to peer pressure there—and, child of my heart, spent more time describing his salad dressing than the other five-and-a-half hours of school.

Not content with his self-reporting, I started to help out in the lunchroom. Call it spying, but in my defense, I'd heard raves about the school's lunch program and I wanted in on that food. I also wanted to meet the other parent volunteers. Were they as food-crazy as me? Ben had told me about the mom who refused to make jam and butter sandwiches ("That's just cake!" she insisted) and the one who put cooked vegetables on every tray, even if a kid was eating salad. I knew some parents were complaining about the new bagel ban, while others were calling bagels more poisonous than donuts. An Atkins-influenced contingent railed against potatoes, rice, and bread, unable to see that PE and two daily recesses kept the carbs from softly padding their young children's active bodies. Sure, we all have our food foibles; doing lunch duty, I discovered, would cast mine into sharp relief.

I didn't set foot in a cafeteria until I was nine; the district didn't permit children to eat at school before fourth grade. Although my mom muttered about a suburban conspiracy to keep mothers in their cars, driving back and forth all day long, she kept it up for a while, and I loved the break in the day, the brief return to the familiarity of home. But when I was in third grade, Mom gladly returned to work and I embarked on a year of itinerant lunches.

Some days, my dad (a priest with a flexible weekday schedule) brought me home, where we sat at the dining room table playing games of double solitaire across our plates. I don't remember my own lunch—probably PB&J—but I remember his vividly: "garbage salad": an assortment of dinner leftovers dumped over a bed of lettuce, topped with shredded carrot, a scoop of cottage cheese, and a handful of peanuts. It didn't appeal to me at all, but still I marveled at the ingenuity of it, that reckless marriage of lunch and dinner on a single plate.

If Dad wasn't free, I carried my brown bag to a friend's house. I walked up the hill to Didi's, where her mom gave us potato chips that we slipped into our sandwiches. I walked downtown with the twins, Rachel and Judy, and their babysitter (their mother, a career woman, was scandalously divorced). Most often, I walked across the street and past the public library to my best friend Jennifer's house. Occasionally there'd be a mix-up and Jennifer would be off on her own lunchtime play date, so I walked alone and ate silently, tense with embarrassment, while her mother bustled around doing chores and making phone calls.

After that year, the school cafeteria was a relief. In the midst of the noise and chaos, in that unregulated place even more stressful for some kids than the playground, I sat every day at the same table, with the same group of friends. I packed a baloney and cheese sandwich, Mom added a Drake's Fruit Pie or Yodel, I bought the subsidized ten-cent carton of milk. As I got a bit older (and taller), I braved the narrow path through the hot lunch line.

"Do you want a burger with that?" the lunch lady would ask me.

"No, just the fries, thanks."

I would take the grease-spotted paper boat out of the lunch lady's hand and move down the line with my fellow fourth graders, keeping my carton of milk and coconut ice cream bar far away from the hot, crinkle-cut fries. I heard the lunch lady call after me, "Does your mother know what you're eating for lunch?!"

I bet my mom did know about my coconut ice cream and French fry lunches (my school had its parent volunteer/spies, too), but she never said a word. It's not that I was a vegetarian (that came later) or a picky eater, or even that I didn't know better. I justified it this way: fries = vegetable; milk = protein and calcium; coconut ice cream = fruit, an accounting that shows that I had already absorbed, at our family table, something of what a balanced, nutritious meal entailed. Mom saw me come home from school happily each day, she saw me eat healthy breakfasts and dinners; I absorbed a small lesson in trust and independence—one I promptly forgot when my son first headed into his own school cafeteria.

———

Instead, when I pulled on my latex gloves and tied my apron strings, it was that old lunch lady I channeled, the one who invoked the controlling, judgmental, "Does your mother know?" I took my place at the fruit and yogurt station and kept my eyes peeled for Ben.

"May I have some yogurt please, with strawberries but no grapes?"

"May I have granolayogurtapple?"

"May I have . . . um . . . yogurt please, and, hmmm? Maybe just a *little* granola?"

"May I have strawberries and grapes? In different bowls? Different bowls, please! Different bowls!"

I filled their dishes quickly, trying to keep track of who wanted what separate and who wanted what mixed. When a wayward grape tumbled into one boy's "no grapes" bowl, his eyes brimmed with tears. I quickly fished out the offending fruit and handed him his bowl, hoping the other moms were as careful with Ben's requests.

I finally spotted him, the last to enter the cafeteria, heading straight for the salad bar. I handed my yogurt spoon off to another volunteer, gestured that I'd be right back, and grabbed a bowl.

"Benno!" I exclaimed, giving him a kiss on the head. "Can I help you get your lunch?"

"That's OK, Mama; Mr. L. always helps me."

Indeed, one of the kindergarten teachers had already filled Ben's bowl with green beans, tofu chunks, baby corn, olives, and celery. "I got it," the teacher said with a nod, "I know what he likes."

I paused before heading back to my yogurt, absorbing this development, but the pang melted when I saw the teacher lean his head closer to Ben's and ask, "So, what kind of dressing do you want today, Ben? Red wine vinegar or balsamic?"

"Balsamic, please!" he answered happily.

He took the bowl in both hands from his teacher and walked to his assigned table. I watched him out of the corner of my eye, resisting the impulse to urge him on. Lunch is only twenty-five minutes, and he can spend longer than that unfolding his napkin. I saw him digging through his little plastic bowl, picking out the olives and eating them individually, taking a sip of water, looking contentedly around the room, chatting with the kids at his table. He'd eaten four olives and a celery stick when the bell rang for cleanup.

I had a moment before the next group of students poured in, so I pushed against the stream of kindergartners leaving the room and headed to Ben's table, pulled off my gloves, and sat down.

"Hey, buddy," I began, feigning a causal tone. "You gonna stay a bit and eat some more?"

He looked up with a big smile, delighted to see me again. "I think I'm done."

"You can stay, you know; it's just recess now. You can join your friends outside in a minute."

"I'm done."

I couldn't help myself; I pressed, "Really? Will you have enough energy for the afternoon? Maybe you should eat another piece of tofu."

He speared a chunk of tofu with his fork, studied it for a long moment, and then put the fork back in the bowl and started to clear his dishes. "I had enough, Mama. Look! Here come the fourth graders!" We watched the older kids together for a moment and then I gave him a quick kiss and sent him on his way. Two-and-a-half hours later, I stood at the school's back gate when he came bounding out, lively as ever, full of news about his afternoon.

Lunch continues to be the top story when Ben and his brother, Eli, come home from school; as they've grown—and because of how they've grown—I've been able to let go of my lunch lady and be more like my mom. Every day, my boys tell me about their meals, making a careful distinction between what was served and what they ate. They have their favorite Chef Ric dishes and both make their own quirky choices: olive and lettuce sandwiches; carrots dipped in salad dressing and sunflower seeds; noodles with a wedge of orange squeezed on top. I listen without critique—after all, French fries and coconut ice cream don't even figure on the menu—satisfied that they're learning how to choose their meals and eat with friends.

Meanwhile, their lunch has become one of my favorite social meals. The kitchen staff, other volunteers, and I swap recipes and stories about our kids' eating habits, and gratefully accept leftovers as we shed our gloves and aprons. I think back to the last time I shared a regular lunch with other parents: playgroup, when my friends and I cracked open plastic tubs and doled out apple slices, crackers, and tortellini for the toddlers while we shared pastries, sandwiches, and salads among ourselves. Most of the kids wandered over for a bite and orbited off, but Ben would park on my lap and eat deliberately while I caught up with my friends and brushed crumbs off his head. Dial back a few years and I was eating school lunch, too: in graduate school, spending more time and money than I could afford, lingering with friends over salade Niçoise; in college, weighing jelly donuts in our hands to find the fullest ones; and in high school, wolfing down hot lunch at a long wooden refectory table before filling up on peanut butter raisin toast from the sandwich bar. I can summon entire periods in my life by recalling the lunches I ate and the people I shared them with. This, I realized, is what I want for my children.

For all my initial anxiety about the school cafeteria, my boys have made it their own comfortable—if noisy—place to eat. If something they love is missing from the salad bar, they'll go to the kitchen and ask for it. Ben offers recipe suggestions to the patient Chef Ric and Eli isn't shy about asking for plain bread and assembling his sandwich from salad bar ingredients. And although I still sometimes think that they're not eating enough, I'm happy that they've absorbed my interest in food and the people who grow, make, and serve it. Lunch is both part of their social experience, and one more thing they are learning at school.

———————————

When he was nine, the same age I first walked into my school cafeteria, Ben faced a bigger challenge: He spent a week with his class in an outdoor education program. At a Q&A before the trip, parents fretted about homesick children wanting to leave and sleepwalking children encountering skunks. Kids who'd been on the program before rhapsodized about bacon at breakfast every day, roast beef sandwiches, and burgers for dinner. I asked the organizers about vegetarian options, and although they listed plenty of choices, they suggested I might want to send Ben with some granola bars and extra snacks. I thought about those skunks and demurred. He packed a lunch (tofu and carrot salad) for the first day, but I counted twelve cafeteria meals before I would pick him up Friday afternoon. I crossed my fingers, gave him a hug, and sent him on his way.

When he climbed into the car after that week away, bursting with stories about games played and songs learned, it didn't take him long to tell me about the meals, especially his lunches, presided over by a counselor called Samurai Sam. Ben made himself a soy nut butter and jam sandwich the first day, then—deciding he didn't like the soy nut butter—a strawberry jam and lettuce sandwich, then grape jelly and lettuce sandwiches the last two days. "It turns out I don't like grape jelly very much," he told me, "but they ran out of strawberry jam."

"I'm sorry, buddy; were you still hungry?"

"Nope."

"Did you have fun?"

"Yes!"

I remember those days of French fries and coconut ice cream. If a lettuce and jam sandwich among friends can sustain him, who am I to judge?

ELI'S SUPER CAKE

In kindergarten, Eli invented a cake. He dictated the recipe to me, and then shared it with Chef Ric, who thought it had school lunch potential. The second graders did the math to scale the recipe up.

We follow his directions to the letter, using our standard pantry ingredients, only mixing the batter slightly longer than ten seconds, and baking it in a 9 × 13-inch glass lasagna pan. We bake the cake for twenty-four minutes (until a toothpick inserted in the middle comes out covered with moist crumbs; cover loosely with foil if cake starts to brown too much), rather than the prescribed twelve, but we do set the oven to 360°F. I recommend you do, too.

DRY

2 cups flour
2 cups brown sugar
1 teaspoon baking soda
2 teaspoons salt
1 bag chocolate chips

WET

1 teaspoon vanilla
2 eggs
1 stick butter
1 cup milk
½ cup honey

Pour wet stuff in. Mix 10 seconds. Pour dry stuff in. Mix 10 seconds.
    Bake at 360°F for 12 minutes.

WHY WON'T MY KIDS EAT FOIE GRAS?

JEFF GORDINIER

Toward the end of 2010, I was invited to join the staff of the Dining section at *The New York Times*. I saw this as a stroke of spectacular fortune, of course, and it seemed to make professional sense. I've spent much of my life writing about pop culture—music and movies, mostly—and American gastronomy has been going through a precipitous growth spurt for two decades or so. Food *is* pop culture, by now, with all the attendant gleam and grime: big stars and big money, high drama and high stakes.

Even so, this career move of mine seemed to baffle a few people. No matter where I went, someone would ask me the same question, usually accompanied by an involuntary spasm of vexation.

"But wait," the person would sputter. "Are you a *foodie*?"

I strive to be polite, so I rarely say out loud what I'm thinking at that moment, which is that "foodie" is such a lazy and odious piece of nomenclature that everyone was supposed to have stopped using it years ago.

Yes, I love to cook, and I can tell you where to find authentic tacos in Yonkers (yes, Yonkers), and I'm enough of a glutton that people who dine out with me have to become skilled at shielding their plates with their hands. But I'm not convinced that knowing all about the provenance of your fennel pollen makes a roast chicken taste any better. The personality type that leaps to my mind when I hear the word "foodie" is the culinary equivalent of the skinny guy in Williamsburg who believes that any person who has failed to listen to the bootleg download of the Decemberists rehearsing a

Vashti Bunyan cover backstage at Bumbershoot *cannot possibly know any-thing about music*.

In my mind, there's a difference between really loving something and being tediously fixated on all the minutiae associated with it.

But I'm leaving out another thing that I don't say aloud, and it's this: Yes, I am a foodie. Or, more accurately, I *was* a foodie.

If we're defining a foodie as a gastronomic snob, I will confess to having gone through such a phase. It happened when I was about ten years old.

It all seems as far away as the Belle Époque, but there was a time in American corporate life when it was not uncommon for a man in the executive ranks to bring his family along on business trips. I was a beneficiary of this practice. My father worked hard and rose quickly in the hierarchy of the cosmetics industry, and by the middle of the 1970s he was traveling to Europe several times a year. Eventually he brought me along.

Although my father would probably vote Democrat before he'd ever refer to something as a "teachable moment," I always got the impression that I had been included in these grand tours of the ancestral lands so that I could learn a thing or two. The ultimate point was not to regurgitate data about how cathedrals were built or what various kings had decreed. I was supposed to come away with something else—a philosophy that could help guide (or goad) me through life. That philosophy could be summed up in one word: access. Through his success, my father had grasped something about the world. He wanted to share this lesson, this secret, with me: You can go anywhere you want to go. Yes, you have to work very hard to amass enough capital, but once you have the cash, you can pass. Nobody's going to stop you.

Thanks to this, my memory banks are full of images and sensations that seem more suited to the diaries of a princeling—or at least a very twee Wes Anderson movie—than to the inner life of a suburban kid. I remember an afternoon in Paris, for instance, lounging around a cavernous suite at the Hôtel de la Trémoille with my brother and sister, swooning over a basket of wild strawberries that we'd scored from a fruit stand on the street below. I remember how the perfect buttery-crisp texture of the Dover sole at the Plaza Athénée, one of the crown-jewel hotels of the Right Bank, gave me the same kind of longing ache that I would later feel whenever I beheld Susanna Hoffs in the "Walk Like an Egyptian" video. (It would be decades before I'd learn that master chef Jacques Pépin had once earned his stripes in the same kitchen.)

My father, a product of the Jersey Shore and still a young man at the time of his corporate ascension, was clearly reveling in his sudden access to haute cuisine. By the time I hit my teens I had dined alongside him in some of the fanciest restaurants in New York, Los Angeles, Paris, and London, and one of my formative experiences with food would involve, of all places, the French Riviera.

I don't know what the circumstances were, but one evening in the early 1980s I found myself riding along the edge of the Mediterranean toward Monte Carlo.

My parents and I were in a car with a worldly and aristocratic Mitteleuropean man. He had something official to do with the company my father worked for, but his primary specialty was the ancient art of knowing the right places to go. He wanted to take us somewhere off the beaten track. Along the highway he signaled for the driver to swerve toward the water. At this point the car made a quick exit and began inching very slowly down a steep, narrow, zigzaggy path that seemed to have been carved into the hillside by wild goats.

It took a long time to make our way to the shoreline. What we found looked like it hadn't changed for decades, maybe centuries. There were wobbly wooden tables under a canopy. There were bowls of olive oil and baskets of fresh bread. You could smell the sea a few feet away and wood smoke rising from a large grill. On that grill were squid and fish that seemed to have come directly from boats that were tied up to a little dock.

The meal was almost a Platonic ideal of what contemporary chefs are talking about when they get all reverent about the virtues of simplicity. We ate charred fish and shellfish straight out of the waters that had produced them. We dunked bread in olive oil. A salad might have been involved, too. The adults had wine. I probably would have loved a glass, myself, but I didn't need the buzz. I was a quiet child, so I doubt my parents even noticed it, but within minutes of our having pulled into this mysterious place, I had slipped into a state of euphoria.

All those trips and experiences wound up leading me to something of a quest, although it's possible that I had been on the quest for a while already. Even in elementary school I was one of those kids who can't resist selecting the richest and most exotic items on a menu. My brother and sister were wired in the same way, and our parents took to boasting about our polite table behavior and our adventurous appetites. Frog's legs, shad roe, liver and onions, wild mushrooms, *finnan haddie* (for breakfast), black pudding (ditto), oysters Rockefeller, cassoulet, baked and fried and steamed clams—if it happened to be fatty, briny, stinky, gout-inducing, or "not something the kids would like," according to the waiter, there was a good chance that one of us would order it.

And we would eat it—every last bite. We loved proving those waiters wrong. My default dish was not weird, per se, but it was absurdly decadent: It became reflexive for me to order tournedos Rossini, a classic that mimics the architecture of eggs Benedict in the service of carnivorous indulgence. Named after the grand pasha of Italian opera, tournedos Rossini usually consists of two or three small stacks on your plate. At the bottom of each stack lies a thin, flat, buttered, toasted piece of bread, which is topped with a tender disk of filet mignon, which is capped by a silken fez of foie gras, which is blanketed by a ladleful of sauce Périgueux, which is laced with black truffles. Looking back, I can see why, at ten, I often worried about having a heart attack.

Elaborate, cream-saucy meals like that established my framework for approaching food, but they did a lot more than that. They introduced me to the concept of pleasure. They taught me that you could, if you had the inclination and a little extra disposable income, maximize a moment of your life—intensify it, elevate it, garland it with truffles. Why not? All you had to say was, "Could I please have the tournedos Rossini?" No one was going to stop you. Not even a snotty French waiter.

Naturally, I planned to pass along that philosophy to my own children, when I eventually had them. I was quite sure about this. Long before I became a parent, or even an adult, I presumed—*knew!*—that it would take no more than a single bite of tournedos Rossini to convert my offspring to a life of gustatory risk and luxury. They, too, would astonish waiters by looking up from a menu to order, with that perfect Gallic inflection, a towering platter of *fruits de mer*. Of this I had no doubt.

I've been a parent for roughly ten years now. It has been, in so many ways, a decade of being humbled. I know parents, usually lodged in the most hipster-chic precincts of Brooklyn and San Francisco and the Pacific Northwest, whose children *will*, yes, greedily dive into a bowl of ma po tofu, or will happily tote an Italian tripe sandwich to school for lunch. I can only look upon those families with a twinge of envious longing.

My children, Margot and Toby, are in countless ways delightful, beautiful, enlightening, and inspiring. I love them beyond expression. But when it comes to eating, they can be so picky that it verges on the pathological. I have heard, at our dinner table in a village north of New York City, protestations that I didn't think were humanly possible. Among them:

"But I don't *like* onion rings . . . !"

". . . I don't *like* bacon . . . !"

". . . mashed potatoes—*yuck*!"

It is my belief that mashed potatoes, like Michael Jackson's "Don't Stop 'Til You Get Enough," are something like a universal language. I simply refuse to believe that there is a person on our planet who "doesn't like" mashed potatoes irrigated with salty, raging torrents of melted butter. The same goes for bacon and onion rings. In other words, *I think my kids are making it up*. I've come to see their pickiness as theater—a subconsciously scripted act of defiance, probably spurred along by the pretentious way that Daddy swans through our local greenmarket on Saturday mornings, saying stuff like, "Kids, *please*, just wait a second while I check out these pickled ramps." I suppose I can't blame them for wanting to get back at me.

And yet, *come on!* I often feel as though I'm trying to hand my children the keys to the kingdom—in the form of chicken-liver crostini, perhaps—and they're looking at me like I'm the fairy-tale warlock who's trying to poison them. Fortunately, there have been moments of progress. My daughter is nine years old now, and whatever psychological ramparts she's put up finally seem to be crumbling with each sighing utterance of "OK, I'll try it."

Because of all its rice, Japanese food is an excellent gateway cuisine; both my son and my daughter now insist that I order them plates of seaweed salad in sushi restaurants, which sends a wave of bliss through me.

And I shall be forever grateful to Bravo and the Food Network: From watching countless episodes of *Chopped, Top Chef,* and *Iron Chef America,* my children have learned that there are other crazy people out there in the world who, like Daddy, seem to think that oysters and morels and snails and chorizo are delicious. (This is an upside of food becoming pop culture. If my kids won't listen to me, maybe they'll listen to Bobby Flay.)

Although my father and I, like millions of fathers and sons, clash (sometimes bitterly) when it comes to politics and culture and sports and clothing and hair and how to operate the toaster oven, I have inherited from him the same impulse to give my children nothing less than the entire world. I want to pass along that secret lesson about access—a lesson that has been reinforced, for me, through my work as a journalist. I've had *pelmeni* in Siberia, hummus in Jerusalem, a raw vegan feast in Silver Lake, Grand Marnier soufflé in Manhattan, barbecue in Memphis, single malt in Scotland, bourbon in the distilleries of Kentucky. My father was right: You can go anywhere you want to go. Save your money and, yes, you can buy a ticket to Spain or Denmark or Japan or Peru, and you can make a reservation at a restaurant where you'll experience elevated and eye-opening flavors and textures and sensations that were, in ages past, offered only to aristocrats.

This can be yours.

I want my children to know this. I want them to be open to it. I want them to discover those elemental sources of pleasure. The more they do, of course, the more I'll suffer a drain on my bank account. I write for newspapers and magazines; I didn't opt for corporate ascension. I love what I do, but I wouldn't be able to afford it if my kids started eating the way I did when I was ten.

And yet I suppose that's precisely what I'm rooting for. I want to bring them into the city to try Prune and Junoon and Tertulia and La Grenouille; I want to take them to Europe so we can track down that seaside restaurant on the road to Monte Carlo. I want to make them tournedos Rossini. It's a strange way to express the depth of my love for my children, but I want them to become so swept away in the lyrical, life-affirming adventure of food that their father gradually, blissfully goes broke.

THE ROAST CHICKEN THAT EVERYONE WILL EAT*

At its best, roast chicken should represent the essence of simplicity. It's the dish you want to make on a Sunday, when everyone is hanging around the house together and there is time to linger in the kitchen, and then at the table, and talk. It goes well with white wine, it goes well with red wine, it goes well with beer. More important, it goes well with children: Even at their most gratingly picky, many kids seem unable to resist the moist, salty white meat of a chicken that has been roasted with care. And as long as you stick to the correct time and temperature, you can improvise in terms of what goes inside, outside, and underneath the chicken. There are countless recipes floating around; this is the way I tend to do it, although I have surely picked up pointers from chefs like Jamie Oliver, Seamus Mullen, and Jacques Pépin over the past couple of years.

SERVES 4 TO 6

1 4-to 5-pound chicken (get a good organic one, preferably from a nearby farm)

A bunch of salt

A bunch of freshly ground black pepper

A tablespoon of smoked paprika or ground ancho chili powder (unless your kids get really freaked out by the slightest hint of spice, in which case forget it)

A cup or two of olive oil

A lemon

A bulb of garlic, with cloves separated and peeled

Copious sprigs of fresh thyme, rosemary, and sage

A stick of unsalted butter

Preheat the oven to 375°F.

Put the chicken in a large bowl. Dust it with a generous amount of salt and pepper, as well as the spoonful of paprika or chili pow-

---

* I feel confident in saying this, although I do hope that the statement is not legally binding.

der. Pour the olive oil all over it. With your hands, smear the salt and pepper and oil and reddish powder all over the chicken so that the skin is evenly covered with flavor. If you can, let the chicken marinate like this for a few hours. If you don't have time for that, don't worry about it. (I never have enough room in the refrigerator, frankly.)

Meanwhile, bring a pot full of water to a boil. When it's boiling, drop in the lemon and all the peeled cloves of garlic. Boil them for 12 minutes or so. When they're done boiling, take them out of the pot with a slotted spoon and place them aside. Puncture the skin of the lemon 8 or 10 or 14 times with the tines of a fork, so that its liquid is freed up, although not just pouring out. (Thanks to Jamie Oliver for this portion of the process.)

Put the chicken in a roasting pan. Stuff all the boiled garlic and much of the thyme, rosemary, and sage into the cavity of the chicken. Now plug up the cavity with the boiled lemon.

Roast the chicken like this in the oven for 45 minutes.

While that is happening, melt the stick of butter in a pan over low heat. Pluck off some leaves of thyme and sprinkle them into the melting butter. When the herbed butter is melted, open the oven now and then and baste the skin of the roasting chicken with a little bit of melted butter, which should help the skin crisp and brown. (I feel as though I might have learned this from Jacques Pépin, although these days my memory is full of holes.)

Every now and then, pour a cup of water into the bottom of the roasting pan to keep everything from drying out.

After that initial 45 minutes of roasting, jack up the oven a few more notches, to 400°F, and roast the chicken at that temperature for another 45 minutes.

At this point you can also drop all sorts of vegetables into the bottom of the roasting pan so that they will get sufficiently mushy and crusty and tasty with all that chicken fat and butter and salt and pepper and olive oil. Halved onions? Sure. Brussels sprouts, garlic, new potatoes, leeks, broccoli, cauliflower? Sure. Any of those will work. Or all of the above. You are free to choose. I like to include little discs of chorizo, which might strike you as a tad over-the-top.

As the chicken and vegetables continue to cook, keep remembering to pour a bit of water into the roasting pan when necessary. And keep basting the skin of the chicken with butter when you feel like it.

Once it has roasted for the full 90 minutes, take the chicken out of the oven and let it sit for a while—10 minutes or so. Remove the garlic cloves and the lemon and consider squeezing hot lemon juice on top of the chicken, but only if your kids will find that acceptable.

Carve up the chicken and serve it with those vegetables, including the garlic cloves, and maybe some rice, mashed potatoes, French bread, black beans, olives, a good salad of fresh greens and vinaigrette.

Dijon mustard is a must. But not for the kids.

OUT OF THE BOX

LISA CATHERINE HARPER

In our backyard, we have an orange tree that entertains my two children for hours. They climb it and hide in it and swing on ropes from it, and sometimes, when the green leaves are thick and glossy and the tree is studded with bright orange fruit, my daughter, Ella, will climb to one of its branching forks, perch there, and pluck an orange from a nearby limb. She litters the ground with her peels and always says the same thing: "Mom, this orange is *so* good. You *have* to try it." She won't let up until I do, and it's always the same, ordinary, extraordinary orange, something, as Truman Capote once said, that nature has made just right.

Our tree gives us more fruit than we know what to do with. We snack on it all winter long, and juice it, and make candied fruit, and *arancello*, and a sublime, bittersweet, upside-down orange polenta cake. When we have picked and eaten all the fruit within reach, and the blossoms for next year's crop are budding like tiny, fragrant constellations, it's my daughter's job to scale the tree's old, winding network of branches and harvest the remaining fruit. She throws the heavy fruit to her brother, who tosses it with a thud into paper shopping bags. We juice the cracked fruit and give the rest away, and when the tree is bare, we have a few brief weeks when we can picnic under its blossoming shade.

For me, the orange tree is a California dream, and everything the fruit of my northeastern childhood was not. No matter how many years I live with them, those oranges still seem to come from a faraway place. Every time I peel one, or juice one, or slice one for garnish, or hand a section to a hungry child, its cool, perfect sweetness silences my imagination. I suspect that when my children are grown, they'll remember this tree and these oranges. Maybe the scent of orange blossoms will become their Proustian trigger, but for now it's ordinary, as simple to them as that carton of juice on my own childhood table.

———————

It's easy to say I eat the way I do because I live where I live. Here, near San Francisco, we have fruit trees in our backyards and farmers' markets in every community. Shortly after I moved to California for graduate school, I discovered that I could get much of my produce at a farmers' market, which was more economical than the local food co-op. Eventually, I moved to the city and it became my habit to shop at the year-round market every week, no matter the time of year or the weather. Long before I became that predictable pregnant woman obsessed with hormone levels and pesticide residue, even long before I met my husband, eating seasonally was simply what I did. If it wasn't at the market, I didn't buy it. No strawberries in December; no apples in July. I learned many things along the way about organic and sustainable foods; about immigration policy and the economics of medium-sized farms; about the farmers and their children. I learned surprising things, too, about the seasonal nature of eggs, pork, and fish. But I loved most the impeccable freshness of the food. While some of my friends and family believed I was a great cook, what I really knew was how to find the best ingredients and then do as little as possible to ruin them.

After I married and we had our two children, our family was a decade-long cliché: mom, dad, and kids wandering the stalls of the local market, sampling and buying our weekly produce and most of our protein. I carried Ella, our first, in a sling while my husband toted our bags. Later, she sat in the stroller greedily hoarding a basket of berries. Soon she toddled along beside us, sampling wedges of fruit. Eventually, she chose her own snacks with tongs and toothpicks and learned to twirl the straw in the honey jar carefully (because we know that farmer is particular about drips). She was gifted a bright red Early Girl tomato that fit perfectly in her small hand, an extra bag of padrón peppers, a single walnut. She loved eating, the farmers loved feeding her, and at home we got her—and, later, her little brother, Finn—to try new food simply by saying, "Michelle/ Pietro/Jamie grew/caught/picked this Romanesco/salmon/radish just for you." They didn't always love the new food, but aside from a frustrating year when my son rejected all non-white food, they ate everything. Our food life was one of the most pleasurable aspects of our family.

Then, one day, when Ella was eight and Finn was six, I woke to The Great Market Rebellion. They declared they were sick of the shopping, the hauling, even the sampling. No amount of bribing or persuading could change their minds, and our idyllic family outing became fraught with whining and foot dragging. Every Sunday morning, they preempted me:

"Do I *have* to go to the market with you?"

"NOOOOO! I don't *want* to go to the market!"

"I. Hate. The. Market. It's *SO* boring."

They wanted to stay home and play. Video games, LEGOs, outside in the pouring rain— anything, really, except the market.

I couldn't blame them. By then, Ella had been to nearly four hundred farmers' markets, all over the Bay Area, on the East Coast, even in Hawaii. She knew carrots grew underground and tomatoes came in a rainbow of colors. She knew what live crabs looked like and that eggs had neon yolks when the chickens ate pepper scraps. She knew there were green and red and purple plums and two kinds of persimmons and which she preferred. She knew bananas could be red, that sugar cane could be slung over her shoulder like a club, and that half-sour pickles were best on a stick in New Jersey. So given the choice, she would prefer to stay home, and would I get her some pistachios? Please?

I surrendered. I left her—and her brother—behind. I was sick of it, too.

As much as I love the possibilities of a well-stocked kitchen, and the abundance of bags so heavy I can barely carry them into the house, and look forward to chatting with the farmers—some of whom I have known longer than my husband—when Ella and Finn rebelled, I had to admit it: Marketing had become a chore. Even when the sun was out, and the stands were full, it was a chore to lug twenty pounds of produce through the crowded market (even with a rolling cart). It was a chore to make sure I had enough cash. It was a chore to unpack and store all the produce, then skim the fine green tendrils of fennel fronds or carrot tops sprayed across my counter and sweep the dirt from the beets and radishes from my floor. It was even a chore to maintain all those good relationships with all those great farmers. Sometimes I just didn't want to talk. Sometimes I wanted simply to get my stuff and go. Sometimes I craved the impersonality of the big box store, any place, really, where nobody knew my name. The market was neither haven nor pleasure. It was just one more thing I had to get done, like the laundry or cleaning the litter box.

I tried, half-heartedly, to kick the habit. I supplemented with fruits and vegetables from a discount grocer, where I do a weekly run for staples like milk and bread, but the produce tasted flat, as though half the flavor had been leached out. I tried shopping at a national chain specializing in fresh, organic, high-end food. The food tasted better, but it spoiled quickly and was expensive in a way that was unsustainable. Finally, I had a box of locally grown, organic produce delivered to my door, but I felt guilty handing over my money to strangers. Sunday morning rolled around and I was dogged by low-grade anxiety. Had I forgotten to feed the kids? Shopping at the market had become such a part of my life that skipping it felt very, very wrong, like I was sneaking around behind someone's back.

In those furtive weeks, I began to realize that my market habit had been ingrained long before I moved west. In my New Jersey childhood we didn't have a year-round farmers' market, nor did we have especially sophisticated food. We ate in ordinary ways on a tightly monitored budget, and I was a reluctant, picky eater. But there were always particular things that we ate at particular times: bagels on Saturdays and pancakes on Sunday mornings; a zippy horseradish cheddar dip at dinner parties; cheesecake on my birthday; and a pumpkin pie that we had only on Thanksgiving, for which I was always silently grateful. In the early fall, we picked apples and bought freshly pressed cider. Once each winter, a farmer delivered a huge ham. And even in climate-challenged New Jersey, there was perfect summer produce. From the nearest farm stand my father would bring home corn, peaches, and strawberries, which we had for a month, maybe two, but they made summer seem eternal and unchangeable—even though it was anything but.

As a kid I just loved the food. Now I think it taught me something about where I was from. The sometimes-local, seasonal-when-possible, never-organic food of my childhood knitted me to my family, our town, and the familiar cycle of the year. Certainly my parents never planned it this way, but in reserving certain foods for certain occasions, they created small rituals to honor home in the middle of all that growing up.

Now, in California, in a very different time and place, it's become our way to eat what comes and goes. We don't have a large family, or elaborate traditions, or many family recipes. But we pick popcorn and squeeze orange juice and shell a new crop of walnuts in season. We know it's summer when there are berries on the breakfast table and that come winter, there will be apples for snacking. In spring we pick lemons from our tree for limoncello and freeze the juice for summer's endless lemonade stands. Sometimes, in the full heat of summer, the kids wonder when the pomegranates are coming back. Months later, they greet bowls of deep ruby seeds with genuine joy. In the middle of winter, suddenly they'll crave the hamburgers we eat only in the summer. At harvest time, they know the heirloom pumpkins that rest on our doorstep are not purely decorative: green Hubbards, flame bright Potimarrons, warty Galuex d'Eysines, signal weeks of risottos and pies. Sharing these things, like the fleeting perfume of pineapple guavas or winter's crunchy Fuyu persimmons, creates our common memory. Most days we come together over ordinary meals, but part of the meal is always connected to the place we live and the time we're living in. It's simply how we've learned to eat in California—and part of how my kids are learning to be Californian. And if we lived somewhere else, we'd eat differently.

———

During that month I stayed away from the market, I learned something else, too. The market has taught me how to think outside the box of our busy calendar days, to understand that the cycle of seasons is part of the cycle of my life, and my children's lives, just as much as sports schedules, homework, and deadlines. At the height of summer, when my memory of oranges is in such deep freeze that I barely notice the tree, I think I will never, ever get enough tomatoes. I grow endless pints of Sweet 100s and Sungolds in a backyard plot and I bring home pounds of heirlooms. I make salads, raw sauces, and tomato tarts; I stuff, roast, and freeze; I blend cold soups almost daily. Then suddenly, one day, I'm done. It has something to do with a turn in the weather, being saturated by a particular food, and the fact that all food has a peak time for eating.

One Sunday night in early October, a freak heat wave had ripened a new crop of tomatoes, and I served gazpacho, a dish the kids could not get enough of all summer long. That night, they took one slurp and made that universal kid face of horror and disgust. Ella shuddered, as if I had served her a bowl of, well, rotten tomatoes. It didn't taste right, she said. She was right. The tomatoes were no longer at their peak, and they were unsatisfying on that cool, fall night. I dumped the gazpacho in the compost. Just like that, summer was over.

The next day I noticed the oranges were beginning to ripen.

This is the real reason I couldn't turn away from the market: I couldn't bear to miss out. The right thing at the right time never lasts long. The market is as constant and changeable as my children. It's always there; it's always new. It's boring and exuberant; a chore and a joy. In a small but important way, that bag of pluots or pile of arugula says *pay attention*. When we wait for our oranges and we eat what the market offers us, we are forced to honor the present. Week by week, I notice what arrives and what passes, and I strive for a small oasis of harmony. Some days, a simple casserole of cauliflower roasted in cream and Gruyère is all I can manage, but the time we spend eating it helps us pay attention to the moment and, if we're lucky, to each other. The market feeds us well, but it also reminds me of how I aspire to parent: Pay attention to each small thing that comes and goes. Know when nature has made something just right.

CREMA DI ARANCELLO

This version of an Italian infused orange liqueur substitutes milk for the simple syrup in the final step, producing a drink that's a little milder than a traditional limoncello. Consider it a grown-up version of a Creamsicle. Don't be afraid of the Everclear. Its higher alcohol content leaches more flavor and color from the zest and makes for a more beautiful and flavorful arancello. If it's legal where you live, use it. This recipe will make enough for about three 750-milliliter bottles, so if you're feeling generous, you can give some as holiday gifts. But once you've tasted it, you might not want to share.

10 to 12 organic oranges
1 organic vanilla bean
1 bottle (750-ml) 100-proof vodka or Everclear
4 cups sugar
5 cups milk

Special equipment needed:
large (1-gallon) glass jar with lid
zester

DAY 1

If necessary, wash the oranges with a vegetable brush and warm water to remove any dust or residue; pat dry.

With the zester, carefully zest the oranges directly into the glass jar. Make sure there is no white pith on the peel. With a sharp knife, split the vanilla bean and scrape the seeds into the jar. Add the vanilla bean pod.

Add the vodka or Everclear to the jar of zest and vanilla. Cover the jar and let sit at room temperature for 40 days, out of direct sunlight. When the color is no longer deepening and the zest looks white, the infusion is finished.

Note: Use the zested oranges for juice, which can be frozen in ice cube trays.

DAY 40

In a large pot, combine the sugar and milk; cook slowly over low heat, stirring until the sugar is just dissolved, approximately 5 to 7 minutes.

Let the milk syrup cool completely. While the milk is cooling, remove the vanilla bean pod from the infusion, then strain to remove the zest. Add the cooled milk to the strained, infused alcohol. Bottle and store in the freezer. Serve ice cold.

BAD AND PLENTY
PARENTAL ANXIETY IN AN AGE OF ABUNDANCE

EDWARD LEWINE

The PTA at my children's school is run with the kind of ferocious zeal the Bolsheviks showed when they took over Russia. I mean this in a good way. Killing the Czar and annexing his Empire are feats no less terrifying than trying to protect and preserve a small elementary school in the New York City Public Education system. Those of us who have neither the energy nor inclination to fight that hard for our children need those PTA stalwarts to fund the library, organize the field trips, and make sure the second grade gets swimming lessons. The rest of us certainly aren't going to do it.

Still, there are downsides to life under PTA rule. Meetings come to mind, but then I rarely attend them, so while I am sure they are tedious, I can't say they much affect me. E-mails are another thing. If there's one thing the panjandrums of our PTA really enjoy, it's a good threaded e-mail discussion. E-mails arrive in small flocks from the school. Class Parents send them, the PTA administration is not shy about them, and then there are the sundry PTA committee e-mails. Lenin would have approved.

I know how this all works from the inside because I myself am a Class Parent, a PTA functionary of the lowest, least-committed sort, charged with passing e-mails to the families in my son's class. I can tell you that more often than not, these e-mails are met with total silence from parents. An outbreak of lice, the theft of forty laptops from the computer lab, overcrowding, budget cuts—they won't get much attention.

But if you want a response to a Class Parent e-mail, if you want a big, messy, emotional response, just bring up one topic: food. Think I'm exaggerating? Let me recount a story. A few years ago a parent at the school died, leaving behind a grieving family to face life without its main source of income. True to form, the involved and caring community (I am not being cheeky, they really are involved and caring) made a few calls to see if the family needed help. The message came back that yes, the family would be grateful if some funds could be raised and funneled to the local pizzeria so the kids and their grieving parent could have an easy dinner a few times a week during the worst of the mourning.

That's when the e-mails started. Pizza? Why pizza? Pizza is junk. Pizza is fattening. Maybe we could buy healthful food for the family and cook it ourselves? Maybe we could hire a caterer to do light and nutritious meals for the family? Finally, it was decided that it was simply too controversial to give food of any kind. The mere thought of pizza was freaking people out. So, we gave them cash . . . in an envelope. It was a somewhat crude gesture and not what they had asked for, but for some of us around here, being complicit in the purchase of pizza was just too much to bear. (My guess? The family used at least some of that money to buy pizza.)

For Exhibit B I draw your attention to the infamous Holiday Party E-mail Thread of 2010. I'm going to make some effort here to protect the identities and feelings of the well-meaning parents who contributed to this throbbing symphony of food angst, because they had no idea that a snarky writer would use their e-mails for fun and profit. But, here goes. The thread began December 9th and sprawled across the following six days to the 15th when it was shut down due to the bad feelings it was engendering. There were no fewer than fifteen different posters, and they generated around five thousand words. That's enough to fill a good-sized *New Yorker* article.

The thread in question was written by members of the Wellness Committee, whose exact portfolio is unclear to me, but who seem to get worked up about food and exercise in the school. (The very existence of this group and its vaguely sinister name ought to tell you something.) The thread begins with a mother who wants to distribute a letter to all classes urging her fellow parents not to serve sugary foods at the inevitable class holiday parties. Remember, it's December 9th. Her letter contains the following statement: "At the risk of sounding like the food police, I would like to request that we all make an effort to avoid bringing in food for the party that is overly high in sugar, highly processed . . . or made with lots of artificial flavors or chemicals."

The e-mails that follow are positive responses to this idea. One mother offers a suggestion that instead of serving cake, the kids could make a drawing of a cake and decorate it, a suggestion that sounds like exquisite torture to me, and I'm forty-four, not eight. The next e-mails involve increasing laments that some parents and teachers in the school aren't sufficiently concerned with holiday fat and sugar. As one Wellness Committee mom puts it, this isn't just about a few cakes. This is about the children's "future health (prevention of chronic health problems at least one-third of the population are plagued with) and developing tastes and eating habits."

OK. But take a walk with me one afternoon down the tree-shaded thoroughfares of my neighborhood and you will see our schoolyard filled with around four hundred children. They are cute. They are clean. They are happy. And I would estimate that at least 390 out of the 400 are thin to normal in weight. A third of Americans may be obese, but not the upper-middle-class kids in my neck of the woods. Have no fear. These kids are eating well. In fact, parental concern with finding natural and pure ingredients is just as great as their concern with keeping their kids thin. This is a neighborhood of people who read labels, decry high-fructose corn syrup, and generally sweat the details when it comes to what their kids eat.

"I do think we need to remember that sugar isn't the only unhealthy thing being served to our children," one mother writes in the Wellness Committee e-mails, "and while it may not appear to be so, people have very strong opinions about this issue. For example, I prefer that my child eat a made from scratch . . . baked good to non-organic grapes grown abroad."

Why are so many educated and high-achieving parents like the ones in my children's school so massively, obsessively worried about what their kids are eating? To find out I called a guy named Brian Wansink. He's the John S. Dyson Endowed Chair in the Applied Economics and Management Department at Cornell University, the author of more than one hundred articles and books, and the most respected social scientist today who studies how people choose what they eat. Wansink told me that I am not making this up: Parents today *are* suffering from acute food anxiety.

"People worry that their kids are too fat," said Wansink, who happens to be the father of three young girls, "but they also worry they are eating too little. And they are obsessed with wanting to have their children eat the right kinds of foods."

The anxiety begins before the children are even born. At the birthing class my wife and I attended before our first child arrived, the instructors spent as much time haranguing us about the miracles of breast-feeding as they did explaining the intricacies of birth itself. No wonder the obstetrics ward, when we eventually made it there, thrummed with the anxiety of new mothers not sure they could pull off feeding their children as prescribed.

The next stage is the most fascinating because it involves worrying that you aren't feeding your children enough. It's the toddler years, a time when parents—who will soon be in a tizzy that their kids are overeating—spend their days cramming food into little mouths, Strasbourg-goose-style: mothers pushing macaroni into clenched jaws; fathers huffing after their kids with Pirate's Booty brandished above their heads. I even knew one mother who insisted her doctor had told her to feed M&M's to her two-year-old because the little mite wasn't large enough.

Brian Wansink explains the urge to overfeed babies and toddlers in terms of the experience of being a parent to a newborn. "When you first get the kid home there is all of this anxiety about the kid not eating and losing weight," Wansink says. "You think, 'My god, the baby is going to die.' That is a tremendous imprinting experience and it causes parents to stuff their small children."

In elementary and middle school, parental anxiety about how much to feed (or not to feed) is seasoned with endless concern about whether the child is getting enough of the *right* foods. By high school you probably can't do much with them anyway, so the whole issue deflates for most families, that is unless one of your children develops an eating disorder, which some of them absolutely do.

When I was a child in the 1970s my family and those of my friends were not overwhelmed with food angst. Wansink agreed that parental food anxiety in its overheated form is a relatively recent phenomenon. "What your kid brings to school as a snack has become a status symbol," he told me. "A lot of these parents are so pressured . . . competing about who is doing a better job as parents. The kids are all taking classes. They are all doing well in school. So, now you have people bragging about what their children are eating. I heard one mother bragging that her child was a vegan. The child was eight years old. It is the new frontier of good parenting."

He's right. Few of us would ever send out an e-mail boasting that we are richer, classier, or better parents than our neighbors. But food is a convenient and deceptively neutral way to get across some of those ideas to other people, a kind of shorthand that allows parents to compete without appearing to do so. Food is also a narrative many of us tell ourselves to make us feel better about being parents. As long as we are feeding our children well, we reason, it doesn't matter so much if we let them watch television because we're too tired to play with them, or we miss their school play because we're working. Parents put a great deal of pressure on themselves these days, and stocking the kitchen with whole-grain, organic, free-range, grape-juice-sweetened goodness gives harried moms and dads an excuse to slack off in all the other parental areas they are supposed to be excelling in and clearly aren't.

Sibylle Kranz, the director of the Coordinated Program in Dietetics at Purdue University, told me there are two major changes in our society that have led to increased parental food anxiety. "Parents used to feed their children exactly what they were eating," Kranz said. "Now there is a new category, children's food. With that change, I think, comes the fact that parents now feel as though they are making a parental judgment every time their children have a meal, rather than just sitting down to eat." The second change, Kranz said, is the rise in childhood obesity. "Parents are aware they have a responsibility. If they don't do the right thing they might be creating another obese child, and they want to avoid that at all costs."

It's the anxiety of plenty, the sort of distortion that takes place when a species, designed to live in conditions of limited access to sustenance, is faced with unlimited sustenance. People in earlier eras were thin because they were always hungry. They didn't need to worry about overfeeding their kids or feeding them the wrong foods. They were lucky if they were fed at all, and so they happily ate whatever came their way. Now we must choose, and every time we choose we are telling ourselves and the world who we are.

Parental food anxiety may help our kids eat better, but it may also be counterproductive and may even lead children to be further out of touch from their bodies than they already are. "Hunger and satiety, they don't count anymore," Kranz says. "The little girl may not be hungry, but Mommy wants her to eat her peas. It is Mommy's expectations that have to be met, not the child's internal needs."

My wife and I are no less prone to food anxiety than the average parent in our neighborhood. We are label readers, portion guardians, and scrooges with holiday sweets, just like all the others. Like most of the kids we know, our kids are healthy, of normal weight, and generally wish they could eat more sweets, but aren't sweating the food thing too much . . . for now. Since they are Americans, it is almost certain that however good or bad we are as parents, they may well grow up to be too thin, too fat, too concerned about food, or not concerned enough. This is a culture that is out of whack when it comes to eating, and our kids are part of that culture, so they are more or less doomed.

"We are now seeing more cases of adult-onset anorexia," Sibylle Kranz said. "That tells you all you need to know about our culture. Mature adults who should know better will starve themselves. Our attitude to food is obsessive, and it goes both ways, eating too much and too little."

There's no way to win. If you are too lax about your children's eating, you could end up with people who are obese for life. As Sibylle Kranz and that mom on the Holiday Party E-mail Thread have both correctly pointed out, the habits our children acquire early on can stay with them for life. On the other hand, being too intense about your children's diets also appears to be counterproductive. We parents are all locked in a contest with each other over who is the best parent when it comes to food. It turns out the best parent may be the one who has opted out of the contest altogether.

Let me leave you with what may have been the most intelligent, insightful, and useful e-mail in the Holiday Party E-mail Thread of 2010. It was written on December 15th, the last day of the thread, by a mother who had clearly been following the discussion and felt the moment was right for an astute observation. "Could I please be removed from this e-mail chain," she wrote. "Thanks."

BANANA BREAD

My family's hyper–ingredient conscious, honey sweetened, whole wheat but still very yummy banana bread recipe.

MAKES 1 LOAF

¼ cup vegetable oil
½ cup honey
2 tablespoons applesauce
2 large eggs (or the equivalent of egg replacer, for vegan version)
1 cup mashed ripe bananas
1 teaspoon pure vanilla extract
1¾ cups whole wheat flour
½ teaspoon salt
1 teaspoon baking soda
¼ cup hot water

Preheat the oven to 325°F.

In a large bowl, beat together oil, honey, and applesauce. Add the eggs and mix well. Stir in the bananas and vanilla, then stir in the flour and salt. Add the baking soda to the hot water and mix well. Add to the batter and stir.

Spread the batter into a 9 × 5-inch greased loaf pan.

Bake for 55 to 60 minutes, until a toothpick inserted in the center comes out clean. Cool for 30 minutes, preferably on a cooling rack, before slicing and serving.

SHARED BOOKS, SHARED TABLES

LIBBY GRUNER

I am standing in the kitchen at dinnertime. I am hungry. I peer into the refrigerator while my husband, Mark, scans the pantry shelves.

"Tuna casserole?" he offers.

"Mariah won't eat it," I say. Our twenty-two-year-old daughter, Mariah, is vegan.

"Plus, cheese. . . ." I trail off. I've been avoiding cheese, though not always successfully, for a while. "Maybe some roasted veggies, with a kale salad?" I suggest.

"I'm too hungry—won't that take forever?" I agree that it will, and we end up, once again, at the burrito place. Our teenage son, Nick, orders his usual carnitas taco, hold all the veg except some token shredded lettuce. He tries, but fails, to convince me that the corn salsa also counts as a vegetable. Mariah's veggie taco salad comes without cheese and sour cream. And Mark and I look at each other over our burritos and wonder how it came to this. Not long ago, it was so different! Once upon a time, we ate dinner—the same dinner—together every night. Family meals were the only shared rituals my husband and I insisted on in our family life from the very start.

It worked for years. In my best memories of family meals, my daughter is in high school, my son still in elementary school. Both are beyond the worst stage of childhood pickiness. She is, alternately, avoiding red meat (she calls herself a "beady-eyed vegetarian," as she won't eat mammals with pretty eyes), an omnivore, a vegetarian. Sometimes she brings a friend or two home with her and they are always surprised to be invited to eat with us, but—often—also pleased. We make large bowls of pasta, salads, vegetables, stir-fries, and soups, and everyone eats together. Then, toward the end of high school, my daughter became a vegan. Cooking for her became difficult, but she still joined us for meals. My son—seven years younger than his sister and a die-hard carnivore—was happy as long as there was a piece of chicken or a tuna casserole on the table.

Nick's still a happy meat-eater, but Mariah's eating has become so increasingly constrained—by concerns about factory-farmed vegetables, and soy, and fat, and by a flirtation with raw eating—that some days it seems as if only sweet potatoes and kale are still on her approved list. I struggle—as does she, as do we all—with how to make a meal we can all enjoy, while still honoring the individual choices we've made about our eating. Some days it works, but often the whole process is so fraught that I give up before we start and offer a "make your own dinner" day—or we end up at the burrito place, where I don't have to plan the component parts.

My husband and I met in graduate school, both of us literature scholars. We courted over meals, as so many couples do: sushi, Thai food, Mexican—talking about books as we also shared our pasts, our own stories, our family rituals. Once we had children, we established only two rituals of our own in our new small family: the family dinner and the bedtime read-aloud. Although books were actually banished from the dinner table, they became intertwined with our meals as we chewed over them in conversation at the dinner table, then imagined feasts as we shared our favorite childhood books with our kids.

My children have never eaten gruel, nor bear meat, nor tongue. They have never picnicked on the banks of a river they've just rowed down, eaten fresh-caught trout in a beavers' den, nor tasted elven *lembas* in Middle Earth. But they have both sat with a book and a snack and cried over the fates of imaginary people. And when they saw Turkish Delight in a British sweet shop they had to have it, hardly believing it was real—and were then bitterly disappointed by the sickly sweet taste for which Edmund Pevensie betrayed his family in *The Lion, the Witch, and the Wardrobe*.

Some books offer us virtual feasts, and even if the actual foods don't appeal, they bring the world of the book closer into our lives, binding us in the rhythms of cooking, eating, and drinking. I remember, in *Little House on the Prairie*, Ma's handprint in the johnnycake as vividly as if I'd seen it myself. When my daughter was young we found the recipe for Laura Ingalls Wilder's gingerbread and happily baked and ate it, bringing the experience of the novel home. But these days, meals in books are becoming a refuge for me, a reminder of what we could have had rather than a model for what we do.

Take one of my favorites, the picnic scene among the animal friends of *The Wind in the Willows*. The Rat, an intrepid river dweller, has brought his new friend the Mole, a homebody, out for a day on the water. As they unpack the picnic basket the Mole nearly collapses in anticipation:

"What's inside it?" asked the Mole, wriggling with curiosity.
"There's cold chicken inside it," replied the Rat briefly; "cold-tonguecoldhamcoldbeefpickledgherkinssaladfrenchrollscress-sandwichespottedmeatgingerbeerlemonadesodawater—"
"O stop, stop," cried the Mole in ecstasies: "This is too much!"

I read the list of foods and think to myself, I couldn't feed my kids with that menu. When did that happen? Why does it no longer seem as purely, simply pleasurable as the Mole finds it to be? Over that picnic basket, Rat and Mole forge a friendship that endures through their various adventures. Later the Badger serves them a bountiful supper that sparks only "that regrettable sort of conversation that results from talking with your mouth full"; they also forage a Christmas meal from the few scraps still available in the Mole's almost-abandoned house.

For my family, I want to provide the kind of bounty Rat does, to serve the kind of meal that generates those truly not-so-regrettable conversations with your mouth full, but it's gotten more and more difficult. At Easter, we often gather friends and family at our house for the first big spring meal of the year. I do my best to provide seasonal sustenance: peas, asparagus, lemon, the pale greens and light yellows of early spring. One year we overdid the symbolism of the Easter egg by featuring two strata for the main course (one vegetarian, one not) and trifle for dessert. It wasn't until we'd finished that we realized we had spent the day basically eating bread or cake soaked in custard—and when we did realize, no one minded. I look at that menu now and think of how far removed custard is from my daughter's diet, and how unlikely my son is to want to sit at the table and talk after the meal's over. We're on our way, I hope, to forging new rituals, but we're not quite there yet.

So instead of the Mole and the Rat, I think about Alice, in *Alice's Adventures in Wonderland* and *Through the Looking-Glass*. The arbitrary rules that govern food in the topsy-turvy worlds she visits remind me of my own family—at least some days. Food is the medium of transformation in Wonderland, but after the first delicious draught of potion (with the "sort of mixed flavour of cherry-tart, custard, pine-apple, roast turkey, toffee, and hot buttered toast"), Alice rarely tastes food in either adventure. More common is her experience at the Mad Hatter's tea party, where she is seated at a messy place and seemingly denied the little food available.

"Take some more tea," the March Hare said to Alice, very earnestly.

"I've had nothing yet," Alice replied in an offended tone, "so I can't take more."

The over-peppered soup at the Duchess's and the tarts at the trial are similarly either inedible or forbidden. Like the child forced to sit at the "adults' table" and then chastised for speaking and for eating the wrong thing—too much, too little, nothing at all—Alice is subject to food rules that seem constantly to change.

In my own family, rules used to come into play most obviously in restaurants, where they also seemed—to my children, at least—the most arbitrary. Some years ago a restaurant meal devolved into tears because I insisted that Nick eat at least one bite of the burger he'd ordered before he had another French fry. This rule made about as much sense to him as "jam tomorrow, jam yesterday, but never jam today"—one of the rules Alice must contend with in Looking-Glass World—so he defied it, eating fry after fry. And, like the Queen of Hearts in Wonderland, I flew into a rage as I saw my authority challenged, leaving my son as bewildered and tearful as Alice at the inexplicability of adult behavior. When it was over, I asked him, "Do you know why that happened?"

"Because you wouldn't let me eat my fries," he answered, reasonably enough.

Now my daughter makes her own rules for food that seem even more restrictive than mine, or than those that govern Alice; they go far beyond the lessons in politeness that the tea party—or our own restaurant meals—might have taught. Avoiding meat and dairy seems straightforward enough until you try to do it on a choir tour in Spain, for example, when restaurant staff, repeatedly stymied, ended up simply offering her limp and uninspired salads, over and over again. "They couldn't even give me plain pasta!" she later told us. Protein and even fresh vegetables seemed out of reach; while omnivores were offered meats and vegetarians got cheese, Mariah went hungry. In some cities, then, she sought out her own, separate meals at hidden vegan and vegetarian restaurants, off the beaten path and away from her travel group. At home, some restaurants are out because they grill the (ostensibly vegan) hash browns on the same griddle with the eggs, or won't guarantee that the side dishes (the only seemingly vegan options) aren't prepared with butter. Rules that govern what she can eat also condition both where and sometimes even with whom, to an extent that does, indeed, divide us at times.

In many children's books, food is also the means by which the characters (and, implicitly, the child readers) learn self-control. The gluttonous rat Templeton, in *Charlotte's Web*, never does actually learn self-control (though even the very youngest readers understand his example as a negative one), but Frog and Toad, in the wonderful *Frog and Toad Together*, do. Toad bakes cookies and brings them to share with his friend. After enjoying them for a while, they begin to worry:

"You know, Toad," said Frog, with his mouth full, "I think we should stop eating. We will soon be sick."

But they find it nearly impossible to stop, the cookies are so delicious—so they box them up and hide them in a closet. When Toad realizes that even then he can "take the box down from the shelf and cut the string and open the box," Frog goes ahead and offers it to the birds outside, saying, "HEY BIRDS, HERE ARE COOKIES!"—a phrase my children still repeat when they want to reach for an extra cookie. As Frog then congratulates himself and Toad on their willpower, Toad says sadly, "You may keep it all, Frog . . . I am going home now to bake a cake."

My son, Nick, took a long time to learn this lesson of self-control. As a younger child he reminded me of Templeton or Toad in his unabashed love of food. It went well beyond simple sustenance, whether he was eating all the fries before the burger, chomping on a shiny gumball fresh from the machine, slurping an ice cream cone as it melted over his hand, or even wolfing down bowl after bowl of tuna casserole. Sometimes we had to take the casserole away so he didn't end up writhing on the floor, legs up, moaning that he was too full. It was up to us to impose the rules of the table, and to help him learn to do it himself. I look at his sister now and wonder if we did it too well, or if she has. While I do still see her take pleasure in food, the rules sometimes seem so restrictive—not just the rejection of meat and dairy, but the scanning of labels, the strictures on fat and calories and sugar. Where do health and pleasure intersect? When does the denial of pleasure itself become unhealthy?

Even in books, the pleasures of food mean many different things: comfort, sensual pleasure, self-indulgence, even greed. In *The Lion, the Witch, and the Wardrobe*, Edmund's inability to resist the Witch's Turkish Delight condemns him to betray his siblings. But the novel is complex: There are all sorts of meals in Narnia, and most of them are happy occasions. Indeed, Edmund's greedy consumption of the candy is as much about refusing community as it is about lack of self-control: a middle child in a time of scarcity, he just doesn't want to share. The communal meals in *The Lion, the Witch, and the Wardrobe*—the meal of freshly caught trout in the beavers' dam, the Christmas tea, the celebratory feast after the battle—are allegorical recollections of the communion table, but they are also family dinners of the sort my own family once shared every evening. Dinner at the Beavers is perhaps the best example of this:

> There was a jug of creamy milk for the children (Mr. Beaver stuck to beer) and a great big lump of deep yellow butter in the middle of the table from which everyone took as much as he wanted to go with his potatoes and all the children thought—and I agree with them—that there is nothing to beat good freshwater fish if you eat it when it has been alive half an hour ago and has come out of the pan half a min-

ute ago. And when they had finished the fish Mrs. Beaver brought unexpectedly out of the oven a great and gloriously sticky marmalade roll, steaming hot, and at the same time moved the kettle onto the fire, so that when they had finished the marmalade roll the tea was made and ready to be poured out.

It's the unexpected dessert, I think, that turns the meal from simply a meal into a celebration, of love and friendship and—again unexpected—comfort. I read this passage now with a sort of sadness that we have lost what seemed to be an uncomplicated celebration of love and nurture through food as we age, as our eating becomes more rule-oriented, more symbolic, more fraught.

Mrs. Beaver's gift to the children doesn't really register as a gift in the moment, of course. The children simply accept it. Most meals in children's books, as in children's lives, simply appear—like Max's supper at the end of *Where the Wild Things Are*, waiting on the table, "still hot." I think about Max's mother when I read those lines, knowing she must have made the supper despite her anger at her son. She disappears from the text, yet she remains a warm and nurturing presence in the background, brought back by the meal, the gift she gives her naughty son. Part of me laments that she never appears—but she doesn't need to, symbolized as she is by the still-hot supper, the tangible expression of her love.

My children read on their own now; their days of picture books have long passed. But we still try to eat together, and I find these stories of shared meals reinforce our own family habit, at least as an ideal. I think that's why we end up going out together, finding some place we can all be at one table, rather than simply fragmenting into a family that grazes alone. I admire the indefatigable mothers preparing the food in my favorite children's books, but I'm not one of them. Did *Little House*'s Ma Ingalls ever tell Pa she just didn't feel like making johnnycake again? The lunch Frances's mother packs for her at the end of *Bread and Jam for Frances* just makes me feel inadequate. Lobster salad sandwiches? Who has time? Is there a vegan version? As I lose myself in the tales again, the imaginary feasts of literature revive me. Those fantasy meals are layered and complex, offering sustenance and comfort, promises and warnings. So, I realize, are the meals at my table—wherever it is.

CRAZY CAKE

The one uncomplicated food gift that both my children will always accept is what, in my family, we call Crazy Cake. I got this recipe from Peg Bracken's *I Hate to Cook Book*, where she calls it Cock-eyed Cake. My mother made it for us when we were children, and I've made it for my children their whole lives, and it's the first thing either of them made for me, too. When Mariah became vegan we didn't have to change a thing about it. It's a delicious, moist, quick, chocolaty cake that can be even quicker if you bake it in muffin tins. Because it's a little sticky, you'll either want to line the tins with cupcake liners, or spray them heavily and let them sit at least five minutes before turning them out of the pans. Delicious warm or cold, you can serve this without ever telling anyone it's vegan.

Preheat the oven to 350°F and spray or butter a 9 × 13-inch baking pan or two 12-muffin tins.

Sift the following dry ingredients into your cake pan or, if making muffins, into a bowl.

3 cups all-purpose flour
6 tablespoons cocoa powder
2 cups sugar
2 teaspoons baking soda
½ teaspoon salt
1 tablespoon espresso power (optional, but good)

Once the dry ingredients are all in the pan, make three holes in the mixture.

Get out the following wet ingredients:

10 tablespoons vegetable oil
2 tablespoons vinegar (cider, plain white, or raspberry)
2 teaspoons vanilla extract
2 cups cold water or cold coffee (I usually use decaf)

Pour the oil into one hole, the vinegar into another, and the vanilla into the third. Then pour the water or coffee over the whole thing, and stir with a fork until everything is one somewhat pale brown color (don't worry, it gets darker as it bakes). Make sure you go around the corners a couple of times and get all the baking soda mixed in nicely.

Stir in ¾ cup chocolate chips. (Or don't, but it will be much better if you do.)

Bake for about 30 minutes (muffins should be done in about 20 minutes), until dark and fudgy looking. The top will spring back when the cake is done.

Best with vanilla ice cream (regular or vegan), but just fine as is.

THE FINAL REDOUBT

THOMAS PEELE

I am hanging out with the chef Dennis Leary.

It is early, god awful early in fact, a few minutes past 6 A.M., on a dreary July morning in downtown San Francisco. The fog and chill seem straight from Twain's supposed line about how the coldest winter of his life was a summer here. Yet here is Leary, one of the biggest food names in one of the biggest food cities in the country, already at work behind the counter of his tiny, open-air breakfast and lunch place, The Sentinel, open but a few weeks. He used to run the kitchen at Rubicon, a big-time celebrity restaurant whose owners included Robin Williams, Robert De Niro, and Francis Ford Coppola. Leary left to open his own small dinner place, Canteen, but that wasn't enough for him, so he went into the breakfast and lunch business, too.

Now he is in a space the size of a walk-in closet, talking in Spanish to two assistants who somehow avoid bumping into each other as they push trays of muffins and coffee cake into an oven wedged against a wall. Leary stops to pound an espresso shot and then reaches over the counter and hands me another in a paper cup.

A couple of women, financial district workers with early hours to keep up with the East Coast markets, hover on the sidewalk in their overcoats, waiting. The Sentinel has already become part of their morning routine.

"Blueberry muffins?" one of them asks, a bit of hope in her voice.

Leary throws her a quick, affirmative smile.

"I like making stuff. I like making people happy, I never get sick of that," he says when we talk later.

Leary plops a muffin in a paper bag for the woman. She takes it out and pulls it apart before she even pays him, steam thick as fog rising from gobs of blueberries. She pays, Leary nods, and the woman is gone.

The Sentinel is as simple as it is small. Leary makes American pastries for breakfast—coffee cake, muffins—and sometimes adds a French touch (brioche) and then retools for lunch sandwiches: lamb and eggplant, barbecued mushroom, pork with figs. Then he is off to his small dinner restaurant, Canteen, which has the sensibility of a diner—a counter, four booths—and the food of the kind of places he left behind: sweet corn and crab gratin with pumpkin seed pesto, or cassoulet with cranberry beans, lardons, garlic sausage, duck.

Leary's ideas about food, he says, are influenced by his mother's cooking, which in turn was influenced by a stay in France before he was born.

"I try to cook food that has a sense of tradition. My mom was a big Francophile, and most of your food memories are based on food your mother made, or didn't make, for you," he says. The years in France, combined with "that cool foodie-ism of the seventies," influenced by Julia Child and Simone Beck, co-authors of the seminal *Mastering the Art of French Cooking*, shaped Leary's ideas of tradition. But, he points out quickly, his mother cooked for a household and he cooks for a restaurant. His mother, he recalls, "brought back not necessarily specific dishes from France but more of a style—an economical style, basically—cheaper cuts of meat, marinades, cooking in wine, certain dishes more ceremonial than others," such as fondue for family birthdays. "The stuff I learned from my mother informs my basic style—not overly complicated, with a nod toward multi-use," he says, Saturday night's steak tartare becoming Sunday brunch's steak and eggs. But balancing the tradition he wants with his ideas of what a restaurant should be is tricky while competing in business, he remarks. Still, he believes he can achieve financial success in the restaurant business without compromising his values about what he believes an unpretentious place to go and eat and talk can mean to people. Even at The Sentinel, he wants it to be about something other than the food.

Leary is wiry, with close cropped, reddish-blond hair and a boyish face. He may like to make people happy, but he doesn't gush over them; there isn't a lot of sweetener in him. He curses a lot, in the intellectually honest sort of way. He is in constant, unwasted motion, always working. But most of all, Leary is a thinker. He likes ideas. He likes books. He likes details. What he doesn't like are those who "fetishize consumption. That is so asinine," he says. "Foodies come in and they say, 'I watch the Food Network all the time.' That is the worst thing to say to me. They might as well be watching the Spice Channel."

To Leary, about whose cooking critics have raved for years, the idea of restaurant eating is not about self-indulgence, or decadence, or experimentation. He has other ideas, plenty of them, but they all seem to revolve around this: *It's not about the food.*

Leary has been called a Luddite, which may not be quite accurate. But his introduction to restaurant work came in Boston as a teenager, where he started as a dishwasher at the Parker House Hotel, and he is, at least, of an old school. Boston restaurants were not places of experimentation and frills—they were where people ate and socialized, got warm on winter nights, dunked fresh bread and rolls into bowls of chowders and soups. His traditions are grounded there, a long way from a typical California restaurant.

In fact, Leary can be almost clinical about food, describing his pastries at The Sentinel as "palatable calories" that give people the energy to get through the day. That's partly a riff on his rejection of "conspicuous consumption—at least as it pertains to food" and also a glimpse into his larger goals: to promote human interaction, even if it is between two strangers who find themselves sitting next to each other.

Food, to Leary, is not an end to itself. It's a beginning, a starting place. It is as if he thinks in terms of a small English village where the pub is at the center of community life, and in between pints and bangers life happens. (But in Leary's world the food is much better.)

Near where I live two restaurants named Gather have opened recently, and when I think of the name, I think of Leary. "I feel like a restaurant is the final redoubt of Western culture," he says. "People don't socialize in church anymore. That's not the glue that holds society together." What he hopes for at Canteen is that people will talk. So Leary has designed Canteen as a kind of refuge, a place where people fortify themselves—not just with food, but with community. The space, in San Francisco's Nob Hill neighborhood, "used to be a shitty little coffee shop called the Titanic Café." The booth-and-counter layout couldn't be changed, but when he scouted possible restaurant locations, Leary saw its potential. "I like diners. I like unpretentious places. I like counters, there is a social element. You put people at a counter and they may actually talk to each other. It is rare that you sit down in a public place and strike up a conversation. I mean, how often do you talk to people on the bus? . . . Maybe, in a restaurant, if it is done properly, you can find something that is socially sort of ramifying."

A few weeks after I spent the morning with Leary at The Sentinel, I meet him on a bright Sunday afternoon at a coffee shop across Sutter Street from Canteen. We sit at a rickety sidewalk table. He is relaxed in jeans and a T-shirt. At his restaurant, a few people linger over brunch. "I walked into the restaurant today, I hadn't been in there all day, and I knew ten people in there," he says. He wasn't a chef making an obligatory tour of the restaurant floor on a busy night. He has drawn an eclectic clientele—one group he mentions is a porn film crew—and even when he isn't working the kitchen he likes to hang around the restaurant. "I wasn't schmoozing, I actually liked them. There were some pretty cool people."

Among the things that make Canteen different and contribute to its intimacy are the books. Let's face it, there aren't a lot of four-star restaurants around that are lined, as Canteen is, with books. The spaces above the booths and around the counter are packed with books, and a question about them dispatches Leary on a riff: "I like books, I like looking at books. [But] books are dying; libraries are dying and that sort of plays into my idea of restaurants. It's not the last option or the saving grace or a citadel, but a restaurant can be a meaningful steward of culture." He wants people to grab a book from his shelves, take it home, maybe bring it and another back. He knows that his patrons could, if they wished, recreate much of California cuisine at home. But that doesn't get them out, talking, glancing up at the spines of the Saul Bellow (*The Actual*) and Don DeLillo novels (*Libra*, *Underworld*) that were above my booth when I ate at Canteen and, perhaps, having a conversation about literature.

Unpretentious is a word that Leary uses a lot as we talk. It is what he wants both his food and his places to be, saying it so often it seems like a mantra. Even with all the books, Canteen is close to resembling a hole in the wall. It is nestled into a slice of an old San Francisco hotel converted into an art school dormitory. It's narrow, the kitchen spilling out of the back into the area behind the counter. The colors are simple greens and blues. When I watched Leary and his staff do prep work one evening, I had to cram myself into a corner and often retreat into a pantry-sized closet packed with crates of onions and garlic to let people pass. It is, as Leary wants, unpretentious, nearly to a fault, the counter topped with what looks like teal Formica, the stools resembling what one might find in an old ice cream and soda joint.

The food, though, is anything but quaint: corned beef Benedict is a weekend brunch specialty; duck breast, halibut, and yellow tail are frequently on the dinner menu. Leary's ever-changing dinner offerings include dishes such as artichoke soup with pickled vegetables and sorrel; roasted oyster mushrooms with porcini flan and beets; pork schnitzel with mustard greens, bacon, and a poached egg; beef tongue with poached egg slices; lamb loin poached in red wine with potato cakes and sauce *soubise*.

Leary takes a sip of coffee, and I ask him the obvious question, changing the subject to The Sentinel: What is one of the best chefs in California doing bagging blueberry muffins at 6 A.M.?

"I am an owner. I would rather be the owner of a fucking hot dog stand than an executive chef working for someone else," he says.

He takes coffee and turns his answer into a statement about Canteen—and what he wants to do with it, too. "When I started Canteen, people made some comments. 'Oh, he is running a diner.' I thought, OK, you know what, it's true, I am making omelets, but they are my omelets."

And he wants his omelets, his blueberry muffins, his places, to be something different from those where everything is about the food.

"I don't want food [that] people have to overthink," he says. "I want people to have a good time, to have a good conversation and want to come back. I don't want a silent dining room."

But at the same time, he insists, "I don't want to serve the same old

Bay Area cuisine, all that knee-jerk arugula, goat cheese, blood orange, fennel salad from some farm they can name-drop. That's boring to me. I want to do stuff that is accessible but different. The way I try to do that is not to read cookbooks, not look at the Food Network, but come up with my own ideas, which takes forever."

Not only does he take forever, as he put it, to come up with his own ideas, he sometimes takes years to execute them. In 2011, three years after he opened The Sentinel, Leary's real reasons for placing it where he did became much clearer. The Sentinel abuts The House of Shields, a very traditional San Francisco bar opened in 1908. It turns out that the bar is what Leary wanted all along and he used the sandwich and breakfast place to forge a strong relationship with the building's owner. When the bar's lease was up, Leary sprung. His renovation of the bar into another of his unpretentious, traditional places was even reported on by *The New York Times*. The building's owner told the *Times* something he had learned about Leary during the years that The Sentinel stood as, well, a sentinel for his true ambitions of taking over the bar. Leary "does what he says he is going to do and he does it right."

Leary took months to renovate the place, throwing himself into the work, and it turned out that running a bar was not any different for Leary than running a restaurant. "A bar is one of the last places where people converse face to face," he would say about The House of Shields.

And finding a way to put people together, be it over plates of duck sausage or glasses of rye on the rocks, is what Leary has always wanted.

———

The cold morning that I met Leary at The Sentinel shortly after it opened, a woman stood in line for coffee cake and then pulled Leary aside to ask him about the soup made with summer squashes she had bought the day before for lunch. She raved about it so vehemently that I would later ask Leary, jokingly, if he set it all up for my benefit. But the woman was genuine, and the soup had touched her. She wasn't a foodie who consumed for the sake of the consumption; she wasn't a Food Network watcher, or a name-dropper. She was an everyday person who had discovered something new. Leary listened to her intently and broke into a wide, unforced smile.

No, I thought, it isn't about the food at all.

DENNIS LEARY'S CARAMELIZED PEAR TART WITH GORGONZOLA CREAM AND BLACK PEPPER SYRUP

SᴇRᴠᴇꜱ 6

PEAR FILLING

7 Comice pears, not overripe
4 ounces sugar
1 ounce butter

PHYLLO CRUST

7 sheets phyllo dough
2 ounces butter, melted
½ ounce powdered sugar

BLACK PEPPER SYRUP

2 ounces sugar
2 ounces Champagne vinegar
1 tablespoon black peppercorns, crushed

GORGONZOLA CREAM

3 ounces Gorgonzola or similar blue cheese
½ tablespoon crème fraîche
Dash of fresh lemon juice

Special equipment needed: 8-inch or 10-inch cast-iron skillet or non-stick pan

For the pears: Peel, core, and thinly slice each pear. Toss in half the sugar and set aside.

For the phyllo: Place one sheet of phyllo on a clean, dry cutting board and brush it with melted butter. Sprinkle a little powdered sugar on top of the butter, then add another sheet and repeat the process until all the phyllo is used. To cut the phyllo, place an inverted plate on top of it that roughly corresponds to the diameter of the skillet. With a small knife, cut around the circumference of the plate and discard the excess. Carefully remove the phyllo from the cutting board (it may stick) and chill in the refrigerator.

For the syrup: Place the sugar in a small saucepan, add a few tablespoons of water, stir well, and cook over medium heat until the sugar begins to turn brown. Carefully add the vinegar, return to a boil, and stir until the sugar is dissolved. Reduce by three-quarters and then remove from the heat. When the syrup has cooled slightly, add the peppercorns, stir, and set aside at room temperature.

For the Gorgonzola cream: Add all ingredients to a food processor and process until smooth. Remove to a small bowl and chill.

To bake the tart: Preheat oven to 350°F.

Place the cast-iron skillet over medium heat, add the remaining sugar and butter, and as they begin to melt, arrange the pear sections in a circular pattern, starting from the center and working toward the rim, overlapping the edges slightly. Make sure that the pan does not get too hot or the sugar will burn. Put the skillet in the oven and bake for 9 minutes, or until the pears are soft and slightly translucent. Place the phyllo circle on top of the pears, press down slightly, lower the oven temperature to 300°F, and continue to bake until the phyllo is crisp and golden, approximately 12 minutes more. Remove from the oven to cool slightly.

To remove the tart: When the skillet is just warm (about 15 minutes), carefully place an inverted plate on top of the phyllo and, in one motion, turn the skillet and plate over so that the tart comes free and the pears are facing up. It may be helpful to loosen the edges of the tart with a spatula prior to inverting.

To serve: Carefully cut the tart into 6 wedges with a sharp knife, place each wedge on a dessert plate, and top with the Gorgonzola cream. Drizzle a small amount of syrup around each piece and serve at once.

ACKNOWLEDGMENTS

Thanks to Jennifer Urban-Brown and Roost Books, who had the vision to give this book a home, and Rochelle Bourgault for her thoughtful edits. Thanks to Tara Hart, who answered every question, and a special thanks to our agent, Elizabeth Evans at Jean V. Naggar Literary Agency, who believed in this project from the very beginning.

ABOUT THE CONTRIBUTORS

Keith Blanchard was deputy editor for the launch team of *Maxim*, the world's largest general-interest men's magazine, and served as Editor-in-Chief until 2004. He is the author of the novel *The Deed*, now in paperback, and has completed a second novel, *Johnny Appleseed*. He's been a columnist for the *Chicago Tribune*, and has written for the *Drew Carey Show* and Comedy Central. Currently he is Executive Creative Director of Story Worldwide, a next-generation content marketing firm. He lives in suburban New Jersey with his wife and three children, and likes deep-sea fishing, playing pool and poker, and long walks in the rain, by candlelight, with kittens.

Max Brooks is the son of Anne Bancroft and Mel Brooks. He is an Emmy Award—winning writer for *Saturday Night Live* and is the author of *The Zombie Survival Guide* and *World War Z*, now being turned into a movie produced by and starring Brad Pitt. He has written several other short stories and comics. He lives in Los Angeles with his wife, Michelle, his six-year-old son, Henry, and their two dogs. Right now his greatest endeavor is to press and boil as much sugar cane juice as possible without losing a finger or two.

Melissa Clark is the author of the novels *Imperfect* and *Swimming Upstream, Slowly*; the creator of the animated television series *Braceface*; and has contributed scripts for *Rolie Polie Olie* and *Sweet Valley High*, among others. She lives in Los Angeles and teaches writing and literature at Otis

College of Art and Design, as well as The Writing Pad. Unlike the other, foodie Melissa Clark, this is Melissa Clark's first foray into writing about food.

Elizabeth Crane is a writer and editor in San Francisco, where she lives with her rapidly growing sons. She can be found every Saturday, rain or shine, at the Noe Valley Farmers' Market, a community farmers' market in her neighborhood. In her fifteen-year freelance career, her writing has appeared in numerous newspapers, books, and magazines, including *Parenting, Brain, Child,* and *Cooking Light;* she is currently editor and chief nitpicker at AllThingsD.com.

Aleksandra Crapanzano is a screenwriter and food journalist. She was awarded the M. F. K. Fisher Award for Distinguished Writing from the James Beard Foundation for her work in *Gourmet;* she has written for *Food and Wine, Saveur,* and extensively for *The New York Times Magazine* and *The Wall Street Journal.*

Gregory Dicum is the author of six books (most recently *The Pisco Book*) and an award-winning journalist who writes frequently for *The New York Times, The Economist,* and others about business, technology, travel, and the environment. He is also the co-founder of MondoWindow, a company that helps airline passengers experience the places they are flying over. His wee son, Xeno Madrone, has complicated matters considerably.

Elrena Evans holds an MFA from Pennsylvania State University, and is the author of the short story collection *This Crowded Night.* She is co-editor of *Mama, PhD: Women Write about Motherhood and Academic Life,* and her writing appears in the anthologies *How to Fit a Car Seat on a Camel* and *Twentysomething Essays by Twentysomething Writers* as well as in *Christianity Today, Brain, Child, Episcopal Life,* and *Literary Mama.* She lives in Pennsylvania with her husband and four young children.

Jeff Gordinier is a staff writer at *The New York Times* and the author of *X Saves the World.* He has written for a variety of publications, including *Details, Outside, Esquire, GQ, Elle, Spin, Creative Nonfiction, PoetryFoundation.org,* and *Entertainment Weekly.* His work has also been included in anthologies such as *Best American Nonrequired Reading, Best Food Writing,* and *Best Creative Nonfiction.* He lives close to the Hudson River with his wife and two children.

Phyllis Grant worked in pastry at New York City's Bouley, Michael's, and Nobu. Eventually she tired of sugar and burning her forearms and never sleeping. Now she lives in Berkeley and writes a blog, *Dash and Bella*, which has been featured in *The New York Times*, *Real Simple*, *The San Francisco Chronicle*, and *Food52*.

Libby Gruner teaches English and Women's Studies at the University of Richmond in Richmond, Virginia, where she lives with her family. Her academic writing has appeared in *SIGNS: Journal of Women in Culture and Society*, *Children's Literature*, and other journals. Her personal writing has been featured in *Brain, Child*, *Literary Mama*, and the anthologies *Toddler: Real-Life Stories of Those Fickle, Urgent, Irrational, Tiny People We Love* and *Mama, PhD: Women Write about Motherhood and Academic Life*.

Deborah Copaken Kogan is the author of *Shutterbabe, Hell Is Other Parents, Between Here and April*, and *The Red Book*. A former columnist for *The Financial Times*, her essays and journalism have also appeared in *The New Yorker* and *The New York Times*, among others. Her cooking is adequate enough for the weekly grind, but it's her techie husband, **Paul Kogan**, an entrepreneur building an eCommerce start-up in New York, who creates the real magic in the family kitchen.

Jen Larsen is the author of *Stranger Here: How Weight Loss Surgery Transformed My Body and Messed with My Head*. She has an MFA in creative writing from the University of San Francisco and currently lives in Ogden, Utah.

Edward Lewine writes regularly for *The New York Times*, *Smart Money*, *Salon*, *Glamour*, *Premiere*, *Stuff*, *Arena*, *Detroit News*, *Newark Star-Ledger*, *The Art Newspaper*, and *Golf & Travel*. He is the author of *Death and the Sun* and lives in Brooklyn with his family.

Chris Malcomb has led workshops for the California Association of Independent Schools, the Bay Area Teacher Training Institute, and the Prison University Project at San Quentin. His work has appeared in the *San Francisco Chronicle Magazine*, *The Sun*, *Narrative*, *Common Ground*, *Red Clay Review*, *Under the Sun*, and KQED Radio's Perspectives series. He earned his MFA in Creative Writing from the University of San Francisco and is the founder of The Mindful Writer, which offers classes and coaching in mindfulness and creative writing.

Lisa McNamara is a professional recruiter and a vocational writer who, in her spare time, bakes for (and gives baking lessons to) those who share her passion for old-fashioned handcrafted pies, cakes, and other soul-satisfying yummies.

Dani Klein Modisett is the creator/producer/director of the live story-telling shows "Afterbirth . . . Stories you won't read in a parenting magazine" and "Not What I Signed Up For." She is also the editor of a book based on her storytelling show, *Afterbirth*. Dani has been a contributor to *Parents Magazine*, the *Los Angeles Times*, and *The Huffington Post*. She has also worked as an actress in film and television and as a comic. Currently Dani is working on a book about how couples stay happily married in the twenty-first century. She lives in Los Angeles with her husband and two sons.

Catherine Newman is author of the award-winning memoir *Waiting for Birdy*, and editor of *Chop Chop*, the nonprofit kids' cooking magazine. She writes regularly about food and families for many different magazines, including *Family Fun, O, The Oprah Magazine, Real Simple, Brain, Child*, and *Whole Living*. She also writes about cooking and parenting on her blog, *Ben and Birdy*.

Thomas Peele's first book is *Killing the Messenger: A Story of Radical Faith, Racism's Backlash and the Assassination of a Journalist*. He is an investigative reporter for the Bay Area News Group.

Deesha Philyaw is the co-author of *Co-Parenting 101: Helping Your Children Thrive after Divorce*. She is also the co-founder, with her ex-husband, of CoParenting101.org. A Pittsburgh-based freelance writer, Deesha's publication credits include *Essence, Bitch*, and *Wondertime* magazines, and *The Washington Post*. Her writing has been anthologized in *Literary Mama: Reading for the Maternally Inclined, Just Like a Girl: A Manifesta!* and *Woman's Work*. Deesha teaches as an adjunct professor in Chatham University's Master of Professional Writing program. She is mom and step-mom to four daughters.

Neal Pollack is the author of the best-selling memoirs *Alternadad* and *Stretch* and several works of fiction, including, most recently, the novel *Jewball*. A contributor to countless magazines and websites, Pollack lives in Austin, Texas, with his wife and son, where they eat unhealthily at too many food trailers.

Barbara Rushkoff is best known for creating the seminal zine *Plotz* and the irreverent book *Jewish Holiday Fun . . . for You!* She got her start by interviewing MC Hammer and has gone on to interview countless pop culture icons. Barbara has written for *People Magazine, SMITH Magazine,* and *Rolling Stone,* was a contributing editor to the arts magazine *Index,* and has contributed essays to *Before the Mortgage, Matzo Balls for Breakfast,* and *A Girl's Guide to Taking Over the World.* She lives in New York with her husband and daughter.

Bethany Saltman lives and writes in the Catskill Mountains of New York State. Her essays, poetry, and interviews can be seen in places like *The Sun, Parents, Buddhadharma, Literary Mama, Witness,* and *Mothering.* She was a student of the late John Daido Loori, Roshi, for many years, and continues to practice at Zen Mountain Monastery. She writes a monthly column, "Flowers Fall: Field Notes from a Buddhist Mom's Experimental Life," in the Hudson Valley magazine *Chronogram.*

K. G. Schneider's writing has been nominated for a Pushcart Prize and published in the *Best Creative Nonfiction, Best Nonrequired Reading,* and *Powder: Women Writing in the Ranks, from Vietnam to Iraq,* as well as in *Gastronomica, Nerve, White Crane,* and *Ninth Letter.* She's a writer and librarian who spent ten years writing for library trade publications—publishing two books and over one hundred technical articles—before trying her hand at literary nonfiction. Librarians and writers alike enjoy her reflections, reviews, and technical and social commentary at her blog, *Free Range Librarian.* She holds an MFA from the University of San Francisco.

Sarah Shey was born in Iowa. Her writing has appeared in *The New York Times, Time Out New York Kids,* the *Philadelphia Inquirer, This Old House Magazine, The Des Moines Register,* and *The Iowan.* She wrote two children's books inspired by the farms and lakes of her childhood, *Sky All Around* and *Blue Lake Days.* Her essays have appeared in several anthologies, including *How to Fit a Car Seat on a Camel.* She is at work on an autobiography, the adventures of a big family who lives on a little farm in Iowa.

Stacie Stukin is a freelance journalist who was born and raised in Los Angeles. Her byline has appeared in *Time,* the *Los Angeles Times, Elle* and *Elle Decor, Yoga Journal, Vibe, The New York Times,* and *Condé Nast Traveler.* She likes to cook and considers herself an old-fashioned general assignment reporter. She has written about yoga, HIV, prisoner rights, design and architecture, organic and unrefined sugar, bling, and buttocks augmentation surgery. She's the co-author of the *Alabama Stitch Book: Contemporary Stories, Lessons and Projects Celebrating Traditional Hand Sewing, Quilting and Embroidery* and has completed an architectural monograph entitled *Richard Manion Architecture: New Classicists*.

Karen Valby is a senior writer for *Entertainment Weekly* magazine, where she writes about books, movies, and TV. She is also the author of *Welcome to Utopia: Notes from a Small Town*, a chronicle of her peculiar and invigorating time in a Texas town of less than three hundred people. She lives in Austin, Texas, with her husband, young daughter, and their assorted animals.

ABOUT THE EDITORS

Caroline M. Grant and Lisa Catherine Harper are the creators and founders of the website Learning to Eat.

Caroline M. Grant is Editor-in-Chief of Literary Mama, named one of *Writer's Digest*'s Best Websites for Writers, and Associate Director of the Sustainable Arts Foundation. She is also co-editor of the anthology *Mama, PhD: Women Write about Motherhood and Academic Life*. She has published essays in a variety of journals and anthologies. She grew up in suburban New York, eating only the produce grown by her father and grandfathers in their gardens and now, with her husband and two young sons, raises what vegetables she can in their foggy San Francisco backyard.

Lisa Catherine Harper is the author of the award-winning memoir *A Double Life: Discovering Motherhood*. Her writing has appeared in places including PoetryFoundation.org, *The Huffington Post*, *Babble*, *San Francisco Chronicle*, *Glimmer Train*, *Gastronomica*, *Mama, PhD*, and *Educating Tastes*. She is currently Adjunct Professor of Writing in the MFA program at the University of San Francisco. She lives in the San Francisco Bay Area with her husband and their two children.

Caroline and Lisa met through Literary Mama and embarked on *The Cassoulet Saved Our Marriage* when their playground conversations about writing and feeding their four young children made their work on this book as inevitable as dinner.